Reflexivity

Sara Miller McCune founded SAGE Publishing in 1965 to support the dissemination of usable knowledge and educate a global community. SAGE publishes more than 1000 journals and over 800 new books each year, spanning a wide range of subject areas. Our growing selection of library products includes archives, data, case studies and video. SAGE remains majority owned by our founder and after her lifetime will become owned by a charitable trust that secures the company's continued independence.

Los Angeles | London | New Delhi | Singapore | Washington DC | Melbourne

Reflexivity
The Essential Guide

Tim May
Beth Perry

Los Angeles | London | New Delhi
Singapore | Washington DC | Melbourne

Los Angeles | London | New Delhi
Singapore | Washington DC | Melbourne

SAGE Publications Ltd
1 Oliver's Yard
55 City Road
London EC1Y 1SP

SAGE Publications Inc.
2455 Teller Road
Thousand Oaks, California 91320

SAGE Publications India Pvt Ltd
B 1/I 1 Mohan Cooperative Industrial Area
Mathura Road
New Delhi 110 044

SAGE Publications Asia-Pacific Pte Ltd
3 Church Street
#10-04 Samsung Hub
Singapore 049483

Editor: Mila Steele
Editorial assistant: John Nightingale
Production editor: Ian Antcliff
Copyeditor: Audrey Scriven
Proofreader: Neil Dowden
Marketing manager: Susheel Gokarakonda
Cover design: Shaun Mercier
Typeset by: C&M Digitals (P) Ltd, Chennai, India
Printed by CPI Group (UK) Ltd, Croydon, CR0 4YY

© Tim May and Beth Perry 2017

First published 2017

Library of Congress Control Number: 2016959679

British Library Cataloguing in Publication data

A catalogue record for this book is available from the British Library

ISBN 978-1-4462-9516-8
ISBN 978-1-4462-9517-5 (pbk)

At SAGE we take sustainability seriously. Most of our products are printed in the UK using FSC papers and boards. When we print overseas we ensure sustainable papers are used as measured by the PREPS grading system. We undertake an annual audit to monitor our sustainability.

CONTENTS

○ REFLEXIVITY

BOXES

ABOUT THE AUTHORS

 Tim May is Professor of Social Science Methodology in the Sheffield Methods Institute, University of Sheffield. He originally trained and worked as an agricultural engineer and, following an evening return-to-study course, studied at the LSE, Surrey and Plymouth universities. In addition to his teaching across a range of subjects, Tim has authored and edited 16 books, including new editions, which have been translated into 15 languages, as well as over one 180 articles, book chapters, research reports and policy briefings. His work has been funded by national and international research councils and the topics of his research and writings cover urban knowledge exchange; policy development and learning; universities, cities and socio-economic development; management and organizational change; research methods and methodology; social and political theory and philosophy of social science.

Beth and Tim are currently co-authoring *Cities and the Knowledge Economy: Promise, Politics and Possibilities* (2017) and a fifth edition of *Social Research: Issues, Methods and Process* (2018) and working on a research programme entitled 'Realising Just Cities'. Tim is also writing a third edition of *Thinking Sociologically* (co-authored with the late Zygmunt Bauman, 2018).

 Beth Perry is Professorial Fellow in the Urban Institute, University of Sheffield. She has followed an interdisciplinary path, undertaking degrees in European Studies and Modern Languages, before completing a PhD in Sociology and Political Science. Since 2000 she has worked in and subsequently led urban research centres, with a focus on the processes and practices of urban transformation.

Beth is currently the UK Programme Lead for the Mistra Urban Futures centre, which has established local interaction platforms in South Africa, Kenya, Sweden and the UK to explore the limits and strengths of coproduction in realising just cities. She holds major grants from the Economic and Social Research Council's Open Research Area and Urban Transformations programmes ('Jam and Justice' and 'Knowledge Matters') and has co-led a large Arts and Humanities Research Council project under the Connected Communities programme ('Cultural Intermediation: Connecting Communities in the Creative Urban Economy'). With Tim May she is currently writing *Cities and the Knowledge Economy: Promise, Politics and Possibilities* (2017) and a fifth edition of *Social Research: Issues, Methods and Process* (2018).

ACKNOWLEDGEMENTS

Tim would like to thank a number of folk who have been sources of friendship and support during what have been a few years of considerable change. For their support of my work now and in the past, my thanks go to Zygmunt Bauman, Dave Byrne, Davydd Greenwood, John Scott, Bev Skeggs, Dorothy Smith, Carole Sutton and Malcolm Williams. My thanks go to the Institute of Advanced Study, University of Durham, where I spent the Spring Term of 2016 as a Fellow and met and discussed ideas with a group of scholars from varying disciplines, as well as to my new colleagues in the Sheffield Methods Institute. To Ken Parsons my gratitude for all those times when we not only reminisce, but also think of times ahead; to the 'Kalkan 7' for the fun, experiences and the holidays; to Vicky Simpson for her support and sense of humour; to Catherine Barlow for her keen eye in compiling the bibliography and index; and to the editorial and production teams at Sage for enabling this book to be published.

Cian, Alex, Calum, Nick and Lewis, my sons and stepsons, have all grown into people whose values carry with them the hope for a better world. To Vikki, my partner and a clinical psychologist who certainly knows a thing or two about what reflexivity means in practice, my love and appreciation for her encouragement.

Beth and I have worked together for fifteen years now. We are currently working on three books together, as well as articles, and have undertaken numerous projects over this time. It has been an extraordinary journey and now we move to a new context whilst continuing our work through recent projects we have been awarded under what we have called the 'Realising Just Cities' programme. My thanks to Beth not only for working on this book with me, but also for how we have sought to hold onto what matters, when circumstances have frequently made that difficult to maintain.

Beth shares this sentiment wholeheartedly. Many thanks to Tim for his friendship and mentoring over the years, sharing his knowledge and insights and for inviting me to join him on this reflexive voyage. Tim encouraged me to step beyond disciplinary boundaries and discover the worlds of philosophy, epistemology and methodology. I am delighted we can continue our explorations together as we make this next move.

My thanks go to Vicky Simpson for support (and dealing with my unwashed cups); to Catherine Barlow and all my co-workers for their insights, support and encouragement; to longstanding and new collaborators from around the world. For emotional and practical support, my thanks to a host of neighbours and friends for providing tea, childcare and parenting taxis. Particular thanks to Tony and Fiona Whyton, for their unique blend of friendship, advice, humour and wigs.

To my immediate and extended family, thank you for understanding and patience. With my brother Matthew I share a love of books and knowledge and have had many inspiring discussions. Bottomless gratitude to my mum, Caroline, and my sister, Kate, for unending care and interest in what I'm up to. To Anya and Myla, of whom I am so proud, my thanks and love for their patience with their tired, old mum and for giving me so much inspiration. And to Marcus, who is so much wiser than he knows, my love, respect and gratitude for an endless supply of the best curries in the world.

We would like to acknowledge the support of the following funders in developing this book: the Mistra Foundation for Strategic Environmental Research which enables our participation in the Mistra Urban Futures Centre; the Arts and Humanities Research Council for 'Cultural Intermediation: Connecting Communities in the Creative Urban Economy' (Grant number: AH/J005320/1); the Economic and Social Research Council for 'Jam and Justice: Co-producing Urban Governance for Social Innovation' (Grant number: ES/N005945/1) and 'Whose Knowledge Matters? Competing and Contesting Knowledge Claims in 21st Century Cities' (Grant number: ES/N018818/1). Responsibility for the arguments in the book remains our own.

INTRODUCTION

━━ CHAPTER CONTENTS ━━━━━━━━━━━━━━━━━━━━

Reflexivity is a wonderful and worrying word. It is wonderful because it signifies intelligence capable of thinking about what it takes for granted and is subject to revision; worrying because it is restless, never content with appearances and in a permanent state in which reality is suspended through scepticism. Reflexivity can lead to uncertainty, as well as contribute to a realistic assessment of the limits of knowledge to advance our understanding. In the latter sense, it challenges the status quo. It can, for example, question how social and political orders seek to hold people to account through invoking ideas of 'reasonable' behaviour and 'rational' actions. Whilst it has this two-edged property, we also find issues of knowledge linked with our being. Hence we find books filling the shelves on how to lead a happy, long and fulfilling life or make money and friends in search of self-fulfilment and personal improvement. There is no shortage of gurus peddling their panaceas for addressing contemporary societal ills.

Ideas on reflexivity reflect the times in which they are produced. Rapid social and technological changes, huge inequalities and the consequences of climate change characterise our times. The form, intensity and spread of these are evident in the ways in which we communicate and how people move across the planet. Yet from these writings we have much to learn. We will chart changes in thought over time and understand how these inform our present situation, as well as the forging of possible futures. Although we live in particular circumstances, we are not imprisoned by them.

We believe that a study and understanding of the role of reflexivity is highly valuable. If we did not think that, we would not have spent our time writing this book! To illustrate this value we draw upon different disciplines – philosophy, sociology, geography, anthropology, history, psychoanalysis, psychology, literature, management and organisation studies, economics and political science – during the course of this journey. Each of the thinkers we examine has been the subject of sustained studies. Our purpose is to examine different arguments in order to convey the richness of histories, but in a way that provides you, the reader, with insights into the role of reflexivity in social life and social research. By the end of this journey we hope it will be clear that we find the features of our existence in a relationship that occurs between others and ourselves, our environments and how we practise in different contexts.

By examining the origins of debates on reflexivity unfolding over the course of history, we address a core set of questions. Who are we? How do we make sense of our lives with and through others? What are the bases and limits of our claims to know the social world? Our wish, as with the book as a whole, is to provide you with the resources to make sense of a range of ideas in terms of their applicability and relevance for understanding modern times and the production of social scientific knowledge. To enhance this aim we use illustrative examples to demonstrate the centrality of reflexivity in social life in general and the social sciences in particular.

WHAT IS REFLEXIVITY?

Before providing you with an overview of the book itself, how can we view reflexivity? Take one example. In a small city, people were used to driving around in their cars without incident. One day, a number of people began to notice small marks appearing on their windscreens. They mentioned this to others who saw the same marks on their windscreens. After a while, the whole population became preoccupied with this new phenomenon. What was the reason? Was it something new that was causing this to happen? The explanation was simple: instead of looking *through* their windscreens, people had started to look *at* them. The pit-marks had always been present and resulted from small stones being thrown up by other cars.

Could this story be used to illustrate an understanding of reflexivity? It is attractive in its simplicity, but problematic. What we have is a distinction between the knower (the driver) and the known (the road), with the driver employing a medium (the windscreen) to observe the landscape ahead. Yet our perception is mediated by ideas and the social landscapes we inhabit – we do not have unmediated access to an unproblematic reality that is then placed beyond question for all time. Specific methods to understand and explain the social world can illuminate, but are not sufficient, to overcome these issues. We need to investigate the interactions between ideas, cultures and practices. Reflexivity is not just about the ability to think about our actions – that is called reflection – but an examination of the foundations of frameworks of thought themselves. The focus is on a second-order question concerning thinking itself and not-taking-things-for-granted.

Reflexivity takes account of the idea that intelligence admits of error, that we may have falsely identified or misrecognised an object, concept or experience. Doubt and a belief in certainty play their role. In these cases the exercise of reflexivity can be said to have a critical function via an examination of the apparently self-evident. Questioning in this way can be seen as a subversive act, particularly among those who hold cherished beliefs in the idea of the Truth. In our troubled times, we can see how challenging accepted truths leads to being cast out of groups or even provokes acts of violence, especially where unquestioning obedience is a condition of belonging.

Different traditions of thought inform how we view the role of reflexivity. At one end of the spectrum, reflexive acts have been understood in terms of their possibility to induce a heightened state of self-consciousness in the service of self-transformation. Being in solitude may be preferred in order to access a purity of thought outside the contamination of a world of chaos and uncertainty. This may suggest a celebration of an isolated individual whose ability to reason is paramount. At the other end of the spectrum, we can see thinkers who have maintained that we can only obtain a true sense of a reflexive self via recognition of our relationships with and through others. Indeed, there are also those who hold we must reject individualism and accept our insignificance in order to find harmony with the world. Views thereby vary between placing an isolated self at the centre of the world and placing and realising who we are within the world as a whole.

What these viewpoints highlight is the importance of how we see ourselves in the first place. In other words, what does it mean to be human and what abilities are ascribed to our condition of being? Issues of ontology, along with the conditions of our actions, are core parts of the journey we take in this book. So much of what we see and do is informed by the spheres of perception through which we make sense of the world around us. The conceptual, physical and social spaces that we carry around with us are constantly in the process of being renewed and inform how we are in the world. Peter Sloterdijk has likened them to air conditioning systems 'in whose construction and calibration, for those living in real coexistence, it is out of the question not to participate' (2011[1998]: 46). Whilst we fashion these air conditioning systems, we do so with the resources handed down to us.

Reflexivity is a guard against what we might call a hypodermic realism: that is, the assumption that there is an unproblematic relationship between us and the world, including social scientific practices and its products, which results in a valid and reliable representation of the world. Reflexivity also guards against the opposite view – idealised openness – that reflects a fluid world in which choices and interpretive flexibility are as numerous as the number of people on the planet. Writings on reflexivity exist on a sliding scale from those which seek to represent the real, whilst recognising such an enterprise must be open to revision, to those for which such an enterprise needs to be debunked. With the latter, studies of the social and physical world must be examined in order to expose the partiality of accounts in terms of their restriction not only to time and place, but also the biography of authors. The result being that if authors are *really* (sic) reflexive, they would recognise the futility of any attempt to 'mirror' reality (Woolgar 1998).

Collectively, the authors and schools of thought we examine in this book provide valuable insights into reflexivity in terms of its applicability both to social life and social science. Views are divided in relation to the role that these writings play in the illumination of scientific practice. Some reject the idea that allegiance to particular ideas of knowledge informs the choices made in research practice (Platt 1996). Whilst such studies can be illuminating, caution needs to be exercised. The tendency can be to reproduce a separation between theory and practice by drawing upon ideas that decisions are somehow free of assumptions, to say nothing of consequences (May 1997). Equally, to place actions outside of time and context according to the supposed immutable laws of human behaviour, governed by a rational calculation of means towards ends, is one of the great problems of modern times that have forged the direction of societies. Instead, we can start by considering the ways in which changes occur in both socio-cultural structures and our everyday agency (Archer 2007).

We may say that reflexivity has a threefold imperative in life. First, an awareness of oneself is necessary for the exercise of any rule or sense of obligation of the expectations that are made and reside within us. Second, our traditional or habitual practices require monitoring as we meet unexpected circumstances and interact with other people who have different practices. Third, guidelines for action may be in conflict with each other thereby requiring deliberation and action. We might say, therefore, that if there is no reflexivity, there no society, because there is no culture which is 'so comprehensive and so coherent in its composition and no structure ever being so commanding or consistent in its organization as to maintain an enduring form of life without making constant resort to the reflexively derived actions of its members' (Archer 2012: 2).

THE STRUCTURE OF THE BOOK

The book is divided into eight chapters. In each we follow a similar structure oriented around the ideas of prominent thinkers of their time, concluding with a reflection that draws us closer to understanding the history and centrality of reflexivity. The chapters generally work in pairs, moving from original ideas and themes (Chapters 1 and 2), through to different forms of reason (Chapters 3 and 4), societal dynamics (Chapters 5 and 6) and social scientific practice and understanding reflexivity in social life (Chapters 7 and 8).

Chapters 1 and 2 set the stage for subsequent debates and act as a springboard for arguments that appear throughout the book. Chapter 1 provides a tour of the relationship between thought and action. Core themes are established that are woven throughout the book, such as the search for certainty, the centrality of reason and the need to locate writers in specific socio-cultural, economic and political contexts, without assuming that their ideas are devoid of contemporary resonance. Chapter 2 considers the relationship between the passions, experience and the social sciences. This highlights the central role of language in not only reflecting but also constituting the social world.

With reflexivity historically framed, we turn to a critique of ideas of reason through an examination of pragmatic and critical approaches. The pragmatist school of thought is the subject of Chapter 3, linked to ideas about how we might know ourselves and others and different forms of knowledge. We continue the theme of language as constituting meanings and the need for intersubjective understandings. Reflexive relations take us into Chapter 4, this time through considering the works of critical scholars and their consideration of the transformative potential of social science. The context of post-war Europe in shaping the direction of ideas on the relationships between the self, the social world and our means of knowing is the backdrop to these debates.

In Chapter 5 we focus on power and action and turn from Germany to France in examining the works of leading social scientists. In the work of feminist scholars and others who have challenged a particular epistemological canon, we then see how certain issues are not only unavoidable, or impediments to social scientific practice, but also a source of strength of insight. With the increasing rise of forms of scholar-activism that challenge traditional boundaries between research and practice, we consequently focus on the dynamics of science in society in Chapter 6. Linking the co-production of society to the co-production of research, we argue that reflexivity is centred in the production, justification and application of social scientific knowledge in contemporary societies. We introduce the dimensions of endogenous and referential reflexivity and their dynamic interaction in shaping social scientific practice in an era of ambivalence and risk.

We have chosen to highlight those ideas which we have found illuminating and helpful in analysing our joint experiences of undertaking research in and for cities over the past fifteen years. In Chapter 7 we make this explicit through focusing on the contexts, cultures and consequences of the environments in which we have undertaken our work. What we mean by endogenous and referential reflexivity is illustrated through accounts from the field across a wide range of areas, from sustainability to cultural economy. Finally, in Chapter 8, we focus on ideas of the self, identity, belonging, positioning and active intermediation as considerations that need to be taken forward in a reflexive, social scientific practice.

We cover an array of ideas in a short space. This is a key strength of the book and an intellectual project which, we hope, comprises both a depth and breadth to inspire you to enquire further. To achieve this aim we have also sought to bring to life questions of reflexivity in ways that connect with the contemporary world. Hence a major contribution of this book is the exemplification of ideas in areas from literature, science fiction, modern social policies, the economic crash, cities, climate change, lying, promising, propaganda, rhetoric, technology, social movements, creativity and higher education, to name a few. Our examples are designed to illustrate the central themes, as well as amuse and inform your own reflections – leaving no doubt about the ways in which reflexivity is central to the making and shaping of ourselves, social research and society.

THE REFLEXIVE DIFFERENCE

There is an implicit and explicit political-economic context that underpins this narrative at different moments in the book. Societies are changing – in positive and negative ways. If social science is to contribute to beneficial transformations for those in most need, then it must be aware of the conditions, contexts and consequences of its own production. This is our call to action. Reflexivity is not a method, as we discuss in the book, but a set of practices that characterise a mature social science. Ours is not a relativist position; we believe social scientific knowledge production is distinctive and that we can know the social world in better ways and inform more inclusive and sustainable futures. We also believe that there is not enough modesty or honesty about the limits of our tools, ways of seeing and claims about our knowledge. Increasingly, work is conducted not only between social scientific disciplines but also with multiple disciplines and epistemic communities in, and outside of, the university as a site of knowledge production.

Social science can benefit from incorporating insights from diverse viewpoints without collapsing into relativism. We must be careful not to allow the search for innovation in methods to go so far that we lose the distinctiveness of social scientific modes of enquiry – there is a rich lineage and intellectual heritage. Concepts, such as co-production, have much to offer if they are deployed in such a way as to embrace, not erode, recognition of difference. For this to occur, reflexivity must be centred. It is for these reasons that we conclude with ideas of active intermediation as the embodiment of a set of reflexive practices. This recognises the changing boundaries between science and society, justification and application, research and practice, and the pressures that shape the conduct of social scientific work. It does not, however, conflate them, or collapse into paralysis, but focuses on the intellectual practices that are needed in seeking clarification.

Those who seek a quick fix or step-by-step guide that can shortcut the work of understanding should read this book – not because it provides the answer, but because it shows why the idea of such solutions are a fantasy. What we offer is an overview of ideas and practices with which the discerning researcher can arm themself. It is a book for all those who know reflexivity matters and wish to enrich their understanding and practice. To this extent we do not provide a set of methods (although you can find plenty of examples throughout!), which we are doing elsewhere (May and Perry 2018). Instead, our journey helps those who wish to provide justifications for the strengths and limits of their claims to knowledge. We hope by the end of the book you will have gained a sense that reflexivity is a fundamental part of social life, and that the social sciences are core to an understanding and explanation of ourselves and our potentialities in living together.

1

THOUGHT AND KNOWLEDGE IN THE HISTORY OF IDEAS

The demand for certainty is one which is natural to man, but is nevertheless an intellectual vice ... to endure uncertainty is difficult. Dogmatism and scepticism are both, in a sense, absolute philosophies; one is certain of knowing, the other of not knowing. What philosophy should dissipate is certainty, whether of knowledge or ignorance.

(Bertrand Russell 2009[1946]: 38–9)

INTRODUCTION

The search for certainty is one of the most enduring themes of humanity. The question of how we might know ourselves and the world we inhabit has driven a range of responses from the Greek philosophers to the scholars of the Enlightenment and on to the twenty-first-century thinkers of our age. The desire to understand what we are, have been and may become – to explore the very essence of what it means to be human – has given rise to a whole industry of reflexive construction in religion, psychotherapy, psychology, philosophy, politics, art, literature, theatre, technology and the social and physical sciences as a whole. The search for certainty opens up a terrain where reflexivity is often seen to operate at its height: between knowing why we act and acting itself, or between thought and action.

How do we grasp an independent, ambiguous reality in an unambiguous form? This chapter aims to address this question and discuss differences emerging between alternative schools of thought. Those are: *rationalism*, which locates certainty and reason within the uncontaminated human mind, via a separation of thought and action; *empiricism* which places trust in the experiences and senses in order to gain true knowledge of the world; and *scepticism* which embraces the limitations of the mind through emphasising doubt and the uncertainty of all knowledge claims. This history will thus reflect different views on how we should make epistemic judgements. Are those derived from a solitary, reflexive view? Or through a consideration of the kinds of beings we are? Or even by combining reflection and experience grounded in historical consciousness and context?

The changing contexts within which these ideas have been developed were highly significant in shaping their content. Many of the thinkers discussed in this chapter lived around the time of the Enlightenment or 'Age of Reason' (1620s–1780s), coinciding with the scientific revolution: René Descartes (1596–1650) lived during the Thirty Years' War and through conflict and uncertainty in Europe; John Locke (1632–1704) experienced the English Civil War and the Restoration, with its new ideas on liberty and freedom; Immanuel Kant (1724–1804) was influenced by revolution, war, plague, the scientific revolution and the experiential elements of religious teaching in Europe. It is unsurprising that a second enduring theme we can take from these authors to inform our understandings of reflexivity is the importance of context, not only in shaping how they saw the world, but also in how we all gain knowledge of and relate to the world we live in. Extending these insights, there are consequences of these ideas for how scholars have not only theorised the making and governing of communities, economies and societies, but also shaped them through their reflections upon knowledge and society (Siedentop 2015).

Certainty, context and the making of society: these are the three themes that run throughout this chapter. Through a brief tour of what is an extensive and rich history – from the Greek philosophers to Cartesianism, British Empiricism, German Idealism and Materialism – this chapter provides a fusion of insights into questions of individualism, autonomy, freedom, authority and society. It is not exhaustive; rather it highlights key thinkers and debates whose works we need to understand as a basis for a deeper interrogation of concepts and contexts for reflexive thought in the rest of the book.

IN SEARCH OF CERTAINTY

It is often assumed that the Greeks were the first off the starting line for philosophical enquiry. The idea of a mechanistic material world, captured and purified through the realm of ideas, found its outlet in elements of Greek philosophy. Plato (c. 428–348 BC) proposed that the separation between knowing and doing could be achieved by the exercise of reason, abstracted from the particularities of everyday experiences. Plato's forms were proposed as higher realities than the material world which we inhabit and through which we come to know the essence of things. Within such understandings, the world of everyday experience is nothing more than appearance and in a state of flux. The constant, understood by the mind, is the realm of ideas: it is a 'universal' that enables us to escape the dim light that pervades the darkened caves of experience in which we normally reside.

Truth is the purity of thought that captures the essence of reality. Hence, the foundations for knowledge were argued to be provided for through a separation of mind and an independent reality. These ideas informed a politics of differentiation between those that know and those that do. The Platonic idea of the 'philosopher king' was to rule over the affairs of people whose actions raised perplexing circumstances that were resolvable only through the exercise of wisdom. In this, we see the seeds of a transcendental philosophy and ascetic attitude in the pursuit of contemplative ideals, deploying the capacity of reason aimed towards a state of spiritual enlightenment, which has continued to appeal across history.

The attribution of all roots of philosophical thought to the Greeks is problematic. Emphasising the extensive links between Northern Africa and Greece, there is a challenge to the epistemological dominance of the West, citing, for instance, the visits of early Greek scholars to Egypt in search of wisdom: 'a rhetoric of denial of Africa's capability was developed to accompany the dispossession of Africa' (Asante 2004). Whilst efforts to ground alternative epistemologies are increasing, through valorising endogenous ways of being and knowing (see for instance, Nkulu-N'Sengha 2005; Nyamnjoh 2012), these often rely on non-written oral traditions, giving rise to ethno-philosophical studies. The dominance of European, white, male writings in most histories of reflexive thought is readily apparent, not only to the exclusion of African, but also Asian or South American perspectives. The necessity of accessing knowledge through written texts makes this a difficult challenge to overcome. The Greek philosophers, Descartes, Hegel and others have also been critiqued for their gendered philosophies (Amóros 1994; Alanen and Witt 2004), whilst women have been excluded from the philosophical canon, as Mary Ellen Waithe has been credited with saying: 'These women are not women on the fringes of philosophy, but philosophers on the fringes of history' (Witt and Shapiro 2016). The legacy of exclusions and inclusions in philosophy and social research is still felt today, hence we are concerned not only with drawing upon, but also challenging, traditional formations of ways of knowing. We shall return to these themes continuously throughout the book. We start first with René Descartes and the birth of French rationalism.

'I think, therefore I am'

René Descartes (1596–1650) was versed in Greek philosophy including the writings of Plato and his pupil, Aristotle, whose writings on ethics included reflexive understandings of human wellbeing. Aristotle rejected the simple separation between knowing and doing and instead held that every object is both matter and form. His view that the mind does not represent reality as such, but participates in the production of knowledge about objects, raised a troubling question: how can the mind be a locus of certainty about the world when it is influenced by the world itself?

Descartes argued that the mind itself provides certainty and does so through a reflexive turn that discovers its own foundations. Recognising that the mind could be misled, Descartes needed to prove that God would not deceive him. Through his extensive works, he derived one of the most famous phrases in the history of philosophy: 'Cogito ergo sum' ('I think, therefore I am'). As he wrote, 'I find the existence of myself as a thinking being an indubitable fact. It is indubitable only because I clearly and distinctly perceive it; that is the ground of its certainty and must equally be a sufficient ground of the certainty of other judgements. I may therefore take it as a general rule that what is clearly and distinctively perceived is true' (Descartes quoted in Stout 1967: 169).

The search for certainty lay in the capacity to reason, which occurred by withdrawing from the world to ground knowledge of reality via a separation between mind and body. For the Greeks, the emphasis was on first working on ourselves before we are able to work upon knowing the truth: self-making through an ascetic attitude *and* working towards the truth were conjoined. Descartes changed this formulation: 'Before Descartes, one could be impure, immoral, and know the truth. With Descartes, direct evidence is enough. After Descartes, we have a non-ascetic subject of knowledge. This change makes possible the institutionalization of modern science' (Foucault 1997: 279).

Descartes' ideas were taken forward and challenged by scholars such as Gottfried Wilhelm Leibniz (1646–1716), who argued that there were innate properties in the mind and who sought a universal language to express all thoughts, as well as by those such as Jean-Jacques Rousseau (1712–78) who saw human nature as a 'state of reason' corrupted by civilisation and that knowledge resides in sensory experiences. For Rousseau, movement in and through nature was necessary to release the mind from the shackles of society, a theme that finds its resonance today. Box 1.1 illustrates this point and highlights that social scientists need to pay attention to the spatial conditions and contexts which might help or hinder reflexive thought (see also Chapter 7).

■■ Box 1.1 ■■■

Mind, body and reflexive thought

Jean-Jacques Rousseau is one of the most important French philosophers of the Enlightenment. Rousseau's 'virtue epistemology' emphasised how our capacity for sensation can be cultivated to develop judgement and wisdom, moving from the passive reception of experiences to the active process of developing complex ideas and morals (Hanley 2012). To this extent he was a predecessor of Romanticism (see Chapter 2). Rousseau believed that civilisation had generated and corrupted human beings from a 'state of reason': knowledge could be acquired not only by experience, but also through the reflections of the solitary mind. For Rousseau 'being' was as important as 'knowing' and that to both be oneself and know oneself required an immersion in nature. Importantly, it was not only intellectual retreat, but also physical withdrawal from the corrosive influences of society, that informed Rousseau's philosophy. We see this most clearly in his *Reveries d'un Promeneur Solitaire*, published posthumously in 1782. Having felt persecuted, criticised and rejected across Europe, Rousseau could only find peace and 'be himself' on his daily solitary walks, as 'my mind only works with my legs'. The purpose of walking was not to value the innate beauty of the natural world (although Rousseau was a keen botanist), but to value himself. Walking enabled meditations on his inner life; the process of being in nature and of movement through nature acted as a sensory catalyst to grasping his own mind. As he put it in the Seventh Walk, 'Sometimes my reveries end in meditation, but more often my meditations end in reverie; and during these wanderings, my soul rambles and glides through the universe on the wings of imagination, in ecstasies which surpass every other enjoyment' (1922: 91).

Many other writers since have discovered an intuitive connection between walking, movement, thinking and writing, for example Henry David Thoreau, William Wordsworth, Virginia Woolf and Friedrich Nietzsche (Nicholson 2009). Contemporary scholars have undertaken early studies to prove the relationship between walking and creative thinking (Opezzo and Schwartz 2014), enabling our minds to wander through images, thoughts and ideas. Others have focused not on walking but on bodily movements, such as the practice of combining meditation with qigong movements in Chinese spiritual practice. In our 'Age of Distraction', the value of deep, slow, semi-automatic and mechanistic movements – mending motorbikes, home-cooking, gardening, kung fu – is not to be underplayed in efforts to resist 'a culture saturated with technologies … [in which] our interior mental lives are laid bare as a resource to be harvested by others' (Crawford 2015: 247). This connection between mind and body challenges the Cartesian dualism. From literature and spiritualism, psychology and chemistry, many emphasise instead the intrinsic interdependence between mind, body and spirit in knowing the self and the world.

The seventeenth century has been characterised as one that switched from 'philosophical egalitarianism' to a 'scientific hierarchy' (Toulmin 2003: 22). Explanation took on a mechanistic viewpoint expressed in terms of laws and underpinned by mathematical formulations

(Kearney 1971). Descartes was attracted to mathematics as a means of providing certainty through impersonal abstraction. With such developments, the role of science in social life was to change – both through the exercise of Cartesian scepticism concerning everyday life and the desire for predictability in a world increasingly questioning of traditional belief. This foundational legacy remains in contemporary ideas of practice: we provide ourselves with certainty through individualised and isolated acts and the power of moral resources lies only within us. Descartes can be seen as the founder of modern individualism, but he also set us on a quest 'for an order of science, of clear and distinct knowledge in universal terms, which where possible will be the basis of instrumental control' (Taylor 1992: 182).

Mind, exchange and interest

These ideas were to be challenged by the work of John Locke. Whilst Locke read Descartes, he was more attuned to medicine and scientific method and experimentation. Building a lineage for British empiricism, he emphasised experience and induction, with knowledge built upon sensory perception acquired through experimentation. At the same time, he extended the reification of the mind, through insisting that withdrawal and reflection on the operations of our minds are still necessary for experience to be translated into knowledge. Like Descartes, this continued to represent an atomistic and individualistic approach to reflexivity, through the emphasis on a personal responsibility for knowledge acquisition.

From this era, the combination of the scientific revolution with the idea of rational mastery of the self cannot be underestimated. Whilst the artisans and merchants were confident in their handling of things, they also sought ideas to make sense of their lives (Hill 1997[1965]): 'Holding the package together is an ideal of freedom or independence, backed by a conception of disengagement and procedural reasons. This has given Locke's outlook its tremendous influence, not only in the eighteenth century, but right through to today' (Taylor 1992: 174). The construction of the individual in this way, along with the beginnings of modern science, has influenced the practices and presuppositions of modern psychology and economics, often by sidelining uncertainty through particular constructions of the individual.

As with Plato, these ideas had profound consequences for how society should be organised. Locke was part of Social Contract Theory which emerged in the work of those such as Thomas Hobbes (1588–1679). Hobbes was concerned with the search for certainty. He explored the possibility of mathematics and experimentation for this purpose, but recognised the need to appeal to the passions and rhetorical persuasion, without succumbing to scepticism. Hobbes started with self-interest and hence the need for a social contract to prevent life being 'solitary, brutish and short'. Such differences have led to observations that in France we find a tendency for authority to be above the individual, whilst in England a person tended to be seen as the source of their own authority (Hawthorn 1976).

Hobbes was concerned with how individuals, living in isolation, would consent to come together and do so under a particular set of obligations in order to form a society. People both made and were the subjects of the content of the contract itself. Self-interest was assumed to be universal, insofar as people were motivated by the same desires: human laws and nature. In this way he brought what appeared to be incompatible elements together in his work as it 'solves the problem of difference because it makes arithmetic, whose method is capable of producing certain knowledge, an integral part of social and ethical analysis' (Poovey 1998: 108). Putting politics and ideas on the infallibility of science together was no easy task. Whilst some political interventions might rely on 'wit', others needed 'infallible rules'. As scientific knowledge grew more precise, so it would grow away from the understanding of the average citizen and the result would be a greater distance between political knowledge and the everyday experience of citizens. Acceptance of the rules would then be an issue for the populace at large, 'hence the only way that political knowledge could be translated into a shared public philosophy was through imposition by authority and acquiescence by the citizenry' (Wolin 2004: 234). Hobbes' work represented an important point in history. He introduced to political philosophy the idea of 'making' in human affairs: the Real is forged and events are made as they are wished – all of which is ably assisted by science. Therefore 'modern rationalism as it is currently known, with the assumed antagonism of reason and passion as its stock-in-trade, has never found a more clearer and uncompromising representative' (Arendt 1998[1958]: 300).

Within the very different traditions of rationalism and empiricism, a clear focus on the natural sciences could be seen. Box 1.2 highlights key differences, illustrated through a literary example, but what these schools had in common was the search for certainty and an unquestioning adherence for the Truth. To seek to find understanding in the actually existing realm of human activity was regarded as a chaotic endeavour. Within this, a clear hierarchy of knowledge could be seen, expressed in the work of Benedictus Spinoza (1632–77) who formulated a philosophy of life, with experience at the bottom, through to general reasoning, and then finally the deployment of intuition for rational insight as its highest expression.

■■ Box 1.2 ■■■■■■■■■■■■■■■■■■■■■■■■■■■■■■■■■■

Rationalism and empiricism in literature

The epistemological positions of rationalism and empiricism, embodied here through the works of Descartes and Locke, have different consequences for the process of scientific enquiry. Rationalism requires a retreat from the world, to seek knowledge via the inner reflections of the solitary mind. Deductive reasoning is used to reach a true conclusion through establishing premises and working from the general to the particular. Empiricism instead involves gaining knowledge via experiences and sensations, from the facts through induction to more general conclusions.

These positions find their unlikely archetypes in detective fiction, through the works of Agatha Christie (1890–1976) and Arthur Conan Doyle (1859–1930). Christie's Belgian detective,

(Continued)

(Continued)

Hercule Poirot, uses his 'little grey cells' to order reality and sit back, close his eyes and reflect on the cases presented before him in order to draw conclusions. The classic armchair detective, he takes physical clues into account, but does not fully trust them, instead drawing on his rational mind and knowledge of human psychology to solve the problem at hand. Sherlock Holmes, on the other hand, is a close observer and gathers empirical evidence at every point. With his magnifying glass in hand, Holmes is scientifically trained and uses forensics and induction to find clues that will lead him to the truth. Whilst often retiring from the field to think, play the violin or otherwise indulge his senses, it is the evidence that directs him towards solving a case: 'Poirot is the French rationalist par excellence whereas Holmes is the English empiricist pure and simple' (Tostevin 2010: 20). Detective fiction presents an interesting window into these concerns, seen also in the works of Edgar Allan Poe, whose stories 'reject the empirical "scientific" mode of knowledge that was doing so much to revolutionise existing technologies and industries, embracing instead rationalism in a refutation of the values of an industrialising American society' (Thompson 1993: 45).

CONTEXT MATTERS

There are two key consequences of the mode of abstracting universal features through the exercise of reason. First, it ignores the contingent factors that influence our lives and allow for a diversity of experiences; second, it produces a dichotomy between the subjective and objective. It also separates the reflexive capacity of our minds from our bodies, as if the latter were too close to nature with its apparent distorting power of mere appearance and desire. Once we admit of the importance of these issues, the idealisations of the rationalists may be seen as nothing more than projections born of particular positions.

Historical consciousness and the senses

Giambattista Vico (1668–1744) challenged the acontextual, rational self as the source of true knowledge. He drew on the works of scholars such as Francis Bacon to argue for an understanding of ourselves which takes passion and emotion into account. Questioning the utilisation of the natural sciences to know ourselves, he argued that the study of human affairs needed history for understanding. It is the mental states of humankind that determine the course of events and so it is there that we should look for our explanations, with every epoch being dominated by 'a "spirit", a genius, of its own' (Vico 1990[1709]: 73).

For Vico, history has a basis in psychology and requires a scientific attitude different from previous understandings. In advocating the humanities Vico was not against science but scientism. Common sense should be a basis of education: 'I may add that common sense, besides being the criterion of practical judgement, is also the guiding standard of eloquence ... There is a danger that instruction in advanced philosophical criticism may lead to an abnormal growth of abstract intellectualism, and render young people unfit for the practice of eloquence' (Vico 1990[1709]: 13). With excessive attention paid to natural sciences in educational methods, Vico concluded that ethics had been sidelined: 'We neglect that discipline which deals with the differential features of the virtues and vices, with good and bad behaviour-patterns, with the typical characteristics of the various ages of man, of the two sexes, of social and economic class, race and nation, and with the art of seemly conduct in life, the most difficult of all arts. As a consequence of this neglect, a noble and important branch of studies, i.e., the science of politics, lies almost abandoned and untended' (Vico 1990[1709]: 33)

In contrast to the rationalists and empiricists, another group of thinkers were influenced by different lines of thought: for example, the work of Charles-Louis de Secondat de Montesquieu (1689–1755). Montesquieu's investigations on climate, communities, laws and customs were based on a sense of self that is not above society, but located within its networks. Consequently, social explanations are needed for given phenomena. Inequality, for example, was sought in the dynamics of society, not in a return to Rousseau's state of 'natural equality' in which civilisation was a corrupting influence and ignorance had only been replaced by an emphasis on scepticism. Human freedom was paramount and that meant an emphasis on how government could be most efficiently organised to secure it. Montesquieu was also interested in the connections between people's opinions and the nature and structure of society. Through systematic study, he sought explanations of how, in ways previously unsuspected, society forms people as 'social creatures'.

Locating issues in social, cultural and historical contexts posed a fundamental challenge to the presumptions of those who sought to position their ideas as somehow free-floating over external influences. Mary Astell (1668–1731), for example, wrote in her *A Serious Proposal to the Ladies* (Rogers 1979) that differences between the sexes should not be attributed to some examined idea of 'nature' or 'reason', upon which so many thinkers had drawn from the Greeks onwards, but to the power that men held over women in society (Griffiths and Whitford 1988). If Descartes had proclaimed reason in all, then it must also be available to all. Francois Poulain de la Barre also built on Descartes' work to argue for the social equality of men and women in *On the Equality of the Two Sexes* (1673) (Witt and Shapiro 2016). Unlike more explicitly misogynistic philosophies, such as those of Hegel, Descartes' work was seen as providing a basis for female philosophers, such as Madeleine de Scudery and Gabrielle Suchon, to claim reason as a basis for equal education for women (Atherton 1994).

Engagement as a matter of fact

In Scotland there were a group of thinkers who continued this turn to the importance of social context in the formulation of their ideas. The 'Scottish school' included David Hume (1711–76), Adam Smith (1723–90), Adam Ferguson (1723–1816) and John Millar (1735–1801).

Hume accepted that custom plays a central role in guiding lives, whilst ideas of what is right and good are informed by the norms of society. Although there are differences between and within societies, people exhibit common dispositions. In contrast to Cartesian rationalism, Hume believed that impressions come from experiences and they inform complex ideas. Experiential content matters and is not dismissed as mere appearance. Whilst Descartes believed that consistency over time was constituted through the exercise of reason within the individual mind, Hume challenged the idea of unity or coherence in the self – all we find when we look reflexively at ourselves are experiences. In this view, whilst we may have a psychological desire to see unity, there is none – things and people are in flux, and there is no 'self' as an unchanging object of our gaze.

Where earlier thought allowed the mind to discern the properties of the world through the search for causes, Hume argued that this was nothing more than habit and we had no warrant in asserting one thing causes another. Instead, we could only observe constant conjunctions: 'there is no known circumstance, that enters into the connexion and production of the actions of matter, that is not to be found in all the operations of the mind; and consequently we cannot, without a manifest absurdity, attribute necessity to the one, and refuse it to the other' (Hume, quoted in Lenz 1966: 171).

In terms of knowledge, it was now believed that 'Nothing can be known to *exist* except with the help of experience. That is to say, if we wish to prove that something of which we have no direct experience exists, we must have among our premises the existence of one of more things of which we have direct experience' (Russell 1983[1912]: 41–2; original emphasis). The door was now open to find the idea of disengagement from nature and society to be not only problematic, but also impossible. The Scottish School reinforced the idea that we find knowledge in experience, but how do we know that something we have seen in the past will resemble the same thing we will see in the future? This issue is further exacerbated given that each individual is susceptible to prejudices in their judgements. In this we see a form of scepticism, which – as we see in Box 1.3 – involves not the search for certainty but the invocation of doubt.

■■ Box 1.3 ■■■■■■■■■■■■■■■■■■■■■■■■■■■■■■■■■■■■

Scepticism and the importance of doubt

In emphasising that much of our alleged knowledge involves beliefs that cannot be rationally justified, Hume has been described as a 'radical sceptic' (Meeker 2013), introducing the idea of doubt and the limits to knowledge. Taken to extremes, scepticism involves a rejection of the search for certainty and suspending judgement and belief. 'Global' or 'philosophical' scepticism denies the possibility of there being any certain knowledge as we may always be misled by our senses, our minds or others. This is not what Hume was proposing. Descartes had earlier raised the spectre of scepticism in his search for certainty through examining dreams, a deceiving God and an evil demon. Cartesian scepticism concerning the possibility of certain knowledge has also been updated through Putnam's (1981) thought experiment 'Brain in a Vat' hypothetical scenario: how do we know we are not simply a brain in a jar, hooked up to a massive computer that is simulating the external world through feeding us experiences and insights? We see this metaphor infiltrating popular science fiction genres, particularly the *Matrix* trilogy (1999–2003) directed by Andy and Lana Wachowski. Here characters learn to distrust everything about themselves and the external world as they move through layer upon layer of deception and artifice, 'exposing us to the uncomfortable worries of philosophical scepticism in an especially compelling way' (Erion and Smith 2002: 29).

Whilst it has strong epistemological roots, the more popular use of the adjective 'sceptic' has different connotations. 'Eurosceptics' are not making any epistemological arguments, but are defined through a sense of distrust or suspicion of the European project. 'Climate change sceptics', on the other hand, purport to question the basis of knowledge claims and evidence of causality – taking aim at the certainty of science and appealing to a wider public distrust in scientific and technological developments (see also Chapter 6). Despite the overwhelming scientific consensus and geographic and partisan affiliations of those involved, climate change scepticism focuses on undermining the credibility of attempts to draw causal inferences and reach certain conclusions via doubt and uncertainty. This draws attention to the fine line between doubt, scientific knowledge and politics – and with it the need for reflexivity about our knowledge claims.

If our sense of who we are and what we know is limited through the particulars of our experiences, then what warrant does any thinker have for the basis of these reflections, limited as they are by the same constraints that befall us all? Is all belief just unbelievable? Hume does not go this far, and instead 'suggests that the unity of personality can be assimilated to that of a republic or commonwealth whose members unceasingly change but whose ties of association remain' (Ricoeur 1994: 128). Hume did not subscribe to atomistic ideas of the reflexive self whose mind's eye captures the Real through disengagement. His argument for the partiality of our knowledge and role of the passions in our judgements may be seen as revealing the necessity to admit to the importance of context in coming to know who we are and what we might hope for. In understanding our actions and perceptions we need to regard engagement as a matter of fact. Indeed, George Berkeley took this even further and argued that material reality was nothing more than a collection of ideas and the only reality was sensation!

Two issues arise from these latter contributions. First, the problem of induction: imprisoned by the particularity of our perspectives, how can we have general knowledge? Second, given this state of affairs, how is society possible? If people have different ideas, experiences and passions, what can they have in common? What norms and values might guide the coordination of actions among such persons? Addressing these questions points to the need to both accept and embrace our limitations. If we cannot rely on the generalising properties of reason to escape our experiences, the latter is all we have. There is no divine purpose of which we are a part. In these respects, Hume's aim was 'to show the house that as humans we had to live in. We anatomise the moral sentiments, in all their ultimate metaphysical arbitrariness, could-have-been-otherwiseness, in order to accept them, endorse them, know what address we are living at. Even the disengagement serves the end of an ultimate engagement' (Taylor 1992: 345).

Hume rejects ideas of 'original contracts' or 'states of nature' in his writings on justice and property, and notes how people have more needs than can be satisfied. He also gave consideration to 'ties of association' in the coordination of life. It is society, with its conventions and rules, which provides a sense of justice in conditions of scarcity. Ideas of a common good were displaced in Hume's writings because the passions, not reason, directed moral judgement. Passions have a role in self-preservation, but equally we have an instinctive sense of what is acceptable and unacceptable as the moral basis of a society. It is for these reasons that the twentieth-century laissez-faire economist Friedrich August von Hayek regarded Hume as undertaking no less than a general science of human nature, in which morals and politics were as important as sources of knowledge. For Hayek, Hume was 'not merely the founder of the modern theory of knowledge, but also one of the founders of economic theory' (1968: 339). If reason had any role, it was simply to determine the best means to achieve what the passions desired. This is manifest now in mainstream economics textbooks which teach that calculation informs the rational pursuit of desired ends in market-based societies. We shall return to this question in Chapter 2 when we consider the concept of the 'Will'.

In the work of the economist Adam Smith, we can see the alignment of this position on moral and economic behaviour: both are informed by individual desire, without any supposition that actions might also be intended to promote the good of society. Humans like to barter and exchange, and unlike animals have a need for each other in terms of different talents and dispositions. The system of coordination that allows this to take place is the 'hidden hand' of the market. A spectator idea of moral good arises in Smith's work in which the person observing the work of another experiences a similar form of virtue in the act itself which does not harm others and is of some benefit to society as a whole. As he puts it: 'Each animal is still obliged to defend itself, separately and independently, and derives no sort of advantage from that variety of talent with which nature has distinguished its fellows. Among men, on the contrary, the most dissimilar geniuses are of use to one another; the different produces of their respective talents, by the general disposition to truck, barter, and exchange, being brought, as it were, into a common stock, where every man may purchase whatever part of the produce of other men's talents he has occasion for' (Smith in Parsons et al. 1965: 105).

Instrumental use to one another is based on an individualistic, subjective moral outlook that others cannot adequately judge. Consequently, the role of government is assumed to be limited. Taking their lead from one of the founders of the Scottish Enlightenment, Francis Hutcheson, Millar and Ferguson were to focus on securing 'the survival of civil society, by a constitutionally regulated system of government without repression and encroachment on liberties spelling the end of the active or participatory virtues and eventually the public political spirit itself' (Strydom 2000: 217). We find a concern with this balance not only in the works of liberals such as Locke, Hume, Smith, Millar and Ferguson, but also right through to the Utilitarians and John Stuart Mill who wrote that 'It is not by wearing down into uniformity all that is individual in themselves, but by cultivating it and calling it forth, within the limits imposed by the rights and interests of others, that human beings become a noble and beautiful object of contemplation' (1974[1859]: 127). In this tradition we find an attempt to reconcile freedom and authority. These writers appear to solve this 'by destroying authority in the name of liberty and replacing it by society, but only at the cost of exposing freedom to society's controls' (Wolin 2004: 314).

ENDURING CONCEPTS: REASON AND SCEPTICISM RETURN

The thinkers discussed thus far held opposing views on how we, as fallible humans, can first know ourselves and then the world: Descartes focused on non-association via withdrawal, doubt, and finally the exercise of reason; Hume reached sceptical conclusions regarding the idea that a science of cognition is anything more than mental projections into a world based on custom. Traditions of thought emphasised different sources of authority in the search for certainty and varied consequences for how society should be organised. At the same time, contexts were changing and concepts being revisited. In Germany, under the influence of change, revolution and plague, idealism was rooting reason back in history, drawing on the writings of Rousseau, Leibniz and Hume. Pietism was also influential, with its roots in Lutheranism and an emphasis upon the experiential elements of religious teaching and in German deism, with its view that the existence of God may be established through reason (Appelbaum 1995).

Reason and being in history

Against this background, along with the scientific revolution, embodied in the works of Isaac Newton, Immanuel Kant (1724–1804) was awoken from his 'dogmatic slumbers'. Here was a thinker who was to restore metaphysics into an understanding of ourselves and the world around us. Kant's 'Copernican Revolution in philosophy was to invert the relationship between mind and world by theorizing human consciousness as the constitutive formal nexus of all possible objectivity and knowledge' (Sandywell 1996: 173).

Kant's ideas are highly complex. He sought to reconcile elements of rationalism and empiricism. He did not adhere to dogmatic metaphysics, but held onto the importance of the mind in relation to the external world and the validity of scientific conclusions. Although agreeing with the empiricists that there are no innate ideas and that the thing-in-itself exists independent of our experience, he also argued that all experience conformed to knowledge. A major contribution was to insist that categories in the mind are essential to make sense of our experiences. According to Kant, we come to understand the world through a set of *apriori* concepts – for example, space, time, causality, quantity and quality. These categories enable us to see the *phenomena* of the world, rather than their true reality (*noumena*). If we apply these categories to our experiences, we can order them in a sense-making activity, taking care not to confuse our perceptions with knowing the thing-in-itself. Kant made a clear separation between concepts and sensations. In this we can see the legacy of the Greeks, in particular Aristotle, who developed a series of philosophical categories without which scientific thought would not be possible.

How we represent things to others in our judgements then matters: it is this taking-into-account of others that increases our forms of representation, which are then neither simply objective, nor subjective. Objects of our consciousness may be produced through how we represent them – the properties of these objects are determined by the intellect. Alternatively, objects may appear within us, in which case they are determined along with the object itself. What is missing, however, is something that appears to stand before all acts of representation. Here Kant introduces the spectre of self-consciousness: awareness of oneself, others and things, but through a clear distinction between the subjective and objective. It is this distinction between sensation and thought that is so influential. As a study on the history of scientific objectivity puts it, 'By the mid-nineteenth century, dictionaries and handbooks in English, French, and German credited Kantian critical philosophy with the resuscitation and redefinition of the scholastic terminology of the objective and subjective' (Daston and Galison 2010[2007]: 206).

In his studies of how the mind constructed the objective world, Kant found his solution in 'a universal subject that, to the extent it was universal, could be the subject of knowledge, but which demanded, nonetheless, an ethical attitude' (Foucault 1997: 279). We may refer to this as the primary principle of human knowledge – the 'I' as in 'I think'. As Johann Fichte (1762–1814), the post-Kantian idealist put it, this 'actually appears within consciousness as something real, although not as a *thing in itself*; for were the I to appear within consciousness as a thing in itself, then idealism would cease to be what it is and would be transformed into dogmatism. Instead, the object of idealism appears within consciousness as an *I in itself*. It does not appear there as an object of experience, for it is nothing determinate, but is determined solely by me, and without this determination it is nothing whatsoever and does not exist at all. Instead, it appears within consciousness as something elevated above all experience' (1994: 13, original emphasis).

Fichte takes the existence of the 'I' as a given, which is not provable in any way, but necessary. He fuses an awareness of the transcendental condition of our consciousness with the moral ideal of autonomy to produce both freedom and self-consciousness together: 'In the sphere of practical philosophy human beings become persons in the full sense of the word by attaining a reflexive knowledge of the world-work of the Transcendental Ego' (Sandywell 1996: 174–5). Fichte's contribution to a transcendental idealism was to extend

Kant's emphasis on consciousness through highlighting the need to reflect on the process of consciousness itself.

The basis of human knowledge is the initial Act of Consciousness and it is through reflecting on this process itself that we bring ourselves into being. As Joseph Schelling, a student of Fichte's, put it, 'this Being which is assumed as prior to knowledge is no being, even it is not knowledge either; it is real self-positing, it is primal and basic willing which makes itself into something and is the basis and foundation of all essence' (1992[1936]: 63). It is for such reasons that Bertrand Russell regards Fichte as carrying 'subjectivism to a point which seems almost to involve a kind of insanity' (1955: 744). Fichte critiqued Descartes' foundational claims, but exhibited an ambivalence encapsulated in his 'adherence to the traditional idea of knowledge as demonstrable and demonstrated on the one hand, and the conclusion to which he himself comes in his own analysis of the theory of knowledge, that claims to know are finally indemonstrable' (Rockmore 1994: 100). This is significant. The foundationalist thrust of his argument comes from the influence of Kant extended through the work of Karl Reinhold (1757–1823) in terms of specifying the grounds for knowledge. Yet from a reflexive point of view, can we both make consciousness possible through the Act and at the same time be aware that we are acting? 'The inconsistency is that if the Act is prior to and a condition of consciousness, we cannot also be aware of its intellectual intuition' (Rockmore 1994: 102).

What we have is a chicken-and-egg situation – what comes first, the 'I' or awareness of the 'I'? How can we have one without the other? 'Since thought needed to be like its object in order to know it, and since reality itself was circular or spherical, thought also must be circular' (Rockmore 1994: 104). Such views were rejected by Aristotle and Kant, but strongly shaped Fichte's ambivalence concerning necessary but not provable first principles, as indicated in his writings on *Foundations on the Entire Wissenschaftslehre* (Doctrine of Scientific Knowledge). In insisting that the first principles of science must be assumed but are not provable, Fichte held a non-foundationalist view: instead of searching for certainty, all we can ever hope for is probability. Perhaps we are not subjects whose reflexive relations to our consciousness enable us to stand at the centre of reality, but are instead finite and caught in circumstances which always elude a full understanding? We will find these issues appearing again and again in this study: for example, in a non-foundationalist view of knowledge which is apparent in the work of Jean-François Lyotard (see Chapter 5). In this respect, as well as in the tradition of German Idealism as a whole, Fichte is a major thinker whose work still resonates with contemporary issues.

As we enter the nineteenth century we do so at a time of French and American revolutions and contestations over their sources and meaning, as exemplified in the writings of the conservative Edmund Burke (1729–97) and the more radical Thomas Paine (1737–1809). They developed ideas on the self into arguments about the roles of government. As we see in Box 1.4, such was the significance of these debates that they continue to influence the organisation of societies today.

■ **Box 1.4** ■■■

Finding the self in society

From his *Philosophical Enquiry into the Sublime and the Beautiful*, Edmund Burke charts a different path from the Cartesian dualists and the principles of rationalism and humanism by locating the source of knowledge in the body and the emotions and passions. This privileging of the 'sense-experience over the intellect' (Jeter 2014) results in a three-step process in acquiring knowledge: the pleasures of the senses; the pleasures of the imagination; and the conclusions of the reasoning faculty. It is this emphasis on emotions and experience that he takes into his propositions for the roles of state and community in the organisation of social life. Burke is perhaps best known for the following statement: 'to be attached to the subdivision, to love the little platoon we belong to in society, is the first principle (the germ as it were) of public affections. It is the first link in the series by which we proceed towards a love of our country and to mankind' (Eberly and Streeter 2002: viii). In this he was referring both to the importance of ties between members in social subdivisions and to the desire of people to seek security in the traditions of authority and morality. It is for these reasons that Burke is sometimes seen as the father of modern conservatism. He was actually rallying against the French Revolution and in favour of a strong role for the aristocracy in ordering society.

More recently, his ideas have been taken as the foundation of the UK Conservative Party's concept of the 'Big Society' in which state functions are delivered by community and third-sector organisations. Jesse Norman, a British Conservative MP, has argued that Burke's ideas underpin the concept of the Big Society, as opposed to Big Government, which is pro-social, anti-statist and conservative. Combining both the rhetoric of community engagement and top-down paternalism (B. Taylor 2013), the Big Society is seen to draw on many other influences – including the radical social action in 1930s Chicago of Saul Alinsky, the cooperative movement which started in Rochdale in 1844 and Robert Putnam's theory of social capital (House of Commons 2011). That one concept can be claimed by such different traditions illustrates the power of rhetoric, language and politics in linking rival ideas of the self to ideas of society, a theme we continue in Chapter 2.

Georg Wilhelm Friedrich Hegel (1770–1831) was one thinker who built on the legacies of Kant and Fichte in terms of thinking about the limitations to knowing ourselves and the worlds we inhabit. In so doing he transposed 'the epistemological limitation into ontological fact: the void of our knowledge corresponds to a void in being itself, to the ontological incompleteness of reality' (Žižek 2012: 149). Hegel invoked relations between reason and history, but without turning us into atomised and isolated subjects whose ethical acts and basis of knowledge rest upon the exercise of practical reason. Human 'being' must be defined, not as something external to people but through the internal relation within and between people. For Hegel, reality is linked to the process of our becoming as rooted in history; reason could become manifest in history which unfolds in dialectic from thesis and antithesis to synthesis. Hegel examined the unfolding of societies over time according to a Spirit: 'This self-contained existence of Spirit is none other than self-consciousness – consciousness of one's own being. Two things must be distinguished in consciousness; first, the fact *that I know*; secondly, *what I know*. In *self* consciousness these are merged in one; for Spirit *knows itself*. It involves an appreciation of its own nature, as also an energy enabling it to realize itself; to make itself *actually* that which it is *potentially*. According to this abstract definition it may be said of Universal History, that it is the exhibition of Spirit in the process of working out the knowledge of that which it is potentially. And as the germ bears in itself the whole nature of the tree, and the taste and form of its fruits, so do the first traces of Spirit virtually contain the whole of that History' (1991: 17–18; original emphasis).

Hegel's *Phänomenologie des Geistes* (1807) was a study of how minds appear to themselves. Kant had argued that reality could never be known as it was, but only comprehended through the a priori categories of thought. These, to recap, are not part of reality, but the means through which it is grasped – the instruments we deploy to understand reality, rather than reality itself. The separation between our being and knowledge of reality forms the basis of Hegel's critique of Kant's epistemology: 'The empirical principle that Kant retained by making reason dependent on "given" objects of experiences is here completely rejected. In Kant, Hegel declares, reason is limited to an inner realm of the mind and is made powerless over "things-in-themselves"' (Marcuse 1969: 48).

For Hegel the starting point for knowing reality is consciousness of that reality. Through examination we can discover the limitations of consciousness; this enables the development of more sophisticated forms of consciousness and so on ... until 'absolute knowledge' is reached. Hence, there is no need for a Kantian 'appearance of reality' as knowledge can be gained of reality itself. Hegel regards knowledge as historically constituted, linking 'being' with history: 'History is the substance of society, since the substance of society is nothing more than continuity. Humanity's being therefore lies in its historicity' (Heller 1984: 28). The 'ideal' is then to realise our potential in reality. We are learning subjects whose knowledge of who we are and what we know is a dialectical process of reflection rooted in history. Hegel acknowledged Kant's achievements and built upon these through 'true forms of thought' expressed in a unity of opposites through the triad of 'subject, object, and their synthesis' (Marcuse 1969: 49).

In contrast to liberal individualists, such as Rousseau, Hegel saw that freedom needs to be acquired and won, through the discipline of knowledge, willpower and the development of self-consciousness. People are socially constituted and so there must be a relation between our internal consciousness and the external sphere of the societies we inhabit: a social means through which we are recognised as 'free agents'. The means is 'possession' and its social manifestation is 'property' (see Ryan 1986). To return to an earlier discussion, there must be some regulatory relation between the seeking of individual ends and the wider society in order that it is both maintained and reasonably stable. It is at this point we find Hegel's critique of atomism, including social contract theory and his reading of British political economy.

Hegel finds his answers in writings on the State and ethical forms of life in ties of association that provide for both unity and the promotion of individuality. The State is a fusion between self-consciousness and its objective manifestation in social, political and economic relations. The rights of the individual and universal reason can thereby be united and the social problems created by competitive societies tempered. What Hegel termed 'civil society' may be moderated by this higher unity, without which there would be an 'alienation of the spirit'. By this, Hegel meant the duality within people to regard their freedom as freedom from the constraints of the material world and to strive to be purely spiritual, whilst at the same time recognising that they are part of that world and thus cannot escape nor transcend it. This suggests that reflexivity is a task that needs to take account of the facticity of existence.

There can be no doubt that Hegel's work has continued importance for our understanding. In his theory of recognition (see Chapter 4), Axel Honneth has taken the insights of authors, including the young Hegel, to make the point that they 'wanted to imagine a future of modern society in such a way that it brought forth a new, open value-system, within the horizon of which subjects learn to esteem each other mutually with regard to their freely-chosen life-goals' (Honneth 1996: 178). Yet Hegel, as with us all, is a product of his time. We can see this in, for example, his writings on the State, where he cannot conceive of the formation of political will as anything other than residing in a monarch, or his misogynistic constructions of 'cunning' as a female characteristic.

Søren Kierkegaard (1813–55), who set the stage for existentialism, felt that allusions to spirit undermined the importance of subjectivity, individual choice, the truth and the role of the particular over the general. He was not, however, the only critic of Hegel. Ludwig Feuerbach (1804–72) was a 'Young Hegelian' who examined the ideas and role of 'religion' and 'God' in Hegel's writings, but in so doing adopted a position opposed to it. Broadly speaking, he argued that God was a creation of human beings and not the other way round, arguing for an anthropological rather than philosophical basis for knowledge: 'Everlasting happiness will begin with the transformation of the kingdom of heaven into a republic of earth' (Marcuse 1969: 267). The figure that stood between Feuerbach's writings and these reflections of Herbert Marcuse was another young Hegelian: Karl Marx.

Making societies

The Industrial Revolution in Britain took place in the late eighteenth century, alongside the French Revolution. This was a time of extraordinary growth in wealth, in which attempts to organise labour were met with the deployment of armed forces in France and Britain to quash uprisings – all of which contributed to the making of the English working class (Hobsbawm 1962; E.P. Thompson 1968). By the revolution of 1848 famines, uprisings and numerous conflicts had taken place. Alternative advocates to this forward march of capital, namely the followers of Claude Henri de Saint-Simon (1760–1825) in France and Robert Owen in Wales (1771–1858), had dissipated. Saint-Simon, with his notion of a science of society expressed in terms of 'social physiology', regarded a moral vacuum as underlying social disorganisation. His influence was to continue in the work of Auguste Comte (1798–1857) and, later, Emile Durkheim (1858–1917). The followers of Robert Owen turned their 'intellectual energies to spiritualism and secularism, their practical energies to the modest field of cooperative stores' (Hobsbawm 1975: 158).

In the face of these circumstances, Karl Marx and his friend and collaborator Friedrich Engels took forward their writings under the influence of German philosophy, French political thought and British political economy. Marx engaged with epistemo-logical and ontological debates and linked the search for certainty to the material conditions under and through which we live. In *The Economic and Philosophical Manuscripts of 1844*, Marx praised Feuerbach as the only person who had taken a critical attitude to Hegelian dialectics. He regarded Feuerbach's achievements as demonstrating that philosophy was nothing but religion expressed in thought. He sought to establish a real science through making the relations between people the principle of his theory and demonstrating that the transcendental is nothing more than that which affirms theology. In the process he regarded Hegel's idea that speculative thought would end in absolute knowledge as 'nothing but the estranged mind of the world thinking within its self-estrangement – i.e. comprehending itself abstractly' (Marx 1981: 129).

Whilst Hegel argued that social relations were dependent upon the 'Idea of the State' man-ifested in reason, Marx argued that consciousness did not create institutions but the material conditions under which people actually lived: 'To Hegel, the life-process of the human brain, i.e., the process of thinking, which, under the name of "the Idea", he even transforms into an independent subject, is the demiurgos of the real world, and the real world is only the external, phenomenal form of "the Idea". With me, on the contrary, the ideal is nothing else than the material world reflected by the human mind, and translated into forms of thought' (Marx 1983: 29). For Marx, it is not spiritual attitudes that shape us and society, but the wealth people have, their labour and the ruling interests in particular epochs. Our reflexive difficulties are not given by the ways we relate to ourselves, but to the world as a whole, structured as it is by the concentration of power in the hands of relatively few: 'In the social production of their life, men enter into definite relations that are indispensable and inde-pendent of their will, relations of production which correspond to a definite stage of development of their material productive forces. The sum total of these relations of produc-tion constitutes the economic structure of society, the real foundation, on which rises a legal and political superstructure and to which correspond definite forms of social consciousness' (Marx 1980: 181).

Marx embarked upon an empirical examination of capitalism and a critique of the nar-rowness of the economic ideas that seek to provide for its legitimacy. Economic exchange is not some 'accidental fact': 'The only wheels which political economy sets in motion are greed and the war amongst the greedy – competition' (Marx 1981: 62). Labour and the need to sell labour to capital, for the extraction of surplus value, oil the capitalist machine for the benefit of the few, not the many. Although Hegel was correct to connect 'being' to social relations and restore history and meaning to the human realm, he was wrong to view this in terms of something called 'will'. For Marx, the implications of this position were clear: 'What is society, whatever its form may be? The product of men's reciprocal action. Are men free to choose this or that form of society? By no means. Assume a particular state of development in the productive faculties of man and you will get a particular form of commerce and consumption. Assume particular stages of development in production, commerce and consumption and you will have a corresponding social constitution' (Marx to Annenkov in Marx and Engels 1953: 40).

Marx moves us from relations of personal dependence in earlier societies to those founded on material dependence and from there to relations of trade, luxury, money and exchange values: 'Exchange, negotiated through exchange value and money, implies a universal independence between the producers, but at the same time the complete isolation of their private interests and a division of labour, whose unity and mutual fulfillment exists as an external, natural relationship, independent of the individuals. The tension between universal supply and demand constitutes the social network that binds the indifferent individuals together' (Marx 1979: 78–9).

Many insightful volumes have been written on the legacies and importance of Marx and Engels for contemporary times (see, for example, Derrida 1994; Gibson-Graham 1996; Žižek 2009; Holloway 2010; Harvey 2014). It is not difficult to find examples in popular media which support the view of Marx as the thinker we should turn to in order to understand the dynamics of capitalism and its effects upon our lives in the twenty-first century. As Mills noted, 'the "social science" in the name of which Marxism is ignored or rejected is, more often than not, a social science having little or no concern with the pivotal events and the historic acceleration characteristic of our immediate times' (1963: 12).

Different traditions of Marxist thought have developed which have implications for our study of reflexivity, given by the dynamic interplay between subject and object. At times his followers have led us to ask, 'if the moral impoverishment of advanced capitalism is what so many Marxists agree that it is, whence are these resources for the future to be derived?' (MacIntyre 1985: 262). This leads to a whole difference in traditions between the more positivist Marx – with the law-like unfolding of history to an end state of communism – and the Marx of *praxis* – whereby the fusion of practice, experience and theory leads to greater self-consciousness, and with that the overthrow of a repressive regime that disadvantages the many and benefits the few. These ideas have been mobilised in support of multiple causes, not least feminism, as writers have sought to make sense of how capitalism produces and reproduces systemic marginalisations and exclusions. We will return to these issues when we discuss social scientific knowledge and action in Chapters 3 and 5.

SUMMARY: REFLEXIVITY ROOTED

We have been though a fast-paced journey to explore the roots of reflexivity. We have examined the history of ideas and their relation to reflexivity in terms of the exercise of reason, the senses, social institutions, customs, and the forces and relations of capitalist production. Writings have oriented around different poles of thought. Ontological concerns about the nature of things are reflected in the different traditions of idealism and materialism; epistemological reflections on the basis for knowledge are addressed through rationalism, empiricism and scepticism. For some, self-consciousness and reason place us at the centre of the world, providing for a duality between the mind and the world or between the subjective and objective. For others, we can see the importance of context, social relations and material conditions in shaping what we are and the basis of knowledge claims.

Each emerging discipline over the course of this history seeks its monopoly on the questions of what and how we know and with what consequences. Yet whilst the search for certainty underpins this journey, the extent to which thinkers and writers are bound up in their own contexts and circumstances is clear. They were influenced in different ways by civil unrest, war, theology and the scientific revolution, and the Age of Enlightenment. A central theme is that of individualism and individuality as thinkers sought to make sense of who we are and why we act. Are we governed by our passions or our reason, our emotions or our intellect? As this period gave way to the Romantic era, these questions took centre stage with a backlash against scientific rationality and an increasing focus on the 'Will' in accounting for human action as a reaction against reason and certainty.

2

WILL, INTERPRETATION AND BEING

━━ **CHAPTER CONTENTS** ━━━━━━━━━━━━━━━━━━━━━━━━━━━━━━

Granted that nothing is 'given' as real except our world of desires and passions, that we can rise or sink to no other reality than the reality of our drives – for thinking is only the relationship of these drives to one another.

(Friedrich Nietzsche in Hollingdale 1977: 228)

INTRODUCTION

In the last chapter we examined the history of ideas and their relation to reflexivity in terms of the exercise of reason, the senses, social institutions, customs, history and, finally, the forces and relations of capitalist production. We distinguished between different schools of thought on how we know ourselves, as human beings, and how these conceptions influenced the methods and techniques deployed to study and know the social world. We saw how 'mind' became a concern as it places a knowing subject at the centre of the universe in the pursuit of knowledge as certainty. Equally, the rise of a positivistic attitude focused on the application of rules and procedures.

This chapter resumes the narrative of how particular debates have influenced the relationship between individuals and society. A fundamental difference arises between those thinkers who seek certainty in the mind, characterising people as rational creatures, and those that seek certainty in method. If we are governed by our passions and can only know the world through experience and sensation, how is general knowledge possible? This question now bridges the nineteenth and twentieth centuries in guiding us through debates on reflexivity. We continue this exploration around three themes: the 'Will', interpretation and Being.

Interpretations of the human condition encompass multi-faceted elements. On the one hand we see the utilitarian focus on moulding social environments around particular worldviews; on the other, reactions against individualism through developing rules and laws to govern and temper our passions and desires. Cutting through such concerns is the idea of the 'Will', explored by writers such as Arthur Schopenhauer (1788–1860) and Friedrich Nietzsche (1844–1900). This leads to a fundamental questioning of the basis of our knowledge, taken up in the works of Max Weber (1864–1920) who was concerned with the relationship between facts, values and interpretations. Weber tackled issues relating to subjectivity and objectivity and his work was influential, along with that of others such as Wilhelm Dilthey (1833–1911), in leading us to focus on abstraction and interpretation in social scientific practice.

With an emphasis on the 'Will' and the researcher as active interpreter, the importance of lived experience and knowing ourselves as 'Beings' is explored through the works of Edmund Husserl (1859–1938), Martin Heidegger (1889–1976) and Maurice Merleau-Ponty (1908–61). Finally, acknowledging ourselves in these ways means that we can know the world only through our interpretations of it. Hence the tools and discursive means of representation take centre stage, with an emphasis on the role of language in mediating between experience and social science, as seen in the works of Alfred Schutz (1899–1959). By the end of this chapter, we will see how reflexivity takes centre stage in an acknowledgement of the partiality of our accounts of both ourselves and the world.

THE WILL AND REPRESENTATION

Rationalism, as advocated by Descartes and those that followed him, emphasised the capacity of reason in bringing about greater progress, with implications for the reflexive framing of social science through deduction. For some, this was underpinned by allusions to a transcendental deity in whose image we should act, abandoning our desires in order to be closer to God. Hence a responsibility to acquire certainty through thought and knowledge, along with a strong sense of duty, were merged. Such a view was rejected by those within the empiricist school of thought, who focused on individuals acting according to their passions and desires, with different implications for how we see ourselves and social scientific methods through induction. One of the key themes for these thinkers was how to reframe the relationship between the individual and society.

Individualism and society

Building on the works of Hume, Jeremy Bentham (1748–1832) was to take this issue seriously. He focused on individual utility, by which he meant the extent to which any object or act would produce notions of benefit, advantage, pleasure or good, and prevent such things as unhappiness or pain (Bentham 2007 [1789]). Within the tradition of liberalism and with a focus on the individual's experience, Bentham proposed an art of governing that focused on happiness as a human goal. This is why he was often described as an ethical hedonist because he believed that the morality of actions would be judged by whether they produced more pleasure than pain. These ideas, whilst subject to extensive critique, gave rise to a focus on utilitarianism as a means of balancing individual freedoms and desires with those of collective society.

These works influenced other thinkers of the time, including Herbert Spencer (1820–1903) and John Stuart Mill (1806–73), both of whom were immersed in the political culture of English individualism. Mill saw that society changed rapidly, but that human nature was a constant from which social science could construct laws. Spencer, on the other hand, held an evolutionary view of society that combined a radical individualism with a collectivist organicism. Layered on top of the discoveries and writings of Charles Darwin (1809–82), this view proved popular among those who sought to justify the worldviews of particular Victorian classes as they cast their moral gaze upon what was assumed to be the lower strata. That, in turn, had an influence upon the development of social policy (Titmuss 1976; May 1991).

Charles Renouvier (1815–1905) was concerned to define what makes humans unique and combine individuality with self-determination and free will. In this work we find a 'Kantian concern with the dignity and autonomy of the individual together with his theory of social cohesion based on the individual's sense of unity with and dependence on others; his preference for justice over utility and denial that the first can be derived from the second' (Lukes 1981: 55). This philosophy is said to have formed the basis for the political culture of the French Third Republic. Yet whilst Renouvier rejected universal laws, others felt this was exactly what was needed to curb the free will, passions and desires of humans. Whilst we may choose our actions, are we free to carry them out? What if passions and emotions lead to poor consequences? How can we regulate free will in such a way that it makes society possible?

Auguste Comte (1798–1857), widely acknowledged as the founder of positivism, paid attention to the social dimension of science with an explicit goal for the reorganisation of society through social progress. With a motto of 'Order and Progress', Comte is famous for his three laws: theological, metaphysical and positive. Where the first seeks explanations in God, the second focuses on abstract entities and the third (for Comte the 'natural state') stops looking for causes and looks instead at the laws governing them. For Comte, science is a *'connaissance approchée'*, which comes closer and closer to truth, without reaching it. From Comte we also inherit a classification of the sciences that informs the epistemic boundaries between these today.

Emile Durkheim (1858–1917) devoted his thoughts to these processes under the influence of those for whom morals were an appropriate topic for the scientific gaze, such as Kant. Like Comte, Durkheim believed that people are governed by their passions and need external moderation. Society imposes limits on human desires and there is no antagonism between the State and the Individual: 'Nothing could be more contrived than this so-called antagonism ... The truth is that the State has been quite the opposite – the liberator of the individual. It is the State which, as it grew stronger, freed the individual from private and local groups which tended to absorb him: the family, the city, the corporation, etc.' (Durkheim 1992[1899]: 57). In well-regulated societies, limits are set on individual propensities and laissez-faire does not bring peace to our lives. Durkheim thus resisted atomistic tendencies disguised as arguments for liberty and the utilitarian forward march of individualism. Morals and ethics matter.

Other thinkers developed views related not to the search for societal consensus, but the analysis of conflict. We see this in the works of Karl Marx and Max Weber, Georg Simmel (1858–1915) and Ferdinand Tönnies (1855–1936), who rejected both general laws of development towards some end state applicable to the human realm and any prescription for human ends in scientific means. What all these efforts to theorise the relationship between individuals and society have in common is the primary recognition that individual actions are informed by passions and desires. What makes us individuals is not just our capacity for reason, but our Will. As unique individuals, how can we then know ourselves, others and the world we live in?

Where there's a will ...

For those constituting the era of Romanticism, progress was not to be achieved through the triumph of reason but recognition of the passions. Poets and novelists were reflecting on a life where reason is not sufficient. Wollstonecraft, Goethe, Wordsworth, Byron, Austen and Dickens, to name a few, dealt with the situated realities of life including those things ruled out by Descartes, such as the body and desire, focusing on emotions in making us who and what we are. Influenced by these reflections, Arthur Schopenhauer (1788–1860) argued that the `Will' governed our lives. Our bodies are situated in time and space and no allusion to a priori concepts can overcome the fact of irresistible drives.

Schopenhauer took Kant's idea of 'thing-in-itself' as being the 'Will': what we can only know is being aware of ourselves as an expression of the will-to-live. From this revelation concerning our own nature, we can infer to the physical world that nature itself exhibits a will to exist. He then forms his 'principle of individuation' as a way of distinguishing between what we are as an individual as opposed to a group. As Bertrand Russell puts it, 'My will, therefore, is one and timeless. Nay, more, it is to be identified with the will of the whole universe; my separateness is an illusion, resulting from my subjective apparatus of spatio-temporal perception. What is real is one vast will, appearing in the whole course of nature, animate and inanimate alike' (Russell 1955: 783).

As complex organisms we adapt to our environments. We seek satisfaction of our wants through different paths of fulfilment and deploy varying forms of representation in the process. To that extent 'the more exact, definite, manifold and varied the knowledge which the animal provides for itself of things, and finally the closer, more persistent and excitable its attention to the things represented, hence the more developed its *intelligence*' (Schopenhauer quoted in Sandywell 1996: 146; original emphasis). The way in which environments are tested and negotiated for adaptive potential signals not a reflection of that environment, but a process of reflexive, transactional exchange: 'from the perspective of a living organism the world is a network of pathways created by its own activity' (Sandywell 1996: 146). Schopenhauer roots us back in nature with bodies and desire, but expressed in the idea of 'Will'. Gaps between our passions, environments and systems open up a space to act upon ourselves in an ongoing process of flux and change. Box 2.1 illustrates how this interpretation of the Will contrasts with more individualised notions, demanding a decentring of the self precisely to know oneself, and one's position in the world, better.

■■ Box 2.1 ■■■■■■■■■■■■■■■■■■■■■■■■■■■■■■■■■■■■■■■

Mastering the Will

When we think of the Will we can distinguish between two different paths. On the one hand the idea of the Will suggests a celebration of the self, a centring that appears to saturate our contemporary existence. Concerned with our own passions and desires, we may follow our Will and justify our actions accordingly. Such a trajectory is amply demonstrated in mass consumerism, in which instant purchases are possible via credit cards which delay payment. Facebook, texting and mobile internet technologies allow us to edit patience from our lives as information, products and friends can be accessed at once. We may defer to an insatiable Will in excusing bodily desires and passions unchecked by our ethics or any reflection on the consequences of our actions.

A celebration of detached individuality is further witnessed through the television revolution of the popular voting show – *The X Factor*, *America's Next Top Model*, *Britain's Got Talent* – in which ordinary people are elevated to stardom via spectators deciding their fate through the

(Continued)

(Continued)

click of a button. Judgement, talent and criteria become secondary concerns to the immediate responses of the voting public. In such acts we see not *the* Will, but an expression of *my* will, in which society becomes geared to the delivery of instant gratification to satisfy our immediate wants and needs. Overconsumption, consumerism, greed and excess are the bedfellows of this path of the Will.

This is not the view propounded by Schopenhauer who drew on Eastern philosophies to focus on self-discipline and the will as a whole. Schopenhauer, as Daston and Galison put it in quoting directly from his work, 'preached a bitter struggle with the will, on the model of Christian mysticism and the philosophy of the Indian Vedas, that would ultimately "rid us of ourselves" and replace the individual subject of willing and wanting with the "will-pure, eternal subject of knowing", an "unclouded mirror of the world"' (2010[2007]: 203). He wrote on ascetic and aesthetic states to find relief from the conflicts that surround and inform us. Here he believed he had discovered, in artistic forms of representation, a general realm of Plato's Ideas. Buddhism, of course, is but one example concerned with the mastery of the self and the aim to decentre our passions and desires in pursuit of a deeper knowledge of the Will.

Kant linked 'I think' to a universal feature of the human mind in order to avoid subjectivism. The same Kantian idea of being pleased 'without interest' with respect to the aesthetic is apparent in Schopenhauer. For one highly influential writer, both viewpoints were disguising particular, subjective interpretations as if they were universal features of the world (Nietzsche 1977). Friedrich Nietzsche (1844–1900) took aim at those who claimed their reflections on knowledge and morality had universal features, instead of seeing their knowledge claims as situated interpretations. He was an adversary of Descartes and was particularly critical of the rhetorical claims of thinkers in which he detected an explicit or hidden hand of God.

For Nietzsche, individuals denied situatedness in the formation of their beliefs and expressed their ideas in language as if it were just a neutral medium through the guise of objectivity. His critique applied beyond Schopenhauer to all those thinkers and philosophers who constitute systems of thought intended to resolve problems in the world: 'The boundless ambition and exultation of being the "unriddler of the world" constituted the thinker's dreams: nothing seemed worth-while if it was not the means of bringing everything to a conclusion *for him*!' (Nietzsche 1977: 34; original emphasis).

Nietzsche believed that claims to reach beyond oneself in the pursuit of absolute or objective knowledge were symptomatic of a 'tyrannical drive' and 'dogmatic endeavour' of the will. It is a particular morality which is nothing more than 'decided and decisive testimony to *who he is* – that is to say, to the order of rank in which the innermost drives of his nature stand in relation to one another' (Nietzsche 1977: 39; original emphasis). Nietzsche annihilated the reflexive self of Descartes, and in so doing connected knowledge to interest through a psychology of the will to power. In the wake of these investigations progress was seen as a false idea: 'onward development is not by *any* means, by any necessity, the same thing as elevation, advance, strengthening' (Nietzsche 1977: 247; original emphasis). Objectivity as certainty is metaphysical speculation born of the exercise of the will where needs and instincts interpret the world. He held that the realm of experience and being in the production of knowledge were fictions based on particular values.

Nietzsche's work, whilst important in rooting the need for reflexivity in how we understand and claim to know the world, is not without its detractors. Kant insisted that duty lay at the heart of the will to truth. Does Nietzsche, in shattering this illusion, leave us open to rule by the evil genius manipulating all around them according to will? If so, how can his thoughts escape this dilemma? This did not 'seem to have kept Nietzsche from thinking and writing'. It did, however, split those who followed him 'into two camps: the faithful and the ironists' (Ricoeur 1994: 13). Furthermore, reducing issues of knowledge, morality and justice to nothing more than interests in society can end up being anti-political: 'for Nietzsche the ultimate vision is that of an aesthetic utopia of wisdom, in which a wise old sage, Zarathustra, reaches a state of autonomy beyond community' (Benhabib 1992: 195). It seems, once again, that a solitary, autonomous view is presented as the repository of wisdom.

Despite these withering assaults on objectivity, Nietzsche's critique was not aimed at the dominant positivist framework of science, but instead at the philosophers' conceptions of their task. Unlike those for whom reflection upon science is ruled out by an unquestioning adherence to objectivism, Nietzsche constructs individuals as illogical in the beginning and that rules out self-reflection as a whole: 'Nietzsche is so rooted in basic positivist beliefs that he cannot systematically take cognizance of the cognitive function of self-reflection from which he lives as a philosophical writer' (Habermas 1989a: 299). His works contributed to the decoupling of methodology from epistemology in separating questions of validity from those of their genesis: 'In the process, epistemology, including the theory of knowledge developed immanently out of the logic of the natural and cultural sciences, could be surrendered to the psychology of research. On this basis modern positivism then erected a pure methodology, purged, however, of the really interesting problems' (Habermas 1989a[1968]: 300).

We can take from Nietzsche a need for the following: a critical examination of dominant ideas in terms of locating our bodies and minds in the world itself as both object and subject of its operations; awareness that language does not just reflect, but constitutes reality and a turn towards the analysis of cultural life in terms of values. He reminded us that we cannot explain what we are and how we should be by facts separated from cultural frames; autonomy does not come in ready-made philosophical packages but through individual and collective efforts in and through the world itself. Whilst he held there are no facts, only interpretations, this is not a termination point: 'interpretation is not (as most people assume) an absolute value, a gesture of mind situated in some timeless realm of capabilities. Interpretation must be evaluated, within a historical view of human consciousness. In some cultural contexts, interpretation is a liberating act. It is a means of revising, of transvaluing, of escaping the dead past. In other cultural contexts, it is reactionary, impertinent, cowardly, stifling' (Sontag 2001[1966]: 7).

FACTS, VALUES AND INTERPRETATIONS

Schopenhauer was not a 'pessimist'. He did not assume that all we have is conflict through an endless clash of wills. Rather, he emphasised that desires, the particularities of experiences and the spectacle of an awesome nature could be managed through an empirical scientific attitude with practices to constitute rules and procedures across continents and time. Science can act to temper the Will, if careful observations are undertaken and if the scientist remains a passive, methodical self who extracts truth. Yet here is an ambiguity, not just between facts and values, but also between the passive scientific gaze and the active post-Kantian self in which ideas cannot and should not be squashed, but explored and interrogated in confrontation with the world itself. The result may easily become 'opposition between allegedly passive observation and active experimentation and a split within the scientist's own self' (Daston and Galison 2010: 242).

Subjectivism places the subject at the centre of the world who exercises their ability to know it according to their own perspectives. Objectivism, on the other hand, focuses on how objects in the world have properties that are reflected in the human mind. In addressing this issue Heinrich Rickert (1863–1936) makes a point that Karl Popper was also to make much later: objectivity is a value required by science in its search for the truth. As he says, 'We must, in fact, assume, if not the existence of an already definite body of knowledge of what values are valid, then the validity of objective values and the possibility that we can approach knowledge of it ever more closely' (quoted in Owen 1997: 86). Rickert stressed that there was a qualitative difference between history and science and that certain values demanded a distance from life. He offered a unifying theory drawing on the works of Immanuel Kant. Whilst Nietzsche denied the possibility of objective knowledge, these issues of subjectivity/objectivity and the values of and for science continued to provoke a number of reflections, not least in the works of Max Weber.

A value-free science?

Max Weber (1864–1920) was an economist, political scientist, sociologist, historian and legal scholar. He was influenced by Rickert's neo-Kantianism and Nietzsche and Marx. With this legacy, Weber's works continue to have relevance to understanding the struggles of contemporary times (Ritzer 1999, 2015). Weber held that from no science could values be derived (Löwith 1993): 'scientific pleading is meaningless in principle because the various value spheres of the world stand in irreconcilable conflict with each other' (Weber in Gerth and Mills 1970: 147). He was critical of those who retreat to both irrationalism *and* the belief that science can provide answers to the problems of life: 'After Nietzsche's devastating criticism of those "last men" who "invented happiness", I may leave aside altogether the naive optimism in which science – that is, the technique of mastering life which rests upon science – has been celebrated as the way to happiness. Who believes this? – aside from a few big children in university chairs or editorial offices' (Weber 1949: 143).

Weber questioned the basis of our knowledge claims and added to an increasing body of work in the sociology of knowledge (Burke 2000). He eschewed relativism, focusing instead on a conception of science as a vocation informed by a Kantian duty to the facts: 'Science today is a "vocation" organised in special disciplines in the service of self-clarification and knowledge of interrelated facts. It is not the gift of grace of seers and prophets dispensing sacred values and revelations, nor does it partake of the contemplation of sages and philosophers about the meaning of the universe. This, to be sure, is the inescapable condition of our historical situation. We cannot evade it as long as we remain true to ourselves' (Weber in Gerth and Mills 1970: 152). He believed that we interpret what is worth being known in scientific work 'with reference to its ultimate meaning, which we must reject or accept according to our ultimate position towards life' (Weber in Gerth and Mills 1970: 143). Weber admitted that the 'deontological' and 'consequentialist' views of ethics were difficult to bring together, but that it was essential to do so: 'the ethic of conviction and the ethic of responsibility are not absolute opposites. They are complementary to one another, and only in combination do they produce the true human being who is capable of having a "vocation for politics"' (Weber1994[1919]: 368].

These debates matter for our discussions on reflexivity. If we accept that we, as social scientists, also have an undeniable Will, that we are born into a pre-existing world and cannot separate our Being from it, that we interpret and give meaning to our experiences and those of others through our language which constitutes the world, don't we need ethics to govern our work and to produce responsible knowledge? What makes good knowledge? Is it produced according only to a rigorous method or does it require sensitivity to contexts of knowledge production and reception in order to have the greatest societal impact? Do the ends justify the means? And what if we cannot envisage the means to which our research might be put – where does our responsibility end? In the wake of the Second World War in post-Nazi Germany, the ethical conduct of scientists was not to be left to chance with a series of ethical principles agreed – the Nuremberg Code – which continue in research ethics guidelines today.

To fully understand Weber's ideas on science and reflexivity, we need to turn to his substantive studies. For Weber, capitalism is not made up of forces and relations of production which assume an alienating autonomy: 'capitalism could only become the "most fateful" power in human life because it had itself already developed within the framework of a "rational way of life"' (Löwith 1993: 63). In *The Protestant Ethic and the Spirit of Capitalism* (1964[1930]) and the *The Theory of Social and Economic Organization* (1985[1947]), Weber charts the increasing rationalisation of everyday life alongside a corresponding disenchantment with the organisation of society and social relations. As illustrated in Box 2.2, this requires morality and emphasises the need for ethics in the process of research to guard against 'Specialists without spirit, sensualists without heart; this nullity imagines that it has attained a level of civilization never before achieved' (1985[1947]: 182).

■ **Box 2.2** ■■■■■■■■■■■■■■■■■■■■■■■■■■■

Governing the Will

We have already seen how some writers believed that laws were required to avoid a descent into chaos through a clash of Wills. For Durkheim, when social regulations cease to control individual behaviours, when there are no norms guiding society, *anomie* results. This is a state of instability in which society provides little moral guidance to individuals. In our day and age, we can see the idea of socially regulated norms not only in relation to the big issues of morality – defining right from wrong through the legal system and statute book – but also through non-legal expectations. Some people feel that society has gone too far – for instance, dictating what we eat, how we parent, how often we exercise, whether and where we smoke – and are critical of the so-called 'nanny state' (Le Grand and New 2015; Magnusson and Griffiths 2015). The tabloid press, often on the right of politics, bandy this term around liberally and refer to undue intervention in areas of personal choice: 'Only nanny state Britain could turn this glorious sunshine into a national crisis' (*Mail Online* 01.07.15); '80% of Britons hate the meddling nanny state' (*Express Online* 19.08.15). Yet for others, society is increasingly individualised and rationalised, and greater rather than fewer moral norms are needed to produce a more cohesive society.

An alternative view is that we have an internal moral compass which defines how we should govern our own Will. Buddha's five precepts and Socrates' focus on virtue, inquiry and knowledge as a route to ethical conduct emphasised the rational mind of the individual as the basis for morality and a self-regulating society. For Socrates, one could never damage another person's soul through inappropriate behaviour, even by taking their life, but could cause irrevocable damage to one's own. Thinkers down the ages have grappled with this issue of moral conduct. Kant's emphasis was on deontological ethics in which actions are prescribed according to their inherent value, not because of their consequences. This led to a focus on absolute moral laws, in which there is a duty to perform particular actions regardless of the outcome. Under this example telling lies which are assumed to have little consequence would be categorically wrong, even in order to reduce any small amount of harm to significant others. His 'categorical imperative' included universal moral laws true under all circumstances and which respect what it is to be 'human'.

In contrast to Kant's moral absolutes, others focus on judging morality according not to the acts themselves, but to their consequences. Bentham, for instance, judged the morality of an action according to whether it caused more pleasure than pain for the greatest number of people. Sacrifice is implied in such a concept, both for the individual and the groups that may need to suffer pain in order for the majority to benefit. In the words of a famous sci-fi hero, 'the needs of the many outweigh the needs of the few' (Spock in *Star Trek II: The Wrath of Khan*, 1982). Spock shares this philosophy with Kirk earlier in the film, and later uses it to explain why he sacrificed his own life to save others. Inherent in such discussions is the question of whether the ends justify the means.

Here we find echoes of Hegel fused with Nietzsche. In Weber's social history of religion we can detect a Hegelian objective 'spirit' (in this case, of capitalism) as a correlate of Kant's abstract concept of a 'categorical imperative' – the duty to act according to a universal moral law regardless of the consequences of one's actions (Brunkhorst 1992). Human meaning and values are declining in the modern world as the calculation of formal rationality overwhelms us and undermines the place of substantive rationality, defined as the 'conscious belief in the absolute value of some ethical, aesthetic, religious, or other form of behaviour, entirely for its own sake and independently of any prospects of external success' (Weber 1964[1947]: 115).

Like those before him, Weber was influenced by his context and drew conclusions from his studies for the workings of society. He found himself in the post-Bismarckian era with a furtherance of the German nation state accompanied by a belief that all politics is, in the last analysis, a struggle for power (*Macht*): 'Weber became convinced that great goals could be achieved only by power politics. For the rest of his life he set a premium upon examining political life without illusions, looking at it as a struggle between individuals and groups with conflicting beliefs and interests, always decided in the end by the reservoir of power available to the winning side and by its greater ability to use that power effectively' (Bendix 1977: 7). With these reflections, his political analysis is informed by a quest to generate a liberal political consciousness in the face of the forward march of modernity. Parallels here are evident with Marx who, after all, took aim at Romantic conservatism and utilitarian ideas.

There is no solace in history, no answers to be found in the results of science, no resolutions in history and reason (Hegel), no transcendence in the actions of people with common interests (Marx), or resolution through the laws of historical evolution (Saint-Simon, Comte, and to a lesser extent Durkheim). History is resolved by 'Will' and in this way Weber is characterised as a theorist of 'fate' (Turner 1981). Whilst the individual may be stifled, it is a condition from which they cannot escape: 'Weber saw historical change as the unintended effect of endless social processes and contingent circumstances ... this world-view is a social liberalism which asks us, given the complexity and uncertainty of knowledge, to behave responsibly – that is, as agents with "personality" who are forced to make choices in conditions of unreliable knowledge' (Holton and Turner 1990: 9). The social scientist, acting responsibly, is left to chart this course, without recourse to an over-extension of the boundaries of their endeavours.

Abstraction and human understanding

How does science proceed? Here Weber turns to the 'ideal type' as a strategic demarcation to enable a separation between scientific means and social ends – in other words, through abstraction, Weber sought to render justice to the practice of science without conflating its consequences for how social life should then proceed. The 'ideal type' was an approximation of particular forms of human behaviour or processes that should not be confused with reality 'in-itself': 'In reality, action takes exactly this course only in unusual cases, as sometimes on the stock exchange; and even then there is usually only an approximation of the ideal type' (Weber 1964[1947]: 96). Here, we can only wonder what Weber would have made of the economic crash in terms of what it told us about the culture of global banking! Our reflexive gaze is alerted to this conflation, which is checked by rigorous methodological distinctions in our studies: for example, between adequacy at the level of meaning and at the level of cause (see Weber 1949 and 1964: 98–103).

As Box 2.3 highlights we are reminded that Marx taught us not to confuse the model of reality with the reality of the model, requiring continuous vigilance about the theories and approaches we use to make sense of the social world. Models are ways of abstracting from everyday life. They are often seen as ways of building upon experiences in particular contexts to produce generalisations that have relevance across time and space. Pierre Bourdieu (1990), to whose work we shall turn later, was interested in ways of knowing the social world not only through statistics but also through our accounts of it, recognising that both are representations: 'to consider regularity, that is, what recurs with a certain statistical measurable *frequency*, as the product of a consciously laid down and consciously respected *ruling* ... or as the product of an unconscious *regulating* by a mysterious cerebral and/or social mechanism, is to slip from the model of reality to the reality of the model' (Bourdieu 1990: 38; original emphasis).

■■ **Box 2.3** ■■■■■■■■

Limits to modelling the social world

Appealing for caution about the assumptions we build into representations of the world, Bourdieu's reflexive sociology is based on the idea that life is an ensemble of social practices. He warned against reification in which the model itself is seen not as a representation or approximation of reality but as reality itself. Weber's 'ideal type' sought to avoid this pitfall. He did not believe that scientific systems could reproduce all reality, or that infinite phenomena and human experiences could be captured by conceptual tools. His ideal type was not a mirror of reality, rather an exaggerated version of it, to illuminate particular dimensions and characteristics. It was seen as the basis for comparison through acknowledging both the need for particularisation and generalisation in social science.

We can see the fallibility of models of economic behaviour in the recent financial crisis, driven by greed and unaccountability in a deregulated banking sector. George Soros, a Hungarian-born American on the Forbes rich list and a supporter of progressive-liberal causes, argues that the collapse was due to the flawed models and assumptions of economic systems without taking their reflexive properties into consideration (Soros 2013). Models of human behaviour remove the realities from the world. As Soros puts it, 'The assumption of independently given conditions of supply and demand eliminates the possibility of any reflexive interaction' (1998: 38).

Questioning the assumptions of economic modelling, the idea of 'perfect competition' or 'perfect knowledge', Soros argues that the principles of fallibility and reflexivity are essential in understanding the roots of the crisis and prospects for recovery (Wade Hands 2013). Far from perfectly operating market systems, Soros sees international capitalism as flawed, failing to acknowledge that participants' views are partial and distorted (fallibility) and that those views can influence situations as they lead to inappropriate actions (reflexivity). Hence he writes, 'the global economy appears to be stabilizing. There is a growing belief that the global financial system has once again escaped collapse and we are slowly returning to business as usual. This is a grave misinterpretation of the current situation. Humpty Dumpty cannot be put together again' (Soros 2010: 105). This is a good example of what Bourdieu was talking about, in which representations of the world through models are ultimately dangerous when we fail to take human characteristics and cultures into account and regulate for the excesses of individualism through the Will.

The importance of distance and the role of abstraction in understanding social life was apparent in the work of Georg Simmel (1858–1915). Simmel saw how human thought synthesises 'the given into units that serve as subject matter of the sciences' (1964[1950]: 5). If we were interested in the behaviour of the Greeks and Persians in the battle of Marathon, a 'true' account would include the behaviour of all those individuals who were involved. Yet what does this tell us about the collective? To speak of the histories of cities, political territories and the feminist movement is abstract, but such abstractions are essential facts of our existence. At the same time, to scientifically analyse characteristics of the individual is to separate out innumerable influences that stretch away in time and space which are just as 'real'. His emphasis upon the development of space and how it produces conflict is evident in his writings on urbanism, where he compares rural conditions of proximity to the complexity and indifference of the city: 'During epochs in which abstraction capable of transcending space is demanded by objective conditions, but is hampered by psychological under-development, sociological tensions accordingly arise with considerable consequences for the form of the relationship' (Simmel in Frisby and Featherstone 1997: 153).

Our lives are forged by abstract and proximate relations. We cannot only focus on individuals, as this would represent an unending search for a knowable reality: 'It relegates it into the infinite and looks for it in the realm of the inscrutable' (Simmel 1964: 7). Differences in cognition come from a 'number of heterogeneous objects of cognition that are nevertheless recognised as equally definitive and consistent. The principle may be expressed by the symbol of different *distances* between such a complex of phenomena and the human mind' (Simmel 1964[1950]: 7; original emphasis). What we take from Simmel is the importance of recognising that we have perspectives from different viewpoints born of distance, each of which is correct in its own way and contributes to a 'totality of meaning'.

At one level the individual may be differentiated from others, but as distance increases, so the individual disappears and a picture of society emerges that 'has its own possibilities of being recognized or missed' (Simmel 1964[1950]: 8).

If distance and abstraction decrease the visibility of the individual, how then, if at all, are totalities of meaning possible? How can we understand written texts which seek just such abstraction from human understanding, yet are taken as historical 'fact'? In the work of Wilhelm Dilthey (1833–1911) this was a central issue. His emphasis on understanding social life, and the meanings for the individuals who comprise it, led him to question the validity of scientific texts and historical writings. In the process he sought nothing less than new epistemological foundations for the human sciences. Understanding both the content and the context of the production of texts and how they were used to create meaning was essential for a theory of human understanding.

To pursue a 'scientific hermeneutics' it is necessary to situate and interpret texts in the social context in which they are produced: to move beyond 'particularity' to the 'general', and thereby 'to rise above not only the particularity of texts, but also the particularity of the rules and recipes into which the art of understanding is dispersed. Hermeneutics was born with the attempt to raise exegesis, the act of critically interpreting text to draw meaning out of it, and philology to the level of a *Kunstlehre*, that is, a "technology" which is not restricted to a mere collection of unconnected operations' (Ricoeur 1982: 45; original emphasis). We must be reflexive to see historical texts as a form of abstraction, yet one which is saturated with unrecognised or missed human dynamics. Situating a text and understanding it through an act of interpretation that connects it with the author and their knowledge at the time of its production is the hermeneutic circle: 'the relation between an isolated expression or work and the pre-given totality of language or literature' (Thompson 1981: 37).

Where Weber looked for scientific causes, Dilthey focused on human understanding or *Verstehen*. A direct relation between the observer and observed was not framed as an impediment to objectivity constituted by the detached mind. Rather, reflexive engagement provided for something over and above the natural sciences – that is, understanding the social meaning of an event for the persons involved. In this way, we move from the explanation of an event as 'the effect of a cause' (Strasser 1985: 2) to a form of study that involves 'understanding what makes someone tick' and how they 'feel or act as a human being' (Taylor 1981: 30).

Dilthey took us from individualistic psychology to an historicist view based on Hegel's objective 'mind' or 'spirit' as indicative of a given age: 'Every single human expression represents something which is common to many and therefore part of the realm of objective mind ... the individual always experiences, thinks, acts, and also understands, in this common sphere' (Dilthey quoted in Outhwaite 1986: 26–7). In terms of issues of values, abstraction and particularisation, such works emphasised how the human sciences can respect both individuality and universality through their ability to locate the 'inner' experiences of people in terms of their history, in contrast with a more positivistic approach of explaining the 'outer' observable patterns of human behaviour through cause and effect.

INTERPRETATION AND BEING

The passive idea of the methodical detached scientist is now that of the active interpreter, engaged in the construction and understanding of social life whose endeavour enables texts to be contextualised in ways in which their authors may not be aware. The emphasis upon interpretation, history and understanding enables a movement from the deficit model of public understanding of science to a science of the public mind through which people can become more reflexively aware of their context. A precondition becomes an understanding of the consciousness that informs human actions. The idea of the self is not the isolated introspection of Descartes, but one of lived experience.

Lived experience

Edmund Husserl (1859–1938) was the founder of phenomenology. He undertook a defence of the 'legitimacy and dignity of the human sciences' (Nuyen 1990) and embarked upon a critique of prior ideas of subjectivity and objectivity. All philosophy could and should be was a description of experience 'to the things themselves'. With this he emphasised that consciousness is always directed towards 'something'. Taking Descartes' act of perception, Husserl added the 'thing' which is perceived and emphasised. '*Cogito ergo sum*' was replaced with '*Ego cogito cogitate*': 'I think, and what I am thinking are the objects of my thoughts' (Strasser 1985: 124).

Knowing is related to a perceiving subject. Husserl moved us away from the idea that consciousness comprises a reflexive relation in order to constitute distance from society as an object. Instead, reflexivity is born in a subject–object relation of lived experience: 'Phenomenology does not locate reflexivity as a higher cognitive faculty of a self-present substance, but rather explores the experiential genesis and intentional operations of lived reflexivity (anticipations, protentional syntheses, corroborations, verifications, negations, etc.) organizing the life of consciousness' (Sandywell 1996: 224–5). In this sense Husserl's concern with perception is to try and grasp 'true understanding' as continuous streams of intentionality that occur within lived reality in which meaning and objects are constituted.

The method is to suspend presuppositions regarding society through 'bracketing'. People are then freed from historical context to uncover a 'true understanding' that is pre-theoretical. Phenomenology thereby asks us 'to question nothing less than our culture, that is, our way of looking at and being in the world in which we have been brought up' (Wolff 1979: 500). As the tradition unfolds it extends itself into a method for knowing the social world, and it is this relationship that explains the enduring attraction of the approach – one extended and modified in the works of Martin Heidegger (1889–1976), Maurice Merleau-Ponty (1908–61) and Alfred Schutz (1899–1959).

In their different ways, Husserl and Dilthey pursued an Enlightenment ideal: the search for 'true' knowledge. Martin Heidegger moved the focus of phenomenology from epistemology to ontology. He was critical of Kant and the distinction between 'being' and 'thinking', taking aim at the whole epistemological enterprise in which the problem is seen in terms of coming to know a world that is external to us. He argued that we are not just observers of an external world mediated through our consciousness, but members of a world who exist as 'beings-in-time'. Heidegger notes how the idea of 'being' has 'congealed into the self evident' (1961[1953]: 81) without critical interrogation, and yet is invoked in terms of formulae: 'being and becoming; being and appearance; being and thinking; being and the ought' (1961[1953]: 79). He found each of these relations wanting. As a result reflexivity is rooted in and through not only an experiential but also a temporal dimension.

With Heidegger's interventions, we move from neo-Kantian preoccupations with interpretation and method, intuition and consciousness to the study of *Dasein*. This is best described as 'pre-understanding': 'the *place* where the question of being arises, the place of manifestation; the centrality of *Dasein* is simply that of a being which understands being. It is part of its structure as being to have an ontological *pre-understanding* of being' (Ricoeur 1982: 54; original emphasis). It is a significant development because it takes aim at the 'transcendental ego'. There is no attempt here to 'solve' the subject–object dichotomy by prioritising the reflexive capacity of human consciousness, because understanding is part of the 'mode of being'.

How exactly does a subject come out of the world that constitutes their very being to then become external to that world? For Heidegger this stepping-out-of-the-world is not possible. It then follows that any methodological injunction that rests upon this ability must be flawed. Only through an encounter with others, or being-with-others, can we discover the world – not to distinguish ourselves, but as a condition of existence in which a world is disclosed to us: 'The claim here is not that the disclosure of the world is a social or *inter*subjective achievement – an assumption which still presupposes subjects, only now as a related plurality. Rather, what Heidegger is insisting on is that the intelligibility of Dasein's closest everydayness is, in each case, characterised by a *constant anonymous publicness*' (Glendinning 1998: 57; original emphasis).

With this latter move Heidegger extends Husserl's 'existential analytics' by insisting that, in order to describe experience, we need to find the being for whom that experience matters. *Dasein* means we are already born into a pre-existing world, focusing on a temporal dimension, raising questions of both responsibility and authenticity. As with Nietzsche, this train of thought hits limits in so far as Heidegger places philosophy in something of an opposition to the social sciences and in particular psychology. That is paradoxical for someone who emphasised the importance of being in the world: 'One might expect, therefore, that the philosopher who finds himself thrown into the world might also find some difficulty in arriving at an adequate state of knowledge. But Heidegger defines the attitude of the philosopher without recognizing any restriction on the absolute power of philosophical thought' (Merleau-Ponty 1974: 278).

Maurice Merleau-Ponty sought to avoid these traps by engaging with the empirical sciences of anthropology and psychology, as well as philosophy. Perception plays a major role in understanding the world. In contrast to the dualist ontology of Descartes, he proposed the body-subject as an alternative. Here, the possibility for a reflexive relation to life emerges through being-in-time and a gap that might exist between where bodies are located in time and the possibilities available to them for the future. These possibilities are then 're-projected' into the present which can become 'an object of potential questioning, challenge, and change' (Bauman 1978: 166).

The act of social science is the act of interpreting people's everyday interpretations. It does not draw upon the problems associated with a representational view of language, but a constitutive one: 'The later Heidegger conceives of language as the house of self-adaptive (*sich schickenden*) "being"; hence, the various stages in the understanding of "being" still retained for him a transcendent relation to a "being" that always remains *itself*' (Habermas 1992a: 209; original emphasis). Merleau-Ponty was interested in how the incarnate subject might transcend the body to understand its actions. In intellectual and cultural terms, this gives rise to the role of language as the connection between Being, the thoughts, the senses and our interpretations of the world. Drawing on both Husserl and Heidegger, Simone de Beauvoir (1908–86) also focused on the importance of lived experience and the ways language reveals the meanings of the world, turning to literature to develop her works and ideas.

From experience to interpretation through language

How then can we categorise things? What constructs do we use to describe things in everyday life and in the work of social science? Language is one tool to bring experience into focus and enables it to be shared and made tangible. The representative idea of language, as seen in Locke and Descartes, views it as a medium for expressing reality and forging ideas into pictures of the whole. Yet there is a different tradition in which language is a means not only of describing but also of constituting the world, and we can turn to critical hermeneutics to understand these relations. Box 2.4 provides a good example of the relationship between critical hermeneutics and the constitutive role of language through a discussion of propaganda.

Étienne Condillac (1714–80) viewed language as an instrument for science in the process of making associations. Ideas, signs and their associations precede language which becomes a passive tool. Johann Herder (1744–1803) criticised this assumption that consciousness precedes language. Language has a reflective quality which gives rise to a different form of consciousness: 'Herder's basic idea seems to be that while a pre-linguistic animal can learn to respond to some object appropriately in the light of its purposes, only the being with language can identify the object as of a certain kind, can, as we might put it, attribute such and such a property to it' (Taylor 1995: 103). The use of language is linked to some sense of 'rightness' such that identifying an object as having properties justifies the use of particular words. This is the semantic dimension in which linguistic beings function. The same may be said of the articulation of feelings. It is not just descriptive, but has the ability to transform a person's life and includes objects of art as expressing those things that cannot be said in everyday language. It is therefore 'the seat of new emotions. Linguistic beings are capable of new feelings which effectively reflect their richer sense of the world; not just anger, but indignation: not just desire, but love and admiration' (Taylor 1995: 105). For this reason language is not only descriptive or representative, but also constitutive: 'language makes possible a whole range of crucially human feelings, activities, and relations' (Taylor 1995: 106).

■ Box 2.4 ■

Language and reflexivity

Propaganda is information used or misused to deliberately promote a political cause or point of view. Without consideration of the position and intent of the authors and their historical context, texts (or indeed visual images) could be taken at face value as representing some objective reality. The portrayal of different races through the ages is one poignant and significant example. From the propaganda wars around the abolition of slavery in the nineteenth century, in which offensive racial text and images were used to associate the enslaved with negative characteristics, to the use of propaganda by the Nazis to promote their doctrines around the Aryan race, we can see how people have sought to construct texts to justify unjustifiable beliefs. Heidegger himself has been deeply criticised for his support of the Nazi regime, his increasing distance and treatment of his mentor Husserl, and his failure to apply his own critical self-reflection to how his own era affected his work (see Shalin 2010).

In the case of propaganda, language is deployed deliberately and with intent to construct particular versions of reality. The relationship between newspapers and the content of their journalism is a milder version of the same. Readers are aware that their favourite dailies are politically aligned – across the globe, different media take predictable stances in relation to different issues, supporting political candidates and disparaging others. They are not simply reporting 'news' but deploying 'facts' to reach often radically different conclusions. Without paying attention to how such biases are deployed and to what effect, the unreflexive reader may treat such news as objective, thereby bolstering pre-existing assumptions and beliefs.

In our everyday existence through the conversations we have with friends, or in our working lives as researchers, we may not intentionally seek to mislead in the language we use or the words we write. We may well consider that academic texts are at the opposite end of the spectrum from propaganda which is deliberately intended to mislead. But can we be sure? A reflexive attitude is essential for such a claim to have any validity.

Alfred Schutz took these ideas seriously and influenced the development of phenomenology. Together with Peter Winch (1990[1958]), who imported insights from those such as Ludwig Wittgenstein into social science, Schutz added to a later focus on the rule-following and meaningful nature of human actions in everyday life. He continued the phenomenological rejection of positivism and was critical of the concept of *Verstehen* (see Outhwaite 1986), insisting this was not a method for 'doing' social science, but what social science should study in terms of how people interpret the social world. *Verstehen* represents the 'experiential form in which common sense thinking takes cognisance of the social cultural world' (Schutz 1979: 29).

The appropriate focus of enquiry for a phenomenological social science is how people produce social life in a meaningful way: 'Commonsense contains innumerable pre- and quasi-scientific interpretations about everyday reality, which it takes for granted. If we are to describe the reality of commonsense we must refer to those interpretations, just as we must take account of its taken-for-granted character – but we do so within phenomenological brackets' (Berger and Luckmann 1967: 20). Weber had failed to recognise the episodic nature of human conduct and hence that causal adequacy was bound by a sociological and historical understanding (Schutz 1973).

This led Schutz to focus on the mediation of first- and second-order constructs as the topic of reflexive concern in the practice of the social sciences. Social scientific knowledge (second order) should concern itself with the explication of the 'natural attitude' by rendering apparent the 'taken-for granted' in everyday life. The 'postulate of adequacy' then holds that social scientific constructs of the social world must be compatible with the first order – that is, 'with the constructs of everyday life' (Schutz 1979: 35). Ideas have to link lived experience with scientific knowledge and scientific concepts, and ideas should account for and be understandable in terms of everyday life: 'Compliance with this postulate warrants the consistency of the constructs of the social scientist with the constructs of common-sense experience of the social reality' (Schutz 1970: 279).

Schutz argued that a focus upon the experiential elements in social life requires a reflexive vigilance so that experiences are not regarded as 'faulty' measured against the scientific categories deployed to explain actions, events and processes. A commonsense stock of knowledge orientates people to apply meaning to their own actions, those of others and the events they encounter. The lifeworld exhibits the basis for primary experience that enables people to orientate their actions through taking its self-evidence, or pre-reflexive constitution, for granted: 'I find myself always within an historically given world which, as a world of nature as well as a sociocultural world, had existed before my birth and which will continue to exist after my death' (Schutz 1970: 163–4).

Schutz presents a clear argument for the study of 'lay' reflexivity through being-in-the world. This is an inter-subjective state of affairs which represents a process of acculturation as manifested through publicly available forms of communication. Recalling Heidegger's insights, interpretative procedures produce meanings oriented towards the context in which they are produced. A separation exists in the social world between the subjective grasp of meaning that we believe is unique to us and the sphere of understanding upon which we draw in order to be in the world with others. We come to know who we are through others by a linking of experience, and in our interactions deploy know-how, habits and pre-judgements. These 'typifications' are deployed in both intimate and more general relations. In the former, familiarity can lead to typification and from there to greater degrees of predictability in terms of how we see those close to us. Symbols become the means by which typifications enter relations and these transcend everyday experience in which no one actually sees the whole situation: 'Nobody in a "we" has a total experience of that "we", since they are in it and part of it. The word "we", in this sense, is a symbol. It signifies, within intersubjective relations and experience, that which transcends inter-subjective experience' (Crossley 1996: 88).

SUMMARY: REFLEXIVITY MATTERS

In further clarifying an understanding of reflexivity, we started with recognition of the 'Will'. This provides a very different perspective on our understanding of who we are, what we know and might become. In the process key positions are questioned – for example, a simple separation between nature and culture, such that the latter provides a vantage point for the explanation of the former and that there can be certainty in explanatory legislation that comes through the exercise of reason over passions by a unitary, reflexive, self. Nevertheless, it is clear that whilst representation has been challenged, the careful, methodical, rule-following self of the positivist and empiricist constructions of scientific endeavour has continued unabated.

Several of the thinkers, such as Nietzsche and Heidegger, place limits on others which they fail to impose on themselves. Nonetheless, from each we take forward important considerations in our study. Nietzsche focused on the role of history in the formation of ourselves and our understandings. Through his works we find a good illustration of what happens if we confuse clarification that comes through engaging with reflections on the world with social scientific practices. If we take a non-reflexive path – whether via empiri-cism or positivism, for instance – we absolve ourselves from working on the ambivalence that resides in engaging with the world.

Max Weber extended these ideas through identifying the tension between an ethic of responsibility for the production of accurate social scientific accounts and an ethic of con-viction that motivates its practitioners to do so in the first place. This means subsuming our own substantive values in a world in which instrumental rationality is increasingly saturat-ing our existence. Not only does this depend on a fact–value dichotomy, but it also exacts a high price in terms of individualising a societal problem. As we have noted before, the social scientist shoulders a great burden if they attempt to take on the dialectic of individual tran-scendence from formal rationality, alongside empathic understanding – unless, that is, we work in institutions whose distinctiveness is to enable interpretation through shelter from these effects (May with Perry 2011). This is why Weber, influenced by Nietzsche, moves toward the need for greater democratic deliberation in the consideration of ultimate ends.

Science is the product of cultural influences: the contexts in which scientists work are informed by those influences and therefore their reflections upon culture itself. Their processes and their products are inherently interrelated. From this we reach the inescapable conclusion that reflexivity matters. Weber injected social scientific practice with both a rigour and a modesty. It requires a reflexive scrutiny in order to not over-extend its insights and an attendance to methodological rigour. When it comes to the practices of a scientific community that inform the analysis of these trends we are left with a two-fold need: commitment to the production of good social science and an excavation of the conditions that give rise to the classificatory practices that frame ways of seeing the world which themselves are informed by prevailing social, political and economic conditions. In analysing social relations in this manner, we find the application of a vision to social practices that is different from the practices themselves in order that it retains a reflexive distance.

As practitioners of social science we have a standpoint, a position from which we conduct our work. This standpoint 'never abandons its secret desire to be the only one worth adopting' (Turner 1990: 115). We will examine this concept further in Chapter 5. However, whilst Weber exposes the illusion that a general standpoint can act as final arbitrator in disputes over ends, he does not terminate social scientific inquiries at the partiality of different viewpoints. This means there is much to learn from mediating between different cultures of inquiry (Hall 1999). We can also learn how abstraction enters into the terrain of cultural understandings in coming to understand who we are and how we are positioned. As Simmel argued, we should not confuse individual-level experiences with the patterns that are formed at a general level; the latter emerge from the former, but are not reducible to them.

In the work of Dilthey we found a concerted attempt to turn to the 'inner world' of the human mind as rooted in history. The argument was that the hermeneutic circle provides something in addition to the physical sciences: understanding. The human act of empathy provides a reflexive relationship that enables connections to experience and undermines the search for causal explanations. Husserl and Heidegger then move us towards social scientific analysis of the realm of 'pre-understanding' via 'bracketing'. In the critique of prior concepts of subjectivity and objectivity, reflexivity is born in lived experience. With an ontological emphasis on being and time, Heidegger rooted us within the world of which we are a part.

From Merleau-Ponty and Schutz we found a sophisticated understanding of what happens when we take culture seriously in terms of its influences on social scientific work and everyday understanding. Schutz left social science with a critique of the 'intellectualist bias' in knowledge construction (O'Neill 1972). When linked with philosophical anthropology (Honneth and Joas 1988), for example, this provides an important corrective to the individualistic assumptions that underpin sociological theories of reflexivity through rooting the 'I' in 'we' and 'thou' relations (Lash 1999). Schutz also had a more sophisticated understanding of the relationship between commonsense and social scientific understandings than subsequent interpretations have allowed (O'Neill 1995); in particular, we can see an emphasis on how scientific reasoning is dependent not on the absolute sovereignty of the knowing subject (Descartes to Husserl), nor their annihilation at the hands of Nietzsche or the logical positivist and those who walk in their paths, but on the 'communicative competence of the community of scientists in general and the larger lay society in which they live and work' (O'Neill 1995: 152).

We have three key elements to take forward in our inquiries. First, history is not an impediment to certainty, but constitutes an understanding from which we cannot escape. Second, the writers discussed here collectively pose a direct challenge to the idea that, through the exercise of reason, we can stand at the centre of the universe to cast our ordering and explanatory gaze upon its appearance and discover its true essence. Third, we need to focus on interpretation, meaning and communication in continuing our guide to reflexivity. Language is not a neutral medium for the expression of ideas but has a constitutive role.

We have a productive line of inquiry for the practice of reflexivity in social sciences and its study in the social world: being in the world means being with others through language. Conducted with a focus on the everyday constitution of being in the world without falling back on past ideas of consciousness, it is possible to develop insights resting upon an ontology of potentials that are given in time. New meanings can develop in this way and the social scientist needs to exercise a reflexive vigilance over the construction of meanings and their own being in the world. This is particularly the case as we consider next not only thinking and being, but also *doing* and the relationship between thought and practice.

3

PRAGMATISM, PRACTICE AND LANGUAGE

━━ CHAPTER CONTENTS ━━━━━━━━━━━━━━━━━━━━━━━━━━━━━━━

All the interests of my reason, speculative as well as practical, combine in the three
following questions: 1. What can I know? 2. What ought I to do? 3. What may I hope?
(Immanuel Kant 2009[1781]: 805)

INTRODUCTION

In our journey so far we have encountered many writers who have considered the relationship between thinking, being and interpreting in order to understand how we can know ourselves and the world around us. In thinking about *thought*, authors have considered the role of reason and experience, passion and desire, interpretation and communication. In this chapter we focus on thinking about *action* and aim to understand how knowledge is related to acting in the world.

Whilst we have drawn largely on European traditions to date, the extensive contributions from North American scholars are highlighted here. We start with an overview of the ideas of the pragmatists, namely Charles Sanders Peirce (1839–1914), John Dewey (1859–1952), William James (1842–1910), Jane Addams (1860–1925) and George Herbert Mead (1863–1931). In these works we see a focus on people's reflexive adaptations in everyday life, and the idea that action as the basis of thought necessitates a different kind of *practical* rather than theoretical reason. If we wish to understand how we, as fallible human beings, can hold different beliefs and yet establish a coherent of body of knowledge, we need to conceptualise the 'self' and interrogate how we might know this self as a basis for knowing others.

The theme of the relationship between theory and practice, knowing and doing is continued in an examination of the work of two twentieth-century thinkers, Gilbert Ryle (1900–76) and Michael Polanyi (1891–1976), whose rejection of Cartesian dualism and elaboration of ways of knowing are central to understanding the relationship between thought and action. With the idea that our self is constituted in a direct relationship to how we are seen by others, we are brought back to the centrality of language as mediating identity and constituting reality. Hence we resume discussions from Chapter 2 concerning the social situatedness of language and the idea that context matters through considering the works of Ludwig Wittgenstein (1889–1951), Peter Winch (1926–97) and Harold Garfinkel (1917–2011).

Collectively, the ideas in this chapter are representative of a vein of post-metaphysical thinking which rejects the dualisms of body and mind, theory and practice, thinking and doing. Throughout the late nineteenth and twentieth centuries scholars began to increasingly question rationality and a foundationalist perspective, turning away from the individual structures of consciousness to examine contextual and situated reason in actual historical practices. It is for these reasons that understanding the pragmatic structures of language and action as part of the contextualisation of reason is so important for our continued journey into reflexivity.

THOUGHT, ACTION AND THE SELF

In North America, the course of the social sciences in the nineteenth century began to take a different path from that of the European rationalists and empiricists. Histories of North American social science have argued that this is because their own revolution, in contrast to that of the French, was considered a success. With the American Civil War and the process of industrialisation, the rise of the social sciences – including anthropology, economics, political science and sociology – can be seen as an alliance between gentry reformers and others held together by an idea of North American exceptionalism. As in Europe, we see a turn towards positivism and historicism, as well as increasing class consciousness (Ross 1992). It is in this context that the writers we discuss below were developing their ideas.

Pragmatism and practical reason

Here we are concerned with pragmatism, a set of ideas developed by a group of young thinkers in Cambridge, Massachusetts, in the 1870s, and first publicly voiced by Charles Peirce in 1878 (Joas 1993). Charles Peirce is widely seen as the founder of pragmatism, although his legacy was eclipsed by William James and John Dewey and his collected papers were not published until 1958. Pragmatists argued that actions rather than consciousness were the foundations of thought, paralleling Heidegger's 'strategic gain' in thinking about the subject: 'Knowing and acting no longer have to be conceived of in terms of subject–object relationships' (Habermas 1992b: 147). The pragmatists shifted attention away from examining consciousness within a subject–object dualism towards consideration of people's reflexive adaptations in everyday life. The starting point of pragmatism is the prejudices that people actually possess in everyday life, not Descartes' abstract method of 'doubting'. The Cartesian solitary ego is replaced by a 'cooperative search for truth for the purpose of coping with real problems encountered in the course of action' (Joas 1993: 19). Under the pragmatists, thought becomes an instrument or tool for prediction, problem-solving and action. Reality is actively created as we act in and towards the world.

The basis of pragmatist thought is to give primacy to practical over theoretical reason. Kant held that there is a world which cannot be known (noumena) and that all we can know are the rules, set down by reason, for how we should go about generating our understandings: 'It is this which makes it necessary to conceive the problem as a relation between two possible objects of knowledge – two worlds – one of which *is* and the other is *not* determinable through our modes of cognition' (Macmurray 1969[1957]: 68; original emphasis). Here, the focus is on theoretical reason characterised by the question 'what can I know?' and the search for certainty. Through reasoning, explaining and predicting, a modification of beliefs may occur as a result of such processes. Practical reason focuses instead on producing modifications in our intentions to act. It is orientated less by the search for certain knowledge than by a value-driven search to understand the desirability of different courses of potential action.

Peirce replaced Kant's ideas of noumena and phenomena with a distinction between what is known now and the infinity of what can be known in time. He introduced modesty at the transcendental level without succumbing to the empiricism that saturates later formulations, right through to Richard Rorty (Mounce 1997). He did this by adhering to the validity of the process of inference in the 'long term' (Apel 1995[1967]: 36). Peirce was a critic of rationalism and empiricism. He argued that our inquiries come from a standpoint or point of view. For Peirce, the question of the meaning of truth relates to those conditions that enable us to develop a framework for interpreting the term itself: 'The concept of truth for Peirce has exactly the function that Kant ascribed to "regulative ideas"' (Thayer 1981: 132). Peirce set the grounds for a 'critical common sense' that drew upon a set of regulative principles to guide scientific inquiry (Apel 1995). His specific doctrine, or regulative idea, was that of 'pragmaticism': 'consider what effects, that might conceivably have practical bearings, we conceive the object of our conception to have. Then our conception of these effects is the whole of our conception of the object' (Peirce quoted in Mounce 1997: 36). From this point of view, pragmatism is first and foremost a method of reflection which keeps the purpose of rendering ideas and their implications for action clear. In these for-mulations we see Peirce refusing a simple separation between theory and practice that is reminiscent of the arguments of Karl Marx. It is for such reasons that he has been charac-terised as the 'greatest American thinker of all' (Apel 1995: 5). His legacy gave birth to the development of 'two pragmatisms' as his work was taken in different directions, for instance through Rorty's anti-realism (Mounce 1997).

Despite his legacy, writers such as Bertrand Russell (1955) paid greater attention to the work of John Dewey and William James. For Dewey, ideas and actions should be judged according to the social situations which give rise to them: 'The world we have experienced becomes an integral part of the self that acts and is acted upon in further experience. In their physical occurrence, things and events experienced pass and are gone. But something of their meaning and value is retained as an integral part of the self. Through habits formed in intercourse with the world, we also inhabit the world. It becomes a home and the home is part of our every experience' (Dewey 2005: 108).

In contrast to top-down metaphysical speculation, Dewey held that we should concern ourselves with the concrete social conditions under which thoughts and actions take place. James also took this view in relation to experience and critiqued the idea of consciousness as a resolution to the subject–object dilemma. For him, experience is provisional and part of a process: there can be no final resting place of verification as it is subject to revision in light of latter points of view and so on. The prior resolution to this dilemma is to seek a standard from which to judge experience beyond experience itself: 'if you then forget that this standard perpetually grows up endogenously inside the web of experiences, you may carelessly go on to say that what distributively holds of each experience, holds also collec-tively of experience, and that experience as such and in its totality owes whatever truth it may be possessed of to its correspondence with absolute realities outside of its own being' (James 2002[1909]: 91).

Pragmatism heralded a different path for the social sciences requiring adaptation, flexibil-ity and openness. Reason is put to work, not as in historic rationalism which tended towards 'carelessness, conceit, irresponsibility, and rigidity' (Dewey 1957: 97), but in 'experimental intelligence' manifest across the sciences, social sciences and the arts. This form of thinking is open to revision and liberating in that it enables us to act in a more directed and less blinkered manner, freeing us from 'the bondage of the past, due to ignorance and accident hardened into custom' (Dewey 1957: 96). Creativity is a central part of the emphasis of pragmatic reflections on the self. Dewey's idea of 'experimental intelligence' is a call to a different way of thinking and conceptualisation of the mind.

In contrast with the ideas of Schopenhauer and Nietzsche, the idea of creativity is not divorced from context as the 'self' is formed in relation to society (see Box 3.1 which explores debates on creative thinking in respect of the relationship between the conscious and unconscious mind). This reflects the common idea that incubation, slow thinking and freeing the mind are essential components of the thought process (Kahneman 2011; Wallas 2014[1926]). For the pragmatists, human intelligence cannot be attained as an end point: 'It is in constant process of forming, and its retention requires constant alertness in observing consequences, an open-minded will to learn and courage in re-adjustment' (Dewey 1957: 96–7).

■■■ Box 3.1 ■■■■■■■■■■■■■■■■■■■■■■■

Thinking differently

Edward de Bono is acknowledged as an expert in the area of creativity. He argues that ideas of the mind, designed by the great Greek three of Socrates, Plato and Aristotle, are out of date for the uncertain and unpredictable world we now live in. Until the Renaissance and the arrival of characters such as Leonardo da Vinci (1452–1519) only God was seen as 'creator' and the generator of ideas and possibilities whilst men merely described or imitated reality. In the twentieth century this idea was firmly refuted as evidenced by the explosion of creative gurus and entrepreneurs seeking to commodify thought processes. De Bono is prime among them, marketing his ideas about 'lateral thinking' through personal training, continued professional development, workshops and seminars. For Sternberg (1999) the scientific study of creativity is suggested to be detrimentally affected by such developments.

Creative or lateral thinking is seen as a problem-solving approach, hence the relationship between thought processes and potential options for action that might arise. But is this a new way of thinking? For de Bono the answer is yes. Seeing the brain as a self-organising system, he contrasts 'lateral thinking' with normal logical thinking, insofar as it suspends the need for reasoning in favour of provocation (de Bono 2009[1970]). Similarly Guy Claxton (1997) laments the decline of slow-knowing and 'unconscious intelligence' in the face of a default deliberative mode of thinking. His Cartesian-inspired 'Hare Brain' is contrasted with the 'Tortoise Mind' which relies on a different kind of intelligence, called creativity or even wisdom, suited when 'the issue is too subtle to be captured by the familiar categories of conscious thought' (Claxton 1997: 3). Genius comes from layers of the mind over which we

(Continued)

(Continued)

have little or no control. Others argue that there is nothing inherently different about creative thinking – rather, that the same cognitive processes are being used as rational thought, even if we cannot readily identify these to ourselves or others (Byrne 2005). If we cannot identify the roots of our thinking, as those interested in the study of creativity would maintain, what does this mean for our role as social scientists? How can we account for and rationalise thought processes to explicate and validate our findings?

Pragmatism displaces the relationship between thought and reality in terms of how truthfully one may be represented by the other. Thinking is now seen as a social rather than a solitary act, which takes place within a 'community of others'. Over time, however, this insight became distorted such that knowledge was seen to be judged in terms of its 'use-value' – the implication being that social practice is the means through which research becomes validated according to how useful it is, rather than whether it is true or false. On this matter, Dewey was clear: 'it is not truly realistic or scientific to take short views, to sacrifice the future to immediate pressure, to ignore facts and forces that are disagreeable and to magnify the enduring quality of whatever falls in with immediate desire' (1957: 130). Instrumentalism, however, does not depart in the face of philosophical argument, but is born in forces that shape knowledge in particular ways. In common with those such as Weber, Dewey developed ideas on cooperative democracy whose relevance remains in the twenty-first century (Honneth 2007).

Female pragmatists played an important role in realising these ideas. Jane Addams (1860–1925) was a philosopher and social reformer who is now receiving greater recognition for her pioneering work alongside better-known male pragmatists. As women were often excluded from university careers, struggling to gain credibility and legitimacy for their work, alternative sites for social action and reform were developed. Addams converted her own house, Hull House, into a hub for local activities and community organising. She supported diverse immigrant groups in Chicago's poorest areas in her efforts to become 'a symbol of the "real" world – a world of work and of people that I longed to reach but could not' (Seigfried 1996: 56).

Me, myself and I

George Herbert Mead (1863–1931) taught at the University of Chicago with Dewey. His belief that science could help address social problems was demonstrated through his association with the City Club of Chicago, the longest-running public policy forum in Chicago. In a classic statement of pragmatism, Mead asked what if philosophy was to take itself out of the ivory tower of its existence and turn 'from its subjective and transcendental idealisms' into 'the world in which we live and move and have our being' (Mead 1938: 514–15). His work was part of the pragmatist tradition in seeing reality not as 'out there', but as actively created as we act in and towards the world. Mead's contributions are central to our understandings of reflexivity through his ideas on the self and our relationships to others, insisting on the inseparability of consciousness from context and interdependence between ourselves and the world.

For Mead, the self is formed through a process of confronting the world of which the individual is a part. It is only by encountering objective conditions that people are able to gain a sense of 'who' they are. A central contribution of Mead was to incorporate the subjective states of individuals into the ongoing flow of social interaction that comprises reflexive relations. His work has parallels with the phenomenological tradition and in particular with Merleau-Ponty, whereby both see the self as a 'socially instituted and temporally mediated reflexive process. It involves the subject "turning back" upon themself (through time), to view themself from "outside" or, rather, as another would view them' (Crossley 1996: 55).

Mead subdivides the self into a 'me' and 'I'. The 'me' is the empirical or social self. It is constituted through social interactions with others and the environment; other people's attitudes and responses are internalised and become part of our own self-identity. People see who they are in part through observing the reactions of others. The 'me' is 'an importation from the field of social objects into an amorphous, unorganized field of what we call inner experience. Through the organization of this object, the self, this material is itself organized and brought under the control of the individual in the form of so-called self-consciousness' (Mead 1964: 140). The 'I' is the 'conversational character of inner experience, the very process of replying to one's own talk'. That implies 'an "I" behind the scenes who answers to the gestures, the symbols that arises in consciousness. The "I" is the transcendental self of Kant, the soul that James conceived behind the scene holding on to the skirts of an idea to give it an added increment of emphasis' (Mead 1964: 141). This aspect of the self is revealed by introspection. A temporal disjuncture between action and reflection reveals the 'I' in a reflexive, memory image of the self, as the 'me' reflects on and judges the 'I' who acted. Box 3.2 highlights this relationship through the example of lying (see also the concept of 'promise' in Chapter 8). Our ability to deceive ourselves and others is at the heart of humanity (Smith 2007).

Dorothy Rowe argues that we lie in response to seeing our 'self' in danger – we lie when our sense of being a person is threatened: 'We all want to be recognised for being the person we are, to have a respected role in society and enjoy good social relations' (Rowe 2011: xvi). Moreover, she argues that as the world gets more uncertain lying is easier than searching for the truth in the face of complexity. If the world is not experienced as the world we imagined, we cannot cope and we cannot act. If these are characteristics of all humans, then what hope might we researchers have in our search for knowledge? When interviewing actors for their accounts of themselves, what confidence can we place in their representations?

■ **Box 3.2** ━━

Constructing the self: lying and reflexivity

The award-winning American cartoon series, *The Simpsons*, has proved a great tool for the communication of philosophy through popular culture (Irwin, Conard and Skoble. 2001). In one episode aired on February 3rd 1994, Bart Simpson is selected to appear on his favourite show, *Krusty the Clown*, but ineptly messes up his lines and wrecks the stage in the process. Despite being on live television, with his actions visible to millions, he exclaims 'I didn't do it!', which then becomes a catchphrase for the nation.

Whereas his Socratic sister Lisa believes that only reason can help her understand and change the world, Bart is bad boy Nietzsche remade (Conard 2011: 64). His identity is constituted through his denial in the face of irrefutable evidence, which supports his identity as a rebel and defines himself in opposition to both authority and truth. Conard concludes that Bart acts out due to a lack of a solid identity or complete self (2011: 77). We can elaborate using Mead's distinction between 'I' and 'me'. The 'me' disciplines the 'I' and reflects on behaviour through anticipating social rules and internalising external norms. Where the 'me' recognises that the 'I' has deviated from those rules, there is a choice – admission or denial. For children, as their social self arises and applies the moral rules of society, they realise they have 'misbehaved'. Lying is a frequent outcome of this internal conversation and sanctioning of the 'I' by the 'me'.

For Bart we could argue that his lie, whilst pointless given the presence of TV cameras, was the result of the sudden realisation by the 'me' that the 'I' had deviated from his actual or preferred actions. Lying is interesting in relation to how we know ourselves and others as it requires the deliberate creation of a false belief in the mind of others, based on a degree of prediction and anticipation of what first 'significant' and then 'generalised others' are thinking. Indeed children's first lies happen in relation to rule violation, to avoid incrimination, protect their perceived interests and present themselves in a positive light (Talwar and Lee 2008).

───

We can conceptualise the 'I' as a 'conversation' within as single person. Language is the medium of that expression that enables a reflexive awareness to conceive of the individual as a 'whole': 'The self acts with reference to others and is immediately conscious of the objects about it. In memory it also reintegrates the self acting, as well as the others acted upon. But besides these contents, their action with reference to the others calls out responses in the individual himself – there is then another "me" criticising, approving, and suggesting, and consciously planning, i.e. the reflective self' (Mead 1964: 145). Reflexivity is at the heart of processes of self-identity formation. However, Mead does not conceive of the mind as a mirror of the social environment, encapsulated in the notion of the 'looking-glass self' (Faberman 1985). His focus upon the collaborative nature of interaction is also important with his emphasis on how 'social interaction "intervenes" in the individual's cognitive development' (Joas 1997: 164).

Mead identifies three stages of inter-subjective activity which develop the self: language, play and game. Mead argues that 'subjects' become 'objects' to themselves via symbolic communication. More specifically, language is the medium through which people speak and hear themselves speak: 'the individual world can exist only in relation to other minds with shared meanings' (Mead 1982: 5). People evaluate their utterances according to the responses of others. Language is not an expression of an inner world made comprehensible through a neutral medium, but our utterances can be a surprise to us and, further, that they provide an insight into what we are through a reflection upon our expressive acts. In addition, we undertake these acts through an understanding of how others might appreciate them which means we convey aspects of ourselves to others using a medium that we share with those others.

Hans Joas regards these insights as significant not only for twentieth-century philosophies of language as found in the works of Mead and Wittgenstein, but further that Herder was 'interested not only in demonstrating the mediated nature of the act of expression, but also in the novelty of each new-found expression. Because of this emphasis, it is legitimate to describe Herder's emphasis on expressivity as a metaphorical version of the idea of creativity' (Joas 1996: 79). For Mead creativity was an important marker in the distinction between the 'I' and the 'me'. Whereas the social self, the 'me', is more conventional and rule-bound, the 'I' is more creative – the 'reservoir of creativity' which Joas (1996) develops in his theory of social action. Importantly for Mead it is the balance between the 'I' and the 'me' that determines personality types and tendencies for individual expression and/or conformism.

The 'play stage' of forming the self involves 'taking the role of others', particularly the 'significant other'. Social interaction occurs through the ability to attribute appropriate meanings to words, gestures and actions. As our selves develop, we relate to a range of significant others – parents, carers and siblings – and here we see an emphasis (shared with Dewey) on the creativity of the individuals in 'the conscious playing through – in imagination of alternative performances of action' (Joas 1993: 249). From this 'play' stage, individuals develop through to the 'game' stage which involves regulated procedures and rules. A notion of the 'generalised other' develops which informs conduct via an expectation of the reaction of others. Signification becomes the means through which the individual and society are inextricably interwoven, with thought itself being 'the conversation of this generalised other with the self' (Mead 1964: 246). We meet the facticity of the world, take account of others and seek recognition through a process of self-formation to gain stability within differing social contexts.

As with Marx, Weber, Dewey and so many others we have encountered, we find a concern in Mead's work for the fate of the individual in the face of increasing impersonal forces. Mead does not conflate change at the level of the self with social change in general, the latter requiring a more generalised and cooperative response to overcome issues. We thus find in his work both an understanding of individual changes through a reflexive process and an acknowledgement of larger, political processes. For Mead it was important to establish 'those social conditions in which formation of the self, rising to the highest levels of capacity for moral decisions, will first become possible for all human beings, and second, the continuous change of all social institutions in order to eliminate all injustices and disadvantages' (Joas 1997: 138).

What we see here is a post-metaphysical understanding of the intersubjective constitution of the self in society. This provides a rich basis from which to generate understanding of the self and reflexivity in society and has led to a rich history of studies (see May and Powell 2008). For instance, Barry Sandywell's discussion of 'phronetic reflexivity' draws upon Greek philosophy, including Aristotle's work, where phronesis refers to 'practical wisdom'. In this instance a judgement upon practical action involves a degree of situational withdrawal that enables reflection to be carried forward into more successful actions: 'Phronetic reflection temporarily disengages the self from practical action; the actor "steps back" or "refrains" from the action; the "loop" hesitation creates is one in which alternatives can be weighed, principles discussed, means and ends communicatively reviewed, advice sought, problems considered from other angles, and anxieties crystallised after being "slept on"' (Sandywell 1996: 320). Here we see the mobilisation of a moral reflexivity with reference to the work of Hegel whom Axel Honneth deploys in his theory of recognition (see Chapter 4).

THOUGHT, ACTION AND OTHER MINDS

Following Kant, the individual had been considered as both 'a *world-generating* and *autonomously acting subject* ... In Kantian philosophy the individuated ego falls between the cracks, as it were, between the transcendental ego, which stands over and against the world as a whole, and the empirical ego, which finds itself already in the world as one among many' (Habermas 1992a: 158; original emphasis). In Mead's work we find neither an interest in utility-oriented action (towards a desired end) nor a Kantian style moral-individual action (transcendental ego). What we have is an examination of the relationship between consciousness and action not in terms of the idea of desired ends as rational action theories so often invoke, but simply because the consciousness that formulates an end does not take place outside of the context of the action itself. Such an approach takes the setting of an end to be the 'result of reflection on resistances encountered by the variously orientated behaviour of a life form whose world is always already schematized in a practical manner prior to all reflection' (Joas 1993: 248). We see how the notion of a 'generalised other' shapes the formation of the self through anticipating the reactions of others. But how can we know the minds of others, especially if we cannot fully know our own?

Knowing that and knowing how

Sigmund Freud (1938) introduced unconscious impulses as that which we do not know, but nevertheless informs who we are and what we do. As such we cannot be reflexively transparent to ourselves! One approach is that whilst we cannot know the minds of others, we can see how people act and the manner in which they do so in the world. The idea of knowing other minds, without resorting to either subjectivism or objectivism, is an important issue not only for the status of the social sciences in society in general, but also for the reflexive relations between how issues are framed, the knowledge produced and what might be hoped for from that knowledge. It is an issue *of* social relations and value.

So what is involved in our description of the actions of others? It often involves the idea that someone is thinking whilst doing. If they are doing so intelligently then their practice is the execution of a set of propositions that have been subject to prior, reflective thought. This solution is part of an intellectualist agenda set by epistemologists in the pursuit of prop-ositional knowledge. However, this is simply not sustainable. It presupposes the prior existence of an act of consideration in which a set of regulative principles are regarded as appropriate or inappropriate to practical problems. Yet there would be so many to choose from! Are we then saying that to act intelligently we must 'first reflect how best to reflect how to act? The endlessness of this implied regress shows that the application of the criterion of appropriateness does not entail the occurrence of a process of considering this criterion' (Ryle 2000[1949]: 31). So why do we invoke theorising and doing as separate processes?

Gilbert Ryle was a British philosopher and leading figure in the 'ordinary language' movement, which paid close attention to the everyday use of language. His seminal work in 1949, *The Concept of Mind*, provided the basis for subsequently overcoming the separa-tion of thinking and doing, through a strong rejection of the Cartesian dualism between body and mind. Ryle's compelling call was to expunge 'the dogma of the Ghost in the Machine' (2000[1949]: 17). He rejected the idea that the mind (Ghost) is a site of reason, was only privately accessible and could be known through introspection, whilst the body (Machine) belonged to the domain of matter, subject to mechanical laws, and could be publicly accessible through observation. For him there was no distinction between the insulated fields of the private mind and actions in space, rather this doctrine of opposition was a 'category mistake'. He illustrates this with a few examples, one of which is a visitor to a university. Upon walking around the university and seeing the administrative build-ings, departments and colleges, the person is mystified and asks 'where is the university?' The error is to take the idea of the university and apply it to those particular things. He suggests the same when watching a cricket match and a spectator is mystified because they do not see 'team spirit'. Theoretical category mistakes include those made by Cartesianism in which abstract thinking applies concepts to 'logical types to which they do not belong' (Ryle 2000[1949]: 19).

Rejecting the ghost in the machine means challenging the hierarchy between physical and mental processes, thinking and doing. We might record a performance artist or sportsperson and note the extraordinary skill that they display. We are not separately recording their skill, nor is there some ghost we do not see. That does not mean it is not happening, but it does mean 'it is a disposition, or complex of dispositions, and a dispo-sition is a factor of the wrong logical type to be seen or unseen, recorded or unrecorded'

(Ryle 2000[1949]: 33). The category error again rears its head. It is due to insights such as these that Daniel Dennett, himself a student of Ryle's, writes: 'Those who still find themselves over their heads on the topic of "consciousness and introspection" would do well to follow Ryle onto the shore of common sense, where the remaining problems are much more interesting than treading water' (Ryle 2000[1949]: xix).

Ryle moves into topics such as the emotions, the will, intelligence, self-knowledge and psychology. He draws a distinction between 'knowing how' and 'knowing that' and commences his inquiries with the following: 'Intelligent practice is not a step-child of theory. On the contrary, theorizing is one practice amongst others and is itself intelligently or stupidly conducted' (Ryle 2000[1949]: 27). The assumption that theorising is a private matter of internal operation is another example of the ghost in the machine. When we describe people as 'shrewd' or 'prudent' or otherwise, we are not imputing a knowledge to them, but refer to their ability to do things: 'Theorists have been so preoccupied with the task of investigating the nature, the source, and the credential of the theories that we adopt that they have for the most part ignored the question what it is for someone to know how to perform tasks' (2000[1949]: 28). We can of course learn 'about something' – how to do a task or play an instrument. We can 'wonder *how* as well as wonder *whether*' (2000[1949]: 29; original emphasis). We do not speak of a person 'believing or opining *how*, and though it is proper to ask for the grounds or reasons for someone's acceptance of a proposition, this question cannot be asked of someone's skill at cards or prudence in investments' (2000[1949]: 29; original emphasis).

What this raises are questions regarding the human capacity for reflexivity at the level of knowledge, aesthetics and ethics. Our contention has been that such matters are not compartmentalised within social scientific and philosophical fields of endeavour, but reflect wider issues that we need to take seriously in order to clarify the place of reflexivity in social life and social science. We might say that they reorientate practices in a dialectical relation between thinking and doing: to practise without thought is to be blinkered and to think without practising is to be stilted. For such reasons we see the popularity of texts on being a 'reflective practitioner' and the 'knowing-doing gap' in organisations (Schön 1991; Pfeffer and Sutton 2000).

Tacit knowledge and contextual understanding

Ryle's distinction between 'knowing that' and 'knowing how' reflects older philosophical stances on different types of knowledge (see Box 3.3). Propositional knowledge, favoured by intellectualists, is knowledge about facts. In this perspective, 'know how' is acquired through a series of 'know thats' which are underpinned by processes of theoretical reason – in other words, follow the right steps and you can learn how to perform a new skill. Others focus instead on the role of ability and disposition in determining whether we can perform certain tasks. The idea of 'know how' rests on procedural knowledge about how to carry out different actions.

■■■ Box 3.3 ■■■■■■■■■■■■■■■■■■■■■■■■■■■■■■■■■■■■

Knowledge currencies

As we make this journey through reflexivity, a single definition of knowledge is being con-tested. Knowledge as true and justified belief, the idea that knowledge is contained in declarative statements about facts, is only one type of knowledge. Theoretical reason is based on this kind of 'propositional knowledge' which can be attained by processes of deductive (a priori) or inductive reasoning (a posteriori). Some have further distinguished between forms of propositional knowledge – logical, semantic, systemic or empirical – that can be drawn on to constitute knowledge as justified true beliefs. Such knowledge can be codified and made 'explicit'. We also have 'procedural knowledge', which refers to the knowledge to do a thing and relates to Polanyi's idea of know-how, and 'personal knowl-edge', which relates to knowledge by acquaintance. Tacit knowledge combines procedural with personal and is hard to codify, often relying on embedded and embodied dimensions. In practice, explicit and tacit knowledge are not definitive categories and can be seen on a spectrum (Botha 2008).

The plethora of efforts to subdivide knowledge is not only a philosophical matter in terms of how we gain understanding about the world; increasingly it is also an economic one. An entire knowledge industry has sprung up around the idea that knowledge is now the source of advantage in a globally competitive market (Scarborough 2001). Strategic advantage comes in coining terms and cornering the market, as seen in de Bono's capture of creativity or even the marketisation of mindfulness for Western audiences through rebranding ancient ideas of meditation and reflection practised for millennia in the East. The knowledge-management industry is based on the idea that knowledge can be codified and extracted to produce economic value. As the importance of tacit knowledge for competitive advantage is recognised, so efforts to commodify it are amplified to achieve 'smart' technological devel-opments (Perry and May, 2015; May and Perry, 2016). Hellstrom and Raman (2001: 139) see that 'it is ironic to find the socialisation of theories of knowledge being faced with its own reification in the form of veritable social epistemological principles developed and sold in the market for management consultants'. Perhaps this is not the type of end use that our socially oriented pragmatists had in mind!

Michael Polanyi was a polymath opposed to a positivist view of science and insisted that all knowledge claims rely on personal judgement. He wrote how there is a 'personal co-efficient, which shapes all factual knowledge, bridges in doing so the disjunction between subjectivity and objectivity' (Polanyi 1962: 17). He contrasted deductive reasoning, empiri-cal exploration and inductive inference with what he called the 'logic of contriving' which 'can never be impersonal' (1962: 328). The tendency to reduce all our knowledge to imper-sonal terms has constrained pragmatism from having its insights developed into scientific methodology. Using a mechanistic analogy, Polanyi showed how we cannot necessarily recognise the identity or functioning of a machine just by understanding its operational principles. These may be seen as *'rules of rightness*, which account only for the successful working of machines, but leave their failures entirely unexplained' (1962: 328; original emphasis). What Polanyi was doing here was pointing out the levels of reality under which things operate. He noted how we can know something through integration of awareness of its particulars – without necessarily being able to identify those particulars.

It is for this reason that he wrote about the importance of tacit knowledge in the vein of the pragmatist tradition. Tacit knowledge itself has been used in all sorts of ways in various fields of endeavour, but may be captured by the idea that *'we can know more than we can tell'* (Polanyi 1983: 4; original emphasis). The act of socialising knowledge continues apace in these formulations. However we choose to communicate our meaning, knowledge must be received to be understood: a gap to be bridged through 'intelligent effort on the part of the person to whom we want to tell what the word means' (1983[1966]: 6). Previously, the argument that projection is not involved in perception had been ruled out on the grounds that we have no previous awareness of the internal processes through which this takes place. For Polanyi, however, 'we have established that projection of this very kind is present in various instances of tacit knowing. Moreover, the fact that we do not originally sense the internal processes in themselves now appears irrelevant' (1983[1966]: 15). He illustrated this in terms of including within tacit knowledge the 'neural traces in the cortex of the nervous system' (1983[1966]: 15). He thus took knowing to comprise both of Ryle's senses of knowing what and knowing how (1983[1966]: 7).

We take some important points from these authors for our journey through reflexivity: that we understand through reference to a whole, that we must challenge a subject–object dualism, and that scientific and artistic genius represents the highest acts of tacit integration. This shifts our reflexive lenses in terms of knowledge and the place of the social sciences in society. As Harry Collins puts it at the start of his study into tacit and explicit knowledge, 'tacit knowledge makes speakers fluent, lets scientists understand each other, is the crucial part of what teachers teach, makes bureaucratic life seem ordered, comprises the skill in most sports and other physical activities, puts the smile on the face of the *Mona Lisa* and, because we users bring the tacit knowledge to the interaction, turns computers from *idiots savants* into useful assistants' (2010: 1; original emphasis).

Differentiating between somatic, collective and relational tacit knowledge, Collins moves us from that which is embodied in the brain and human body (somatic) to that in society (collective), to how people relate to one another (relational). Humans are special in that they have a collective tacit knowledge not shared by animals or objects that enables them to organise things. He calls this difference 'Social Cartesianism' (Collins 2010) and places society at the centre of our understanding of knowledge. Collins takes us in the direction of the social basis of knowledge which, in social studies of science and technology, tends to emphasise the cultural and social contexts of discovery over the scientific content and justification of what is produced (Norris 2014).

Do these insights provide a basis for how we might take a further step away from consciousness and how we know the minds of others? Polanyi joins Peirce, Heidegger, Mead, Addams and Merleau-Ponty in a critique of an abstracted form of knowledge that positions the knower outside the world, yet simultaneously claims to be representative of it. This is the basis of the 'whole rationalist thrust of reflexive testing of the grounds of knowledge' (Taylor 1995: 9).

LANGUAGE, MEANING AND EVERYDAY SPEECH

Once we situate the individual within the world of which they are a part, reflexive understandings of the self and knowledge move our focus away from an atomised individual. A subject, as a being-in-the-world, becomes the topic of investigation in order to know something or have experience of the world. The realm of experience must be self enclosed if it is to be subject to investigation through rationalist or empiricist forms. These are then reflexively tested and those experiences are about something in a world separate from the subject themselves. Husserl tackled this through intentionality: ideas and experiences are about something. Kant showed that Hume's formulations cannot work and there are certain conditions that are needed to provide coherence to our activities: 'Plainly we couldn't have experience of the world at all if we had to start with a swirl of uninterpreted data. Indeed, there would be no "data", because even this minimal description depends on our distinguishing what is given by some objective source from what we merely supply ourselves' (Taylor 1995: 11). What avenues are then open to social scientists?

Language games

Recalling Herder's insights, we need to attend to the constitutive role of language to produce meaning in socially situated persons. Practical reason may be constituted in the use of language in social life. Here we find two stages: first, a reflective stage that arises in our dealings with the world around us and, second, language as a new reflexive stance in relation to things and persons around us. In the second we orientate ourselves, as Mead suggested, towards ourselves and others as speech does not simply report, but reflexively constitutes our relations, including with ourselves. We find no private language known only to ourselves which reports a separate reality, but publicly available forms of language use. The means of coming to know ourselves and others can be studied in situ through how we express ourselves in terms of the cultural repertoires available to us. As the Russian psychologist Lev Vygotsky put it, 'the relation of thought to word is not a thing but a process, a continual movement backward and forth from thought to word and from word to thought … Thought is not merely expressed in words; it comes into existence through them' (quoted in Shotter 1993: 108–9).

Ludwig Wittgenstein moved positions from providing the armoury for logical positivism to adopting a position that was radically different. In his earlier work he had set out the status of a transcendental scientific language in which conditions for statements about the world are made (Wittgenstein 1922). Language thus stands for something – it is a picture of reality. Yet he subsequently stood in stark contrast to the school of logical positivism, arguing that language provides meaning and is meaningless without context. This shift was in part a reaction to his experiences of Habsburg Vienna at a time when 'cultural and political decay was papered over by the meaningless catchphrases of newspapers, by the empty ethical formulations of intellectuals and by worthless political appeals' (Silverman and Torode 2011[1980]: 35). In his later work Wittgenstein argued that words do not stand for things and represent reality, and nor do they express the intentions of their authors, but do have resemblances. In this way Wittgenstein (1953) finds in ordinary language the means through which our forms of life are constituted.

Wittgenstein and ordinary language philosophers, such as John Austin (1976), attacked the idea that a single name refers to common objects. They observed that there are many reasons for calling something by the same name, and instead of referring to such things as 'essence' we should instead embrace the messiness of everyday language use. How we learn to speak and are socialised into a culture, or what Wittgenstein called 'language games', comprise not just speech but practice: they are one and the same. Players of one game cannot criticise another without first learning the rules. This moves our focus from whether language accurately reports an independent reality to different forms of expression that share similar characteristics. It also means a change in direction: Kantian issues concerning the conditions of knowledge are now replaced by a study of language use.

We have seen in our journey how language does not simply mediate an external reality, but is constitutive as an action in the world. Wittgenstein shifted the epistemological focus upon truth and moved us towards the use of words. The outcome was a displacement away from the questions that may impose themselves upon us as a result of the human condition and circumstances towards *how* we use words. As Ernest Gellner puts it, an extraordinary facility thereby arrives: 'Scales fall off our eyes: we can see the solution of the problem of freedom in the rules governing our use of words such as "free", of the problem of probability by observing our use of words such as "likely", and so on' (1987: 158). That rejection moves us away from a theory–practice relation into the realm of situated reason, with the result that we terminate in a place where there is nothing beyond it and no place to imagine oneself outside of it. We are in the world and our questions come from that point of view. Language is deployed, theory is governed by it, and what we have is a form of therapy in terms of proper use accompanied by a situated reflexivity: 'The ordinary is all that we have, and as itself it provides enough of the mysterious to keep us fully absorbed. Situatedness is the place of life, and not a limited condition *within* life that we can inspect; it is integral to what we see with, and therefore cannot be seen' (Simpson 2002: 159; original emphasis).

▄▄ Box 3.4 ▬▬▬▬▬▬▬▬▬▬▬▬▬▬▬▬▬▬▬▬▬▬▬▬▬▬▬▬▬

Rhetoric and language games

In Condor et al.'s excellent (2013) review they use the Aristotelian definition of rhetoric as the practical art of effective communication and persuasion. As soon as we recognise that we are being persuaded, critical hermeneutics becomes necessary to see texts as both situated in and constitutive of their contexts. As researchers, it draws attention to the need not to take statements at face value. Their review covers the topics of political rhetoric: from climate change to terrorism and race; the use of rhetorical language, such as metaphor, proverb, slogans and humour; and the appeal to commonsense values such as change, choice and community. For some, the same thinking lies behind private deliberation and public oratory in terms of the constitution of the self and processes of self-consciousness. Indeed Francis Bacon is said to have seen rhetoric as interpersonal negotiation. For others rhetoric, like lying, is a thought-avoidance strategy in a complex world; labels are 'devices for saving talkative persons the trouble of thinking' (Morley 1886: 142, in Condor et al. 2013).

Rhetoric has very real effects and we see how language constitutes our understanding of the world. Hopkins and Kahani-Hopkins' (2004) analysis of the social category constructions mobilised in texts by groups of Muslim activists in Britain is a case in point, as to whether Islam and the West are presented as compatible or incompatible categories (see Condor et al. 2013). Political decision-making has also been the subject of analysis, with politics as the presence of beliefs in contradiction with other beliefs. Leaders such as Tony Blair have come in for particular study in terms of the effective use of rhetoric to achieve political aims (Fairclough 2000). Rhetoric and identity politics is a particular area of study around race (Billig 2001), gender (Stokoe 2000), poverty, religion (Figgou and Condor 2007) and sexuality (Summers 2007). Condor et al. conclude that studying rhetoric requires high levels of reflexivity and go further in suggesting that all writing is rhetoric! This must also apply to academic texts. Is Lyotard correct in asserting that scientific communications are language games of persuasion and dissuasion? Do we not, in making our arguments, also wish to influence the minds of others, by appealing to different knowledge claims?

Jean Francois Lyotard (1924–98), whose ideas we shall return to later, took Wittgenstein's legacy further and saw science as linguistic game-playing across scientific communities to support one's own and support/challenge the ideas of others. These games may be denotative, prescriptive or technical – focusing on what is true or not, what is good or bad, or what is efficient or inefficient. Words are tools to build our houses and concepts do not need to be easily defined as there is a plurality of language games at play. To illustrate this Box 3.4 considers the example of political rhetoric. The use of language is bound up with our own identities in terms of how we are seen and wish to be seen by others. Talk and text constitute strategic communicative action and are not just expressions of inner psychological states.

Intersubjective understanding

Peter Winch continued the analysis of words as tools for inter-subjective understandings. His emphasis was against causal accounts for human actions, instead focusing on the need to understand context to understand action. Therefore any further advance in reflective understanding 'must necessarily presuppose, if it is to count as genuine understanding at all, the participant's unreflective understanding' (Winch 1990[1958]: 89). Words now become the tools through which inter-subjective understanding is achieved and the topic, not resource, for social science. Methodological and theoretical problems arise in a conflation of the understanding between social scientists and the persons they are studying and the understanding and issues that arise in society. Ryle's call to common sense becomes the study of how that is produced: 'There *are* problems of understanding, but they are not problems between a (sort of) scientist and lay person, but of the sort that arise amongst members of the society themselves, where different kinds of people and different ways of doing things themselves present assorted problems of intelligibility' (Hutchinson et al. 2008: 35; original emphasis).

Efforts to understand different cultures by social scientists are thus limited by the understanding of the social scientist who seeks to impose their own standards where that is inapplicable. Winch's call to rule-following actions is thus not a matter of finding the rules and then explaining the behaviour, but on the contrary of recognising that rule-following understandings are already part of the social life and also, therefore, the very fabric of social scientific practices because they are social. Such a call closes the theoretical/practical reason gap that makes up explanations of human actions and with that phenomenological reference to the subject: 'A major corrective ... to the Schutzian programme is to insist upon the relevance of what Wittgenstein termed "criteria" for practical utilization in everyday life. Criteria are defeasible, conventional evidences for the constitution of phenomena, and they are inextricably linked to the differential distribution of practical interests in social existence' (Coulter 1983: 123).

Harold Garfinkel (1967) was another who refused to separate everyday theorising in social life and social science, seeing reflexivity as a feature of life itself. Drawing on the insights from both Peirce and Wittgenstein, Garfinkel emphasised how everyday language and actions cannot be understood without being situated within the social context in which they are uttered and produced because meanings vary between contexts. To address this social scientists produce metaphors in order to theorise as to how objects are constructed in the social world. Nevertheless, these do not reflect the practical means through which recognition and production take place in everyday life, and result in a disjuncture between the 'concreteness' of everyday activities and social scientific representation. The result is that 'real society' only comes into being 'as the achieved results of administering the policies and methods of formal, constructive analysis' (Garfinkel 1991: 13). To accurately represent meaning-production within the lifeworld, context-dependence must be recognised as the starting *and* finishing point of social analysis. The recommendation is not the imposition of a method or theory, but to start with the ways in which people interpret everyday meanings (Hutchinson et al. 2008).

Meaning is given in the situated and practical aspects of everyday life without reference to any 'phenomenological residua' in social thought (Coulter 1979). Both the setting in which action takes place and the account of that action are fused in the routine, reflexive monitoring of conduct undertaken by actors within the life world. Reflexivity is the basis of order in everyday life and provided for in accurate descriptions of accounting procedures used by 'members' within social settings: 'The central recommendation is that the activities whereby members produce and manage settings of organized everyday affairs are identical with members' procedures for making those settings "account-able". The "reflexive" or "incarnate" character of accounting practices and accounts makes up the crux of that recommendation' (Garfinkel 1967: 1). Reflexivity contributes to social order and is displayed through situated and public activities that are open to analysis. Reflexivity is seen as mundane and so it questions those traditions where we find an 'epistemological hubris that seems to accompany self-consciously reflexive claims'. Its study of 'constitutive reflexivity proposes no unreflexive counterpart', and instead is part of the 'infrastructure of objective accounting' (Lynch 2000: 47).

The scholastic point of view, or the intellectualism that Ryle took aim at, is removed from the stage (Garfinkel 1991). Reflexivity does not privilege a position of social scientific insight but is a mundane feature of everyday life. Language does not stand above the world but is constitutive of it. The transcendental ego is not providing meaning through the word but the word provides meaning through participation in forms of life. Words are not about reference to an object world, or expressions of an atomised subject, but inter-subjective achievements of understanding through the rules that inform language use. To know a form of life is to know these rules that allow for intelligibility and that 'know-how' is the topic for social science. Utterance is not some partial manifestation of an ego's private language in reference to an object world: 'Reflexivity could then, without any apparent difficulty, be assimilated to a subtle kind of reference, the reference to the world-event of utterance. The utterance was then aligned with the things in the world of which we speak' (Ricoeur 1994: 51).

This alignment between things in the world and speech favours a study of the practical achievements of constituting meaning in everyday speech. Following these ideas we cannot presume a reflexive self seeking to establish truth according to rational criteria, and there is no fundamental difference between social scientific explanations and lay understandings: 'If it is possible to lay bare the constitutive ordering of the world that experimental subjects owe to their own interpretive rules, then the process of translation between them and the observer can be done away with' (Habermas 1990[1970]: 110). In terms of the relations between knowledge and social change, forms of life that are bounded do not appear to be amenable to change, but only to understanding through full immersion in their particular lifeworld. However, this language-based corrective to the intellectualism of the theoretical vision of disengaged reason over the practical may have gone too far in expunging phenomenological insight (Ricoeur 1994). Meaning is found in utterance as any reference to the ego vanishes from our analytic terrain, but 'it relates reflexivity to the utterance considered as a fact, that is, as an event produced in the world', and so 'reflexivity is not intrinsically bound up with a self in the strong sense of self-consciousness' (Ricoeur 1994: 47).

Reflexivity may arise between self and other as interlocutor. Whilst intuitive appeal undoubtedly enables us to reside in the world without continual referral to the conditions which enable our actions, to elevate this to the plane of a general analysis of society is problematic. Mead's idea of self took account of this difference without a linguistic flattening of the social field. As the philosopher and anthropologist Ernest Gellner puts it, 'People had not asked philosophic questions because they had made a mistake about language. They asked them because they are unavoidable: they imposed themselves by the very nature of our situation' (1987: 158). That issue is side-stepped through a study of the ordinary use of words and an assumption that this is a better means of study, and so 'Deviation from ordinary use is *ex officio* "unintelligible", unless "it is given a sense"' (Gellner 1968: 201; original emphasis). As Gellner (1987) notes, this shares similarities with currents of existentialism which want to make things easier, not harder, against the spirit of those such as Kierkegaard.

SUMMARY: REFLEXIVITY EMBEDDED

In earlier chapters we saw how an increasing focus on the role of consciousness and history and alternative conceptions of the human sciences arose. An emphasis upon ontology taught us about epistemological limits, whilst history is not just something we learn by dates but an interpretive act which concerns what we have been, are now, and informs what we might become. The realm of democracy is a matter of concern, not just to check the rule of powerful interests, but also to enable a plurality of views born of values unsaturated by instrumental reason. Jane Addams thus emphasised the importance of cooperation and understanding within a democratic and egalitarian spirit. A distinction between the content of science and its consequences needs to be maintained in a deliberative, democratic space in order that it is not manipulated by those who conflate their interests with its outcomes and science does not spill over into scientism. The reflexive self is not a subject rooted in consciousness in which mind predominates over matter. We are beings with bodies that are part of us and which do not exist separate from us; we seek an adjustive relationship between ourselves and social environments. What we encounter as society is not an object constituted by a knowing subject, but a process of self formation through a relationship between subject and object.

In this chapter we have taken a journey to examine how the operational principles of everyday life become the social scientific descriptions of that life through an emphasis on ordinary language philosophy. Situated reflexivity is not a resource for scientific study but part of the topic that is studied. To counter the charge of subjectivism requires understanding forms of life whose meanings are inter-subjectively constituted in everyday language.

Through these writings we have seen how any residual phenomenological insight is abandoned: 'the problem of language has taken the place of the traditional problem of consciousness: the transcendental critique of language takes the place of that of consciousness … In consequence, linguistic philosophy no longer grasps the connection between intention and action, as does phenomenology, in terms of the constitution of meaning contexts' (Habermas 1990[1970]: 117).

The knowing in a socialised consciousness comes through an encounter between self and other that pragmatism constituted as praxis which is a core component in liberation ideas: 'One of the gravest obstacles to the achievement of liberation is that oppressive reality absorbs those within it and thereby acts to submerge human beings' consciousness. Functionally, oppression is domesticating. To no longer be prey to its force, one must emerge from it and turn upon it. This can be done only by means of the praxis: reflection and action upon the world in order to transform it' (Freire 1970: 33).

Is social scientific knowing different in kind to everyday understanding, and does this give it insight as well as being a focus of contestation in society over ideas and practices? If social scientific knowing is different in kind where does this lead reflection? Is it to bring something to awareness in order to examine the basis of its authority to accept it along with other circumstances, or does such awareness lead to a dissolving of what was previously accepted as true knowledge (Gadamer 1977)? To this extent, social science may be a form of reflexive hermeneutics in which the meanings of how we are constituted in society are uncovered.

Whilst we have had propositional and practical knowledge, what then of critical knowledge and reflexivity? This would require an awareness of the social and cultural backdrop to social scientific work which, whilst not determinative, is influential. In the above we see a period in which two world wars occur and we enter the Cold War. A search for certainty continues, and with that a belief in science as the saviour. If scientism is the bounded repository of a particular concept of reason, what is left of the reflexive relation of learning from the past and forging the future? Recognising that science itself is a social activity, what forms of justification exist that enables its practitioners to have the privilege of insight free from the constraints that saturate the lives of non-practitioners? Let us turn to those who took these issues seriously.

4

CRITIQUE AND TRANSFORMATION

━━ **CHAPTER CONTENTS** ━━━━━━━━━━━━━━━━━━━━━━━━━━━━━━━

A critical theory of contemporary society must include an account of the relation of status subordination to class subordination, misrecognition to maldistribution. Above all, it must clarify the prospects for emancipatory change for a time in which struggles for recognition are increasingly decoupled from struggles for egalitarian redistribution – even as justice requires that the two be joined.

(Nancy Fraser in Fraser and Honneth 2003: 59)

INTRODUCTION

We have highlighted the constant interaction between theory and facts. Different authors have considered the relationship between the content, context and consequences of knowledge production (May with Perry 2011), revealing strong variations between those focusing on theoretical reason and those with a pragmatist or empiricist outlook. The search for certain knowledge and the denial of the possibility of attaining it have been key themes, along with the need to recognise the relationship between the constitution of propositions about knowledge and the social context in which they are generated.

In this chapter we continue our journey through turning from theoretical and practical to *critical reason*. Here we consider not only the implications of knowledge for and in action, but also a particular form of action – namely critique aimed at the transformation of existing social, political and economic relations. We wish to consider those traditions and practitioners whose aim is not to produce affirmative strategies to address social injustices, but transformative ones. Research results feeding back into social life are not a problem for those researchers who fall within a critical theory tradition. On the contrary, the value and adequacy of research lie primarily in how it informs political actions without reflecting the dominant rationalisations of the status quo. Critical researchers do not accept a simple distinction between theory, facts and values, and possess constructions of the self with associated ideas on reflexivity, critique and transformation.

Under the broad heading of critique we can place a wide range of literature: from those informed by the works of Marx, Freud and Weber, via those working with poststructuralist and critical realist ideas, to those inspired by feminist ideas and research. There are overlaps, differences and similarities within and between these approaches. We focus particularly on the works of those associated with the Frankfurt School of critical theory in the twentieth century. The story starts with the first-generation scholars inspired by Marx and latterly by Sigmund Freud (1856–1939), amongst them Max Horkheimer (1895–1973), Theodor Adorno (1903–69), Herbert Marcuse (1898–1979), Walter Benjamin (1892–1940) and Eric Fromm (1900–80). We then examine the works of Hans-Georg Gadamer (1900–2) and the contributions of Jürgen Habermas. We also note the interventions of Axel Honneth, Nancy Fraser and Rainer Forst, whose work shapes how we think about the relationship between the self, society and how we know, act in and seek to *transform* the worlds of which we are part.

Through the generations we see how the emphasis has shifted – from a concern with dialectics to the conditions for social action and communication, and finally to the importance of ideas on recognition, redistribution and justification. Yet enduring themes appear: critique is a central part of transforming societies, change is possible through the pursuit of an engaged and critical social science and fundamentally, the a priori recognition that we are *interested* humans who filter knowledge through our prior experiences and understandings. That recognition accompanies the need for a constant vigilance in terms of the contexts in which we act and work alongside the content of knowledge concerning the possibilities and limits for how we can know and change the social world.

CRITICAL THEORY

To the extent that any theorisation of societal mechanisms and means of conducting social relations does not accord with dominant ways of viewing society and social relations, it may be said to be critical. The critical theorists' work drew on a rich legacy. Horkheimer explicitly sought to avoid the melancholy of Heidegger through placing hope in the realisation of the liberating elements of philosophy. He gained this from the young Karl Marx and the possibility of progress in science from the later works of Freud (Wiggershaus 1995: 39). To pursue this possibility there were figures that stood between Hegel and Marx – including Schopenhauer and Nietzsche – who needed to be engaged with in order to recover the promise of Marxism.

Despite the dominance of logical positivism, the entire positivist approach was seen to have failed to examine the conditions under which capitalism develops and is reproduced. Interpretivism, as expressed in the work of those such as Mead and those inspired by him, including Erving Goffman (1971, 1984[1959]) and those working in symbolic interactionist traditions (Rock 1979), was inadequate because of an exclusive focus on processes of self-understanding, agency and self-consciousness. Positivism was rejected for conflating reason – necessary for the purpose of transcending existing conditions in order to ascertain alternative possibilities – with instrumental reason: that is, the exercise of calculation for the determination of means towards ends (Williams and May 1996). Forms of rational calculation, confused with critical reason, serve to reproduce the status quo, as is the case with those who seek to understand consciousness as nothing more than a symptom of given social conditions.

Traditional understandings of what we mean by 'theory' refer to the division between the realms of ideas and practice and the notion that the objective world is a mirror of reality about which we can gain knowledge based on self-evident propositions. Critical theory draws on how knowledge is related to critique and social emancipation, hence knowledge is not a mirror of reality but a form of social criticism embedded in historical and social processes. Critical theory maintains that relations of domination inform meanings, claims and demands – the task therefore is to seek alternatives to forms of oppression and control via understanding oppositional cultures. The term *critical theory* is normally reserved for a particular set of ideas associated with what become known as the Frankfurt School of Social Research and its followers, who have modified and extended its original insights, aspirations and agendas through interdisciplinary work.

Marxist roots

The Frankfurt School was established with the aim to develop Marxist Studies in Weimar Germany, based on a strong critique of modernity and capitalist society emerging from the post-World War I context. Their work focused on a number of areas, including: explanations for the absence of a unified working-class movement in Europe; an examination of the nature and consequences of capitalist crises; an exploration of the relationship between the political and the economic spheres in modern societies; accounts of the rise of fascism and Nazism as political movements; and studies of familial socialisation and sustained critiques of the links between science and positivism. Under the directorship of Max Horkheimer, appointed in 1930, the focus moved to the interdisciplinary integration of the social sciences, drawing on psychological, political, social, cultural and economic factors. To examine these trends required an explanation of the connections between the individual and society through the relations of knowledge, reflexivity, action and transformation in the face of the assault of instrumental reason. Theory under Horkheimer was interdisciplinary, reflexive, dialectical and critical. It was also grounded in a consideration of the role of culture that, until this time, had not been highly valued in Marxist circles, hence studies of music and literature became part of its work. Box 4.1 questions the influence of offline and online media, shaped by partisan corporate giants and non-human algorithms, on how we understand the world and can hope to know it. This shows the continuing relevance of critical theorists' fears of culture and the media today. It also partially explains digital social movements and the rise of hyperlocal, independent, creative commons websites and social media forums which are developing in opposition to mainstream media. It is hoped that this 'new media' have a role to play in fostering public activities and spaces of dissent (Roberts, 2014).

▬ Box 4.1 ▬▬▬▬▬▬▬▬▬▬▬▬▬▬

Reflexivity in a media society

'Candyfloss! Nearly 100% proof sugar! No nutritional value! Get tooth decay with snacks that lasts mere moments!' Not such a great advert is it? The candyfloss metaphor was apt for Adorno and Horkheimer for the way in which the mass media, film companies, broadcasting firms and publication houses of Hollywood peddled their wares – promises of sweet nothings numbing the minds of consumers to the reality of their broader social-economic oppression. Benjamin was more hopeful that political enlightenment could be achieved by progressive cultural creators reorientating cultural production, but shared with Adorno and Horkheimer an interest in alternative oppositional cultures. Habermas reacted against the rise of late capitalism, the culture industries, the power of corporations, and the transformation of citizens into passive consumers of goods and services. Behind his idea of the public sphere – and diagnosis as to why it was not realised – lies a critique of how corporate media deny citizens a voice and inhibit political culture and access to honest information. Access to information via cultural means of distribution is central. For Habermas poorly informed citizens, without access to the same information as elites, cannot fully participate in decision-making or in the public sphere. Multiple factors mobilise against this, including a lack of transparency and the mobilisation of concepts of expertise to devalue citizens' knowledge. Environmental decision-making is one such example (Haklay 2003).

This requires reflexivity about the use of scientific language to bound claims to knowledge by those that profess as expert. Social media add to the problem. In Eli Pariser's *Filter*

Bubble (2012) he outlines the extent to which large companies such as Google and Facebook not only gather information on the public, but also filter information according to anticipated preferences. Debunking the idea that the internet is a tool of democratic advancement through making more information public and connecting individual citizens to a world wide web of free information, he outlines how our perceptions and knowledge of the world are filtered, often without us knowing, based on prior preferences. This 'invisible algorithmic editing of the web' controls which information we have access to. As we increasingly experience the world through a digital lens, are our views of that world becoming more and more biased, without us even knowing it? How does the information we have access to influence and shape our positions on, processes towards and even results from research?

In Nazi Germany they found themselves under threat, with the result that its members, including Theodor Adorno, the psychoanalyst Eric Fromm (1900–80), Max Horkheimer and Herbert Marcuse, emigrated to the United States (Adorno and Horkheimer returned after World War II). Walter Benjamin, who was associated with their work, also fled the Nazis and was making his way to North America when he committed suicide rather than be captured. Benjamin influenced not only the Frankfurt School but also many others, including the poet, playwright and director Bertolt Brecht (1898–1956). In the United States these scholars experienced a self-confident bourgeois liberal-capitalism, with its apparent ability to absorb and neutralise the realisation of a proletarian consciousness through the ideologies of individualism and meritocracy.

The Frankfurt School was concerned with the need to emancipate social science from 'ideological blinders' through bringing to awareness the conditions of individuals' own knowledge of the world (Anderson 2000). The social world is constructed and not given, and only a reflexive social science can provide an account of its own origins. Taking insights from Kant, Hegel and Marx forward, questions were posed about the potential for critical reflexivity and historical investigations undertaken into the failed promise of the Enlightenment project to achieve emancipation, including constructions of the individual in relation to their environment. The processes of ideological incorporation became the social scientific focus. Herbert Marcuse, a source of inspiration for the student riots of the late 1960s, drew attention to the dehumanising effects of capitalism, advocating revolt in the face of an exploitative and objectifying social-economic system in his book *One-Dimensional Man*. Here, the 'technical-administrative control' of society (Marcuse 1968) became a key focus: 'the productive apparatus tends to become totalitarian to the extent to which it determines not only the socially needed occupations, skills, and attitudes, but also individual needs and aspirations. It thus obliterates the opposition between the private and public existence, between individual and social needs. Technology serves to institute new, more effective, and more pleasant forms of social control and social cohesion' (Marcuse 1968: 13). Marcuse, who was at Freiburg at the same time as Heidegger, was critical of the idea of 'authentic existence' for not taking actually existing conditions seriously.

Adorno and Horkheimer concluded that 'the individual is wholly devalued in relation to the economic powers, which at the same time press the control of society over nature to hitherto unsuspected heights ... The flood of detailed information and candy-floss entertainment simultaneously instructs and stultifies mankind' (1979[1944]: xiv–xv). This is representative of the underpinnings of a critical theory, which in contrast to traditional theory 'says that the basic form of the historically given commodity economy on which modern history rests contains in itself the internal and external tensions of the modern era; it generates these tensions over and over again in an increasingly heightened form; and after a period of progress, development of human power, and emancipation for the individual, after an enormous extension of human control over nature, it finally hinders further development and drives humanity into a new barbarism' (Horkheimer 1972: 227).

For these thinkers the issue of reconnection and the potential of an emancipatory and critical science met with investigations of the relations between science and the Enlightenment. Scientific endeavour is usually constituted as the separation between humans and nature. Descartes provided us with this legacy through his insistence that reason was the basis from which we can judge truth. However, as we have already seen the Cartesian legacy has been subject to extensive critique over time through, for example, the assumption of separating mind and body and reason and emotion. The critical theorists took this one step further. They saw 'science' itself as accelerating capitalist development through a desire to form a technical-administrative apparatus to manipulate the social and natural worlds. This domination is disguised and based upon an irrational subject who fears freedom and emancipation.

Irrational fear underpins the desire to control and manipulate the world. That being the case, what hope is there for the relations between social science and reflexivity at an individual level in terms of explaining the effects of society upon action, and at a collective level the potential for societal transformation? Our termination point can easily become denunciations of the potential of the subject as epiphenomenal to the productive apparatus of capitalism, exacerbated through the dualism that is carried in everyday life between thought and action. A turn to such determinations easily saturates the possibilities for reflexivity at the level of agency. Such a move may occur at the level of an inhuman system that separates people from themselves and each other through the effects of instrumental calculation.

Lest this is seen as a hopeless or pessimistic outlook, it is worth restating that these thinkers rejected the separation of thought and being, or theory and practice (Horkheimer 1972). Critical theorists despaired of the popular hostility to theory as if it had no import for the 'practical realities' of the world: 'Among the vast majority of the ruled there is the unconscious fear that theoretical thinking might show their painfully won adaptation to reality to be perverse and unnecessary. Those who profit from the status quo entertain a general suspicion of any intellectual independence. The tendency to conceive theory as the opposite of a positive outlook is so strong that even the inoffensive traditional type of theory suffers from it at times' (Horkheimer 1972: 232). Theory and critique are the first steps to transformation, through taking seriously the unity between science and social activity. Change is therefore not only necessary, but also possible and inevitable – reflected in Adorno's reinterpretation of Hegel through the idea of 'negative dialectics'. History is not simply the unfolding of a predetermined path with a known and definite end point, rather a contradiction between what is and what might be as we move from necessity to contingency. This requires a retrospective orientation, as we can only see what has happened, but not what might happen next.

Freudian influences

Where does this leave us in respect of the ability of the individual to be reflexive concerning the conditions under and through which they act? What does this mean for the role of critical reason and the social sciences in the constitution of such understanding? To answer these questions requires an investigation into the social subject under capitalism to chart a course between the process of incorporation and the potential for radical change. A critical psychology has the potential to study the need-dispositions and the 'personality forms and character structures produced by the social relations of capitalist societies' (Honneth and Joas 1988: 107). This focus moves away from an understanding of the solitary ego in the social world to the *self-misunderstanding* person who fails to see the causes of her or his own symptoms. The unconscious, and its relation to self-realisation, are key elements in the potential for this reflexive process. Here is where the work of Sigmund Freud (1856–1939) influenced the work of the Frankfurt School. Marxist social analysis was accompanied by Freudian psychoanalysis, in part as a response to the search for explanations as to what made people turn to fascism in the 1930s in Germany.

The interest in Freud was apparent in socio-psychological studies on the structure of modern personality types carried about by Adorno and his associates in 1950 (Adorno et al. 1950), as well as in the writings of Willhelm Reich on the relationship between sexuality and capitalism (Ollman 1979). However, if Freud's work was to serve the needs of critical theory, it required modification. Psychoanalysis may be seen as the practice of amelioration through a psychological reductionism which seeks individual adjustment to unjust conditions. Conceptually speaking, it starts from the individual and tends to play down social conditions and constraints. In practice, it may easily become a psychoanalytic task to adjust the individual's needs to the dominant system as if it were both the cause and effect of that system. As Box 4.2 illustrates, psychoanalysis may be a tool of conformism or a 'course in resignation' (Marcuse 1966). In the same way that mass entertainment inhibited people from seeing the reality of the circumstances in which they were trapped, the concern was that psychoanalysis would lead to an individualistic perspective in which people would be encouraged to adapt to and cope within an unjust system rather than seeking to transform it. Fromm was clear that social conditions result in new anxieties and that there is a relationship between agents and structures in ways that are irreducible to an individualistic perspective. This raises a broader issue of the relationships between people and the systems they are located within.

For these reasons Marxists had dismissed psychoanalysis as unworthy of attention, and further a distraction from the primary purpose of overthrowing an unjust economic system. Yet if the individual has emotional needs that lie behind conscious actions and processes, a study of these conditions is essential: 'If reality is the guide by which Marxists shape their tactics and programmes, then psycho-analysis is a signpost of first importance' (Osborn 1937: 285).

■ Box 4.2 ■

Individual reflexivity and systemic injustice

The critical theorists were wary of psychoanalysis. Problems are often portrayed as the result of individual weakness or failure without any consideration of socio-economic and structural factors. The stigmatisation of people receiving welfare benefits is one example: 'Whether or not these areas are in fact dilapidated and dangerous, and their population composed essentially of poor people, minorities and foreigners, matters little in the end: the prejudicial belief that they are suffices to set off socially noxious consequences' (Wacquant, 2007: 68). That poverty is not a question of individual choice but the result of deep-seated and complex structural conditions is less controversial than other topics that are infused with the same individualism. For instance, in Dr Robert Lustig's *Fat Chance* (2013) he argues that obesity is not a choice but brought about as a result of a toxic, poisonous and obesogenic environment. Rather than focusing on personal responsibility and individual diet plans, what is needed is action to prevent the capitalist system, represented by the sugar industry, from prioritising profit over health: 'in order to pull ourselves out of the ditch we have to understand how we drove into it' (Lustig 2013: xiv).

Individualism encourages people to see themselves as the source of their own salvation, diluting attention away from broader injustices. With the increasing popularity of, for instance, mindfulness, cognitive behavioural therapies and self-help groups, the emphasis is on taking personal responsibility and coping to adjust to society *as it is* and on carving out spaces of supposed individual autonomy and freedom.

Scholars such as Colin Wright (2013) explore how psychology and the neuroscience of resilience are producing a subject supposedly adapted to crises who can 'flourish' under neoliberalism. Informed by Foucault's work on biopolitics (see Chapter 5), he critiques the rise of 'Happiness Studies' as a neoliberal interpretation of utilitarianism. In so doing, he seeks to recover psychoanalysis by drawing on the work of Jacques Lacan (1901–81) to challenge the injunction to be happy in consumer culture. The dangers of not doing so are great. The 'pernicious culture of blind hope' directly contributed to the financial collapse of 2008: in 'a milieu in which fundamentally affective states like "confidence" literally translate into trillions of dollars, it is all too easy to place undue faith in positive thinking. In other walks of life, such zealous and rigid attachment to an idea in the face of all rational evidence to the contrary, would be more than sufficient for a diagnosis of delusional mania … Capital, it seems, has institutionalized cruel optimism at the highest levels: the problem is still prescribed as if it were the solution' (Wright 2014: 798).

In the psychoanalytic turn in critical theory, Eric Fromm is a central figure. It was he, along with Karen Horney (1855–1952) and Harry Stack Sullivan (1892–1949), who founded the neo-Freudian 'culturalist school'. Karen Horney was to analyse the psychological character-istics of women under patriarchy, and Harry Stack Sullivan is seen as the founder of ego psychology as influenced by Mead and growing sociological evidence on the formation of the social self. For Fromm, however, it was material relations and struggles that were para-mount to his earlier thought, in which objective struggles within modes of production in a society characterised by class fractures remained the foundation for explanations that others overlooked. He examined the relationship between the individual and totalitarian-ism, and held that the capacity for love and freedom is inextricably bound up with socioeconomic conditions.

With these insights he moved from the instinct theory of Freud to provide a more socialised version of psychology. For Fromm, we take our forms of character from society itself: 'The social character results from the dynamic adaptation of human nature to the structure of society. Changing social conditions result in changes of the social character, that is, in new needs and anxieties' (Fromm 1999: 253). Fromm thus continued with the theme of the relations between thought and being – expressed in relation to the acts of possessing and consuming in advanced industrial societies, with their poverty of fulfil-ment measured against the conditions of being. He spelt out the basis of a more just and content society that included: the prohibition of industrial and political brainwashing; closing the gap between poor and rich nations; liberating women from patriarchal domi-nation; a guaranteed minimum income in order to meet the needs of food and shelter; and separating the conduct of research from its application in industry and defence (Fromm 1997[1976]: 152–9).

Disputes were apparent between Fromm and those such as Adorno concerning outright condemnations of authority and the former's emphasis on the idea of 'goodness' as a bour-geois concept. Horkheimer expressed the view that Fromm was too keen to please people and his publication of a series of 'popular works' did not help these sentiments (Wiggershaus 1995: Ch. 3). Fromm wrote of a different conception of the individual from that typified in Adorno and Horkheimer's (1979[1944]) *Dialectic of Enlightenment*. Adorno and Horkheimer sought to provide an account of subjectivity within a materialist conception of history, but then appeared to saturate the potential of the subject to see the conditions under and through which they acted in the face of the ever-greater attractions of candy floss entertainment. Fromm reached towards Freud and instinctual drives for an alternative approach. In *The Fear of Freedom* he wrote, 'The future of democracy depends on the reali-zation of the individualism that has been the ideological aim of modern thought since the Renaissance. The cultural and political crisis of our day is not due to the fact that there is too much individualism but what we believe to be individualism has become an empty shell' (1999[1942]: 233–4).

Adorno resists Fromm's social psychology that merely follows history with its ebbs and flows, and utilises Freud's metapsychology and instinct theory to expose the false condi-tion in history. Subjectivity is reified because our activities are manipulated by abstract economic laws that are the product of a particular system. The point of a critical social science must be to take these relations seriously by highlighting 'the "intrinsic tension" between the need for the structures of society, which are open to reflection, and the ways they inhibit subjectivity and its desire for freedom' (Bronner 1994: 183). Yet the question remains, where are we to search for this openness to reflection?

RECOVERING THE PROMISE OF REASON

Inspired by Karl Marx and Sigmund Freud, the first generation of the Frankfurt School were deeply influenced by the struggles and torments of the Nazi era which influenced their ideas and writings. Others writing at the time included Hans-Georg Gadamer (1900–2002), who studied with Heidegger and was concerned to resist the hegemony of science and technology through a vigorous defence of practical and political reason. His purpose was to challenge the supremacy of the scientific method and emphasise instead taking responsibility for one's own decisions rather than idolising a narrow idea of an 'expert'. Gadamer was an important figure in our history of reflexivity. Although not explicitly aligned with the Frankfurt School, his arguments later in his life with Jürgen Habermas – over whether an objective position was possible from which to critique society – shaped generations of thinkers to come. Jürgen Habermas was an activist in 1960s Germany involved in student movements, a witness and participant in burgeoning social group formations. Like his predecessors, he was influenced by the fate of his country at the time (Anderson 2000). Critical of where the common sense of the people had led Germany during the 1930s and into the war, he was concerned to recover the promise of reason, of procedural rationality, and defend liberal democracy. It is to the ideas and differences between these two thinkers, building on the lineage of philosophical thought, that we now turn.

Truth, method and prejudice

Hans-Georg Gadamer was a hermeneutic philosopher influenced by Heidegger, Plato and Aristotle among others. From Heidegger, he took insights about our being-in-the-world and the need to see interpretations about the world as grounded in presuppositions. In his seminal work, *Truth and Method* (1975[1960]), he makes a central contribution to our understanding of reflexivity through elaborating the idea of prejudice as a precondition of understanding because it belongs to a historical reality. This contrasts starkly with the scientistic tendency to expunge prejudice from the terrain of its procedures in order to arrive at scientific Truth.

Taking these insights into textual translation, the act of a reader in the present is to link with a past – an 'I' to 'thou' relation – which moves from interpretation to the concrete present by drawing upon the traditions of the past. This is not about subjectivity, but the placement of the individual within a past–present interpretive process. What is termed 'prejudice' is actually fundamental to human understanding: 'Philosophical hermeneutics takes as its task the opening up of the hermeneutical dimension in its full scope, showing its fundamental significance for our entire understanding of the world and thus for all the various forms in which this understanding manifests itself: from interhuman communication to manipulation of society; from personal experience by the individual in society to the way in which he encounters society ... to the revolutionary consciousness that unhinges the tradition through emancipatory reflection' (Gadamer 1977: 18).

Gadamer felt that truth and method were not harmonious. Hermeneutics was not a process to interpret and understand, but to understand *how understanding is possible*. Consciousness is affected by history, and rather than impeding understanding, pre-understanding is central to it. Truth is not reducible to method – it cannot be defined by strict criteria or guidelines but represents a set of experiences in which people are engaged and changed. This notion of 'self change' is an important building block for our understandings of reflexivity: in the particularities of research practice it becomes an alteration in the state of a researcher themselves. Truth means moving away from oneself towards something larger, returning then to oneself – a process in which the grasping of meaning simultaneously changes oneself. We illustrate this further in Chapter 7 in relation to our own research practice. Whilst for Adorno a negative dialectics open up a sphere of reflection on the systemic properties of an unjust system, in Gadamer's approach reflexivity arises in a 'fusion of horizons'. Between situated and perspectival positions of knowing, there is no 'view from nowhere' (Nagel 1986) but only productively mediated relationships between what is close and what is far away.

Gadamer saw interpretive encounters as reflexive, and in so doing corrected Wittgenstein's emphasis upon language as a series of games that involved performance and repetition. The inculcation of prior judgement, for example into learning, is part of education, and is backed up by sanctions that bound particular accepted interpretations: 'The prejudgements in turn are the preconditions of possible knowledge. This knowledge is raised to the status of reflection when it makes transparent the normative framework in which it moves' (Habermas 1990[1970]: 169). When those prejudgements are rendered transparent in the process of reflection, the recipient enters a more mature state in which the personal authority of the educator is transplanted with the objective authority of tradition.

Here Gadamer's views are in conflict with the Frankfurt School's approach to ideological critique aimed at emancipation due to a reliance on tradition: 'The act of recognition, mediated by reflection, would not have altered the fact that tradition as such remained the only basis for the validity of prejudgements' (Habermas 1990[1970]: 170). Therefore, how does reflection relate to tradition except in terms of a repetition of previously established forms of authority? Gadamer's apparent favouring of prejudice, legitimated by tradition, 'is in conflict with the power of reflection, which proves itself in its ability to reject the claim of traditions' (Habermas 1990[1970]: 170). After all, it is tradition in the lineage of critical theory that needs to be overcome for the purpose of transformation. Whilst that limits hermeneutic insight, it also needs to be utilised and then transcended in order to open up a sphere of critical reflexivity.

Communicative reason

Of all contemporary scholars, it is Jürgen Habermas (2001) who has inherited the Frankfurt lineage and continued to write prolifically, developing his own distinctive contributions through modifying and critiquing the ideas of those who went before him. He is at odds with Gadamer whom he criticised for his focus on tradition, lack of attention given to the operation of power and attitudes towards method. The previous generations of the Frankfurt School 'surrendered themselves to an uninhibited scepticism regarding reason' (Habermas 1992b: 129) and failed to apply the standard of critical reflexivity to their own work, adopting a privileged standpoint to explore ideology. The result was an either/or choice between the public realm of instrumental reason and the desire for expressive fulfilment which may be found in the aesthetic dimension that exhibits a relative autonomy from the demands of modern capitalism (Adorno 2013). Adorno, under the influence of Benjamin, found that in high art, rather than empirical studies, seeing this as the sphere that encapsulated 'the last refuge of critical practice in a world completely dominated by total administration' (Aronowitz 1992: 308). As Adorno became increasingly anti-scientific, he found himself in a position that rejected the attempt to grasp social totality in the name of reason.

Unlike Adorno, Habermas formulated a basis for critical theory in language and sought to recover critical theory and reason from the philosophy of consciousness which, he argued, was still apparent in the legacy of the Frankfurt School. Underpinned by critiques of his predecessors, Habermas' works have charted a post-metaphysical route in which the spirit of the Frankfurt School remained, albeit with a stronger emphasis on inter-subjectivity that draws upon Schutz's idea of the lifeworld and Mead, Wittgenstein, Austin, Peirce, Chomsky, Piaget and Kohlberg, among others. As Habermas moved the terrain of his investigations towards language, he did not give up on the methodological implications for the social sciences through a retreat into the aesthetic dimension, like his predecessors, and combined this with a historical study of reason and intersubjectivity. This was informed by the fundamental belief that we are all participants in the societies of which we are a part (Habermas 1994: 100–2).

Drawing on the traditions of the American pragmatists is important for Habermas. In terms of the potential for reflection, he recognises that Peirce, as well as those such as Dilthey, saw the self-reflexive character of knowledge measured against the ambitions of those sciences that wish to legislate over what counts as knowledge. Yet he is critical of each. For Habermas, Peirce did not appreciate that the process of scientific inquiry forms itself on the basis of intersubjective communication beyond instrumental action (Habermas 1989a) – Dilthey went too far in relinquishing the dialectic of the general and the individual 'which is grounded in communication in ordinary language' (Habermas 1989a: 183). According to Habermas, Dilthey and Pierce, like Gadamer, accepted too much of the bias of an interpretation of science which views facts independent of interpretation.

Reason, as we have seen, has had a rough ride through history, and many initially placed their belief in its liberating potential and reflexive possibilities. Then, with Nietzsche, Weber, Horkheimer and Adorno amongst others, reason is abandoned: 'The reason that was meant to be our self-salvation – to be, in Kant's words, man's freedom from his self-incurred tutelage – has become the means of our imprisonment. It has become the instrumental rationality, the bureaucratic rationality that governs contemporary society' (Critchley 2012: 42). Whilst urging social scientists to start with the meanings that people attach to environments, scholars evoked a determinism that, as we saw for Weber, fell back on a call for an ethic of personal responsibility in the face of uncertainty and the never-ending struggle for power. Horkeimer and Adorno found themselves following a path in which reason and domination could not be separated. This is symptomatic of the more general problem of viewing society and social relations in terms of a subject–object dualism that takes contemporary forms of 'subjective' reason and critiques them from the point of view of 'objective' reason which has fallen into disrepute (Habermas 1984: 377). It was inevitable that the end result for those Frankfurt scholars was pessimism, manifested in the 'reification of consciousness'. Habermas sought to provide a new basis for reason, by drawing upon hermeneutics whose 'understanding aims at gaining from traditions a possible action-oriented self-understanding for social groups and clarifying it' (Habermas 1990[1970]: 164).

Habermas's aim has been to recover the potential of the sphere of 'communicative reason'. Communicative reason provides a means through which to identify empirically the historical development of rationality structures, as well as an attempt to problematise rationality to modern spheres of life – money, power and bureaucracy – to demonstrate its effects on how we live together. Communicative action is linked to communicative rationality as its central plank, a condition of 'unconstrained communication'. Communicative action, as the terms implies, means that language and action are linked in conveying meaning, establishing social relations and expressing feelings. Habermas moves to the sphere of communication and the conditions necessary to reach a common understanding when action is co-ordinated by validity claims in speech acts (Habermas 1981). For Habermas every speech act contains three validity claims: *truth* about an external objective world embodied in the discourses we employ; *rightness* in relation to the intersubjective social world according to norms and moral imperatives; and *truthfulness* in relation to our internal subject world, for instance whether our utterances match our actions.

Habermas's ideas are based on his diagnosis of late capitalism in terms of his conceptualisation of society as comprising the 'system' and 'lifeworld'. As new systems emerge over time, they are increasingly separate from those structures which contribute to social integration. As systems become more differentiated, they rely less on structures of social integration and more on systemic mechanisms. These are not anchored in the lifeworld and become norm-free objectified structures. The consequences are clear: 'in modern societies, economic and bureaucratic spheres emerge in which social relations are regulated only via money and power. Norm-conformative attitudes and identity-forming social memberships are neither necessary nor possible in these spheres; they are made peripheral instead' (Habermas 1987: 154). The utilisation of systems theory appears to enable Habermas to create a duality between an independent lifeworld and the operation of power in a sphere that provides for an intersubjective, post-metaphysical move to generate reflexive understanding.

Culture and socialisation rely upon communicative action which cannot take place through the mediums of power and money. Commodification, commercialisation and bureaucratisation generate 'disturbances, pathological side effects in these domains' (Habermas in Dews 1992: 172). Again, the consequences are that '[t]he reproductive constraints that instrumentalise a lifeworld without weakening the illusion of its self-sufficiency have to hide, so to speak, in the pores of communicative action. This gives rise to a structural violence that, without becoming manifest as such, takes hold of the forms of intersubjectivity of possible understanding' (Habermas 1987: 187). Reification of consciousness does not arise, as it does for those trapped in Cartesianism, from the forward march of instrumental rationality. It comes from the ways in which the norm-free and purposively rational co-ordinating mechanisms of system reproduction continually undermine the potential of communicative reason. The conditions for communication remain absent due to the distorting effects of money and power, and manifested through the paradox of increased state intervention into the making of 'free-market' capitalist societies.

As Habermas recognises (1984: 328) one might then ask how we can link this into the everyday use of language. He seeks to use these ideas to arrive at a general classification of 'linguistically mediated interaction' (1984: 329) – the issue here being, in order not to repeat past mistakes concerning reason and rationality, that what should be examined are not the motivations for action, but the relationship of these to the structures of the lifeworld itself. It is the lifeworld that is presupposed as the background to actions: 'Communicative action takes place within a lifeworld that remains at the backs of participants in communication. It is present to them only in the prereflexive form of taken-for-granted background assumptions and naively mastered skills' (Habermas 1984: 335). We are bound together by the rationally motivating force of communicative reason that is embedded in the background to our everyday utterances: 'The concept of communicative rationality does not just apply to the processes of intentional consensus formation, but also to the structures of a state of pre-understanding already reached within an intersubjectively shared lifeworld. The latter demarcates in the shape of a context-forming horizon the respective speech situation; at the same time, as an unproblematic and prereflexive background it plays a constitutive role in the achievement directed toward reaching understanding. Lifeworld and communicative action thus relate to one another in a complementary fashion' (Habermas 1991: 223).

With Habermas we move towards what becomes a weak subjectivity which 'refers to a symbolically structured lifeworld that is constituted in the interpretive accomplishments of its members and only reproduced through communication' (Habermas 1984: 398). He defines it as 'that form of social interaction in which the plans of action of different actors are co-ordinated through an exchange of communicative acts, that is, through a use of language orientated towards reaching understanding' (Habermas 1981: 44). With the communicative competence of social actors in mind, Habermas (1981) distinguishes between 'action orientated to success' and 'action orientated to understanding'. Action orientated to success is measured by rules of rational choice, while action orientated to understanding takes place through 'communicative action'. There is not, as Weber had maintained under the influence of those whom Habermas seeks to correct, a state of competition between two modes of action in the lifeworld: towards success and understanding. The competition that does exist is between *'principles of societal integration* – between the mechanism of linguistic communication that is oriented to validity claims – a mechanism that emerges in increasing purity from the rationalization of the lifeworld – and those de-linguistified steering media through which systems of success-orientated action are differentiated out' (Habermas 1984: 342; original emphasis).

■■■ Box 4.3 ■■■■■■■■■■■■■■■■■■■■■■■■■■■■■■■■■■■■

Standpoints, standing and scholarship

The second-generation scholars were deeply influenced by their time and the growing and changing nature of social movements. Student riots, environmental protests, women's and civil rights movements sprang up in Europe and the USA, giving rise to new strands of thought and reflection for the critical theorists. Habermas saw new social movements as struggles in defence of the public sphere. They were ways to regain forms of communicative action and share information as a precondition to changing the way in which public discourse is structured to create informed and aware publics. New social movements represented conflicts at the seam between system and lifeworlds (1981), not about capitalist labour struggles but about decolonising the lifeworld, reasserting communicative rationality, and building the public sphere. There have been critiques of this thesis but contemporary work indicates the continuing relevance of Habermas's ideas (Schlosberg 2006; Schlembach 2015). Edwards (2009) suggests that the concept of 'colonisation' is relevant in understanding global capitalism and resistance to neo-liberal policies, and further that his ideas continue to articulate with social movement theory.

Critical theorists were simultaneously analysing and seeking to transform society. For Fraser this meant active engagements with the feminist movement from a distinct 'standpoint'. Whilst a standpoint is perspectival – about a point of view – academic 'standing' in relation to social movements is more relational (Croteau et al. 2005). The term 'scholar activist' is often used to refer to those who directly engage with social movements. Some focus on the difficulties in maintaining these different roles: 'Academia can become a velvet

(Continued)

(Continued)

cage that makes it extremely difficult for individuals to make meaningful contributions to social movement efforts' (Croteau 2005: 20). Yet others remain committed to trying to balance both roles.

Paul Chatterton at Leeds University combines activism and social change in research and pedagogy (Chatterton 2008, 2013). Others use activist or militant research to engage with political movements around migration or climate change (Huschke 2014; Russell 2014). For Russell the task is to reimagine the university as a machine not only for the imagination but also for the active production of other *worlds*. In a similar vein O'Flynn and Panayiotopoulos (2015) see the role of the scholar activist as to bridge the gap between movements of social justice, developing counter-hegemonic narratives and a collective strategy for social justice. There are multiple challenges and difficulties in undertaking scholar-activist research, especially for those who are early on in their careers (Suzuki and Mayorga 2014), whilst a range of writings, sharing tools and approaches have arisen in recent times (Flood et al. 2013).

For the materialisation of communicative action, mutual and co-operative achievement of understanding amongst collective participants is required. All parties must understand the meaning of communication requiring a 'public sphere', a discursive space outside the influence of elites in which other issues can be freely discussed and defined in order to restrict elite power (Habermas 1989b). Like earlier scholars in the Frankfurt School, Habermas was critical of how hegemonic interests dictated public opinion and relations, arguing that new social movements and public spaces were needed in an era of mass democratisation to challenge the rise of consumerism and the stage management of the political process. Through mobilising 'situated solidarities' with social movements and alternative forms of reflexive practice (Routledge and Driscol Derickson 2015), interest is not only unavoidable but also necessary to bring about social change. It is through the different strands of his research programmes that those such as Selya Benhabib (1986, 2006) have found elements in his work that can provide the basis for a wide-ranging normative critique of society, as well as the seeds for progressive action. Box 4.3 illustrates these issues further, and reinforces our central contention that reflexivity about the conditions and practices of engaged scholarship is an essential pre-condition to knowing and acting in the social world.

CRITIQUING CRITIQUE

The first generation of the Frankfurt School gave way to the second, led by Habermas, during the 1970s. Whilst the most well known and significant of the scholars of the second generation, intervening frequently in public debate, Habermas was not alone; he was accompanied in his intellectual journey by those such as Karl-Otto Apel, Alfred Schmidt (1931–2012), Albrecht Wellmer, Oskar Negt and Claus Offe. He himself said that he never intended to continue the tradition of a school and at times had little to do with the Institute itself (Andersen 2011). What has now become known as the Third Generation of the Frankfurt School is associated primarily with the works of Axel Honneth, to whom we can add the insights of those such as Nancy Fraser, Agnes Heller and Seyla Benhabib who build upon and move beyond the foundations set by Habermas and his predecessors. In so doing, however, intellectual breakpoints between these 'schools' should not be overestimated; one concern they share is around the basis for critique itself and the need to remain reflexive about our knowledge claims.

Recognition and redistribution

Schools of thought are 'complex and dynamic phenomena we construct to bring order to the real-world messiness of publications, dissertations, conferences, patterns of citation, institutional affiliations, research aims, grants, dust-jacket blurbs, critical book reviews, and so on' (Andersen 2011: 44–5). The scholars we are interested in here are international, frequently outside Germany and influenced by the social unrest of the 1960s and 1970s, the politics and nationalism of the 1980s and 1990s and the implications of globalisation and technological advancement. It was also markedly more female than previous generations, a topic we shall also return to in more detail in Chapter 5.

Just as Habermas had positioned his work in relation to those who went before him – 'history of theory with a systematic intent' (Andersen 2011: 19) – so did his works feature in the critiques and alternatives of those that followed him. Habermas saw that we are socially integrated within the lifeworld through our intentions or background understandings of the lifeworld. System integration, on the other hand, is about 'functional interlocking or stabilization of the consequences of our actions' of which we are not necessarily aware (Habermas 1993: 166). For Axel Honneth this is a 'fiction' which 'results not only from Habermas' evolution-theoretic explanations of the emergence of modern societies in terms of the uncoupling of system and lifeworld but also from the terminological constraints into which he falls with his distinction between two forms of integration of social action' (Honneth 1991: 299).

Honneth argues that his predecessors have not paid enough attention to the *social* dimension of social theory. His conception of history is based on the struggle for recognition by social groups which drive human development and are essential for it to flourish. There are also those who believe Habermas's earlier work was a source of inspiration, until the turn towards a 'positivistic re-hashing' of the systems theory of Talcott Parsons (Bauman 1992: 217). The same issues are reflected in the comments of those who are otherwise sympathetic to his work. As Thomas McCarthy puts it, whilst Habermas is critical of Marx for succumbing to particular definition of science, we are left wondering 'whether in flirting with systems theory he does not run the danger of being seduced by the same illusion in more modern dress' (McCarthy 1991: 139).

A similar point is made by Nancy Fraser (1989). In particular, the idea that system integration is non-consensual and social integration is consensual does not stand up to the realities of social life. Whilst this enables Habermas to make a distinction between strategic and communicative reason, it fails to see how the capitalist economic system relies upon a moral-cultural dimension (see Skeggs 2004; Sayer 2005). Apparently distinct domains of labour and interaction and system and lifeworld are in fact highly problematic. For example, when it comes to gender relations, feminist research on families has demonstrated how they are 'thoroughly permeated with, in Habermas' terms, the media of power and money. They are sites of egocentric, strategic, and instrumental calculation as well as sites of usually exploitative exchanges of services, labour, cash, and sex – and, frequently, sites of coercion and violence' (Fraser 1989: 119–20). Families, for Fraser, are institutions which straddle the lifeworld and the system and are not the domains of free and equal communicative action.

From the above point of view, Habermas repeats the Marxist problematic which reduces reproduction to production. He places an emphasis, through communicative reason, on a public sphere that is highly gendered which cannot assume to bracket inequalities, but must be a space for their elimination (Fraser 1997). Quite simply, a reflexive, communicative space free from distorting effects that enable deliberation on contemporary conditions is built upon a duality between system and lifeworld that does not exist in reality. Habermas locates in communicative reason a universalism in which we cannot but assume the existence of a common basis in the lifeworld. This neo-Kantian weak transcendentalism is depended upon not only for the coordination of actions, but also the relations between our subjective selves and an overriding inter-subjectivity that takes places against this background and emerges in dialogue. The cognitive basis of language that he deploys is one in which we do not simply convey a content in terms of what we say, but also refer to its application.

If representation, communication and action are equally important, as Habermas suggests, does this weak construction of our subjectivity in the name of inter-subjectivity push the former too far out by weakening reflexive capacity at the individual level? Moving away from ideology critique in which the subject of history is placed in the proletariat and in Hegelian-style reason as unfolding in the Real, Habermas provides a basis in the social world for understanding the concepts of social science. Yet if we base social science on the bringing to awareness of the relations between the necessity of background assumptions in terms of the facticity of the social world measured against the distorting effects of an intensifying capitalist order, then the validity of cultural knowledge falls within the domain of intersubjective communicative reason. Whilst that rescues a critical social science from the domain of philosophy of consciousness where it led Adorno to see possibility in aesthetics due to the saturation of social life by instrumental reason, what does this say for its practice and insights?

In terms of recognising the realities that inform daily life in order that the findings of social science resonate with its meanings, Habermas moves away from contextual to universal issues through procedural concerns. Here we find matters of validity not being matters of choice, but grounded in communicative, intersubjective reason. He is only too aware of the importance of tradition and variation in forms of life and life histories (Habermas 1982), but how far does this approach then clash with the contextual meaning that phenomenologists brought to our attention with consequences both for our understanding of reflexivity and the methodology of the social sciences? It has been argued that the transcendence and idealisation contained in the work of Habermas can be reconciled with Garfinkel's emphasis on practicality and indexicality (McCarthy in Hoy and McCarthy 1994: Ch. 3). However, Habermas's concern with procedural matters has the possibility of overlooking the substantive concerns that inform our lives and are part of the subject matter of the social sciences. This is taken account of in his work through an analysis of the distorting effects of systemic issues on communication itself and we have seen the limits of that approach. What if these same issues are actually part of the meaning constitution of language and the lifeworld? Its basis in communicative reason is then placed in doubt and there is a need to take account of contextual considerations as they are part of the interpretation of meaning in our lives. The situated reflexivity which is emphasised by ethnomethodology in order to produce order is a contextual achievement of practical reason. Whilst abstraction from the particularity of circumstances is part of the work and insight of the social sciences, how far should this go?

Reflexivity in critical theory

Ideology critique is a key theme for these thinkers and that informs possibilities and difficulties in understanding reflexivity. Ideologies are false beliefs that are assumed to be true because all members of society believe them. For Habermas this is a 'false state of reconciliation' (Finlayson 2005: 11): whilst people believe the social world is rational and supports human happiness and freedom, the reverse is true. Nonetheless these falsely held beliefs – ideologies – lead people to support institutions and accept their current existence. For Marxist social theorists change would not, however, simply come about by replacing false beliefs with true ones, as people cling to their beliefs even if this is irrational. Hence identifying why and how people act against their 'true interests' was the practical problem to solve.

In the works of Horkheimer and Adorno this led to a reflexive deadlock in which theory could not lead to human freedom if rationality was the root of problem. Adorno lost a belief in emancipation being delivered through theory and that collective political action was difficult, if not highly unlikely. Yet it gives rise to another problem – as we discussed in Chapter 2 – of what prevents the ideology of the critical theorist being anything more than a will to power linking knowledge with interest? How can a critical scholar claim to set their own theories outside the influence of a false belief system, certain that they are not as susceptible to the same problems as others? 'The deeper and more sinister the illusion-forming mechanism is supposed be the less credible is their claim to remain unaffected by it' (Finlayson 2005: xx). Indeed, one of the charges against the Frankfurt School has been their subjectivity, commitment to their own critique of capitalism and failure to consider the positions from which their ideologies are launched.

For contemporary critical theorists, interest can be seen as strength in addressing social injustice as an explicit end point of critique. Reacting against the abstract nature of previous intellectual debates, their work is focused on particularity, contextuality and pluralism. Honneth's work on recognition embraces 'other' voices of reason, whether in 'the public domain of pluralistic, multicultural sociality, in the domain of world-disclosive aesthetic experience, or in plumbing the unconscious depths of the self' (Andersen 2011: 51). His normative stance is what allows engagement with the complex contexts of application and focus on subjective experience. Similarly Fraser sees theory and reason as political; critical theories take up partisan standpoints informed by social movements to change the injustices in society. This has meant that the task for critical theorists is to understand the pathologies of injustice and map routes to overcoming them.

The debate between Nancy Fraser and Axel Honneth (Fraser and Honneth 2003) concerning the priorities of recognition over redistribution may be comfortably formulated as the musings of philosophers by those predisposed to a defence of the status quo as if it were the outcome of some natural process. Yet these authors go to the heart of issues concerned with the subject – social context and transformation. Honneth (2007: Ch. 9) moves from the classical aim of making our needs transparent to their articulation through language, from the idea of individual consistency to narrative coherence and the invocation of general moral principles to a greater sensitivity to the contexts in which we live. Similarly, Nancy Fraser (1997: Ch. 7) takes issues associated with multiculturalism, anti-essentialism and radical democracy in feminist thought, and asks how issues of equality and difference might be formulated without surrendering to an indifference to the importance of political economy. If we take these insights into concerns with justice and how social institutions recognise and exclude people, the forms of justification deployed can themselves be subject to critique to open up a critical, diagnostic and evaluative pluralism that engages with fundamental issues of contemporary times (Forst 2014a).

For David Harvey the route to overcoming the pathologies of modern times means 'charting the path' and investigating the dynamics of capitalism in order to 'show why this economic engine should be replaced and with what' (Harvey 2014: 11). This is a call that influences urban scholars working in the critical tradition, as we illustrate in Box 4.4, serving as the conscience of their own engagements and sources for critical self-reflection, from a standpoint in which change is actively sought. In *Fortunes of Feminism* Fraser advocates for redistribution to overcome inequalities and power imbalances, and like Benhabib is concerned that previous scholars had not adequately proposed strategies for social change. For her, an affirmative-transformative distinction is '*not* equivalent to reform versus revolution, nor to gradual versus apocalyptic change.

Rather, the nub of the issue is the level at which injustice is addressed: whereas affirmation targets end-state outcomes, transformation addresses root causes' (Fraser in Fraser and Honneth 2003: 74; original emphasis).

■ Box 4.4 ■

Reflexivity and critical urban theory

Cities are sites in which the dynamics and dualisms discussed thus far in this book play out and take root. Branches of critical theory deal not only with queer studies, Western epistemological dominance, race and gender, amongst many topics, but also with cities. Key protagonists in this respect are Neil Brenner, Peter Marcuse and Margit Mayer (2012). In *What is critical urban theory?* Brenner draws on the traditions of the Frankfurt School to develop a critical urban theory which 'insists that another, more democratic, socially just and sustainable form of urbanisation is possible, even if such possibilities are currently being suppressed through dominant institutional arrangements, practices and ideologies' (2012: 11). A critical *urban* theory therefore reflects the legacies of the Frankfurt School in several key ways by insisting on: the need for abstraction and theoretical arguments about urbanisation under capitalism; the contextual and historical situatedness of knowledge; the rejection of instrumental, technocratic and market-driven forms of urban analysis; and the desire to excavate the alternative, radical, emancipatory, latent yet suppressed possibilities for urban transformation (2012: 19).

Brenner develops four propositions which simultaneously shed light on how we know and research the city and how 'urbanisation [can be integrated] into the intellectual architecture of critical theory as a whole?' (2012: 22). Critical urban theory is *theory* – in that it abstracts and falls short of suggesting what actions ought to be undertaken or route maps for change. Theory is seen as being practical in that it deconstructs and theoretically reconstructs modern cities, but it does not offer a formula for social change. It *critiques instrumental reason* through focusing on how practice informs theory: 'praxis is a source of power for theory, but cannot be prescribed by it' (Adorno, 1998: 278, in Brenner 2012). Theory emphasises the gap between the actual and possible and it is in this process that alternatives are revealed with implications for practice. It is only because theory has not been realised under conditions of contemporary capitalism that it remains theory and not practice: 'there is no theory that can overcome this divide, because, by definition, it cannot be overcome theoretically; it can only be overcome in practice' (Brenner 2012: 18).

Most importantly, Brenner makes explicit the reflexive underpinnings of critical theory, namely that all social knowledge is embedded and there can be no standpoint outside the time/space of history. Critical urban scholars must locate themselves in the city, in relation to the evolution of modern capitalism, and consider what enables their own critique. In this respect, Brenner notes, as others have before him, that the central task is to understand what makes understanding possible: 'the meanings and modalities of critique can never be held constant; they must, on the contrary, be continually reinvented in relation to the unevenly evolving political – economic geographies of this process and the diverse conflicts it engenders' (2012: 19).

SUMMARY: REFLEXIVE RELATIONS

Critical social science must be aware of the contexts of its production in order that these do not become part of the expert apparatus that stifles human creativity through the increasing rationalisation of everyday life. It is a particular perspective that prioritises instrumental knowledge over the inclusion of alternative values and norms. The scholars whose works we have examined added to the view that knowledge is a social product and that has consequences for understanding the self, but 'epistemic practices have to be comprehended in their sociocultural contexts. In this sense, the theory of knowledge is part of the theory of society, which is *itself* embedded in practical contexts' (McCarthy 1994: 244; original emphasis).

Whilst critical theorists may be characterised as having put critical reason in the same ditch as rationalisation, their legacy remains a rich resource. It is for such reasons that Habermas was to find a basis for critique in communicative reason, whilst always reminding us of the question critique for what? In the process of the formulation of his ideas, however, we find limitations. Earlier we noted how those such as Humboldt recognised that language depended upon performance for its reproduction. However, perhaps Habermas pushes us too far away from langue to parole with the result that we overlook the very bonds that unite us through an over-emphasis on procedural rationality. As Bernstein puts it, *'The assimilation of meaning to validity is what makes the idealization of communicative reason a meaning-destroying mechanism. The meanings destroyed are those that belong to language as a system'* (Bernstein 1995: 219; original emphasis).

This chapter has returned us to particular themes. We are reminded of the importance of context, the transformative potential of knowledge, and the relationship between ideas of the self and the limits to which we can know the social world. With Habermas's focus on communicative as opposed to instrumental reason, we see again how language is central in playing not only mediating but also constitutive functions. We may agree that the self is constituted through language, in terms of the relations between the subjective and the objective, but what is missing is an account of the resonance that exists between the personal and the public domain of communicative reason which attempts to overcome the issues associated with subjectivism (Taylor 1992: 510). If we allow that the world-disclosive features of language are fundamental to understanding in the world, and we admit to the role of emotion and affect and a wish to be recognised by others, then we might say that this process is a reflexive one in which the struggle for recognition involves, in interaction, a process of intersubjective re-cognition with and through others (Honneth 2007; Wetherell 2012). What this requires is a greater understanding of subjectivity but without the procedural formalism apparent in Habermas's work. We need the connection of which Taylor speaks between the subjective and inter-subjective and from there to the forms of social solidarity extant in a given society.

By examining the constitutive role of language in social life, we are led down two potential paths when it comes to reflexivity. One takes us down the road of humanism and the other to a yet uncharted territory: 'if one of the fundamental uses of language is to articulate or make manifest the background of distinctions of worth we define ourselves by, how should we understand *what* is being manifest here? Is what we are articulating ultimately to be understood as our human response to our condition? Or is our articulation striving rather to be faithful to something beyond us, not explicable simply in terms of human response?' (Taylor 1985: 11; original emphasis). What is suggested here is an extension to tradition in which human beings are placed at the centre of understanding, or are displaced through a trans- or even post-human endeavour that requires a change in thinking about what it is to be human and our subjectivity (Braidotti 2013).

The other way to think about these issues is to move into the terrain of a form of anti- or at least not pro-humanism. This means taking the role of power in and through social relations not as simply distorting, as in Habermas's weak form of subjectivity and his emphasis upon inter-subjectivity, but as constitutive of ourselves and our lives. Whilst Habermas finds the insights of ordinary language philosophy important for the development of communication action, it is also limited: it has no hermeneutic input in terms of the translation between language games, and like hermeneutics can become idealistic. Whilst Gadamer (1975[1960]) was correct in overcoming Wittgenstein's limitations by connecting language use with history, he also shares a failure to see the ways in which language 'serves to legitimate relationships of organized force' (Habermas 1990[1970]: 172.; see also Holub 1991: Ch. 3). With this in mind, we now turn our gaze to relations between power and the subject.

5

POWER AND ACTION

The body is moulded by a great many distinct regimes; it is broken down by the rhythms of work, rest, holidays; it is poisoned by food or values, through eating habits or moral laws; it constructs resistances.

(Foucault 1984a: 87)

INTRODUCTION

Those writing in the tradition of critical theory took us so far in our examination of the relations between social scientific knowledge, reflexivity and social transformation. Yet to understand the consequences for action of a critical-emancipatory social science we need to travel further. Whilst knowledge may be necessary, it is insufficient for freedom – this would entail not only a knowledge of one's interests, but also the power and opportunity to transform conditions, along with a predisposition to do so (Bhaskar 1986). From this point of view we might note that '[t]he most powerful explanatory theory in an open world is a non-deterministic one' (Bhaskar 1998: 64).

We turn first from Germany to France and the works of critical post-war social theorists. Influenced by the same socialist, republican traditions in a country which was coming to terms with constitutional government and the ideologies that had motivated resistance, a number of writers began working in the same 'relatively autonomous intellectual field' (Robbins 2012: 176). Michel Foucault (1926–98) made a vast array of contributions across a number of diverse fields, but it is his work on power and subjectivity – and the consequences for knowledge production – that we examine here. Pierre Bourdieu's (1930–2002) formulation of a critical reflexive social science sought to contribute to the 'realpolitik of reason'. Using the works of these two pivotal late twentieth-century social theorists as a springboard, we interweave discussions of the writings of other contemporary scholars: Judith Butler (2005) adds to ideas on the subject and Paul Ricoeur (1994), Slavoj Žižek (2008a) and Zygmunt Bauman (2001) contribute from other perspectives. In particular, we focus on feminist-inspired writings of those such as Dorothy Smith (1996) and Sandra Harding (2006). Their embrace and utilisation of standpoints in social science to produce more authentic and valid accounts of the world is significant.

The present concern is a split between the world as it is given and how it might be, or to express it another way, between the power to get things done and the political sphere in which it is decided what needs to be done: 'Critical theory was free of such a worry in its youthful *Sturm und Drang* phase' (Bauman 2014: 123). Yet it is easy to end at a paradox: if all arguments are situated then we have no grounds upon which to adjudicate between them – and thus there are no 'reasons' to accept them. This leads to a reflexive predicament (Lawson 1986) where the 'performative contradictions' of different lines of thought and the supposed opposition between narrative and science (Habermas 1990[1970]) act to saturate social life with power. This chapter therefore focuses on two questions: what can we say about the subject upon whom a critical social science will draw, and what implications does this have for the practice of social science? Our purpose in this chapter is to continue with the theme of reflexivity through our examination of these questions in relation to power and action.

POWER AND THE SUBJECT

In questioning the idea of the author and dispelling the myth of an all-knowing subject who pronounces on reality, a number of writers in the 1960s and 1970s became associated with what has become known as poststructuralist thinking. Here we find a range of thinkers who have added to the critique of scientific representation (May and Powell 2008: Ch. 11). This is an era in which the end of subjectivity is announced, and a new form is also founded in computer interaction and increasing technological intervention in the body with consequences for identity (see, for example, Barnett 2009). Politically and intellectually, elements of these writings seek to activate differences, alongside a focus upon the textual construction of reality, in order to expose aspirations to universal knowledge (Ashmore 1989). As we previously noted, Jean François Lyotard (1924–98) builds on the legacy of Wittgenstein and writes that science is but one language game among others. Philosophy is simply a legitimating discourse to reinforce the status of science (Lyotard 1984[1979]). To be reflexive in this sense can also mean a turn towards a deconstruction of textual authority in the social sciences, which means exposing rhetorical claims to objectivity as nothing more than situated accounts. Echoes of Nietzsche are evident.

The limits to knowledge

Michel Foucault came to realise 'how the Frankfurt people had tried ahead of their time to assert things that I too had been working on for years to sustain' (Foucault 1991a: 117). He positioned his philosophical reflections to build on, but move beyond, those that preceded him. For Foucault, Western philosophy left a legacy that was to be filled by subjects such as psychology, concerning 'consciousness' and 'thought': 'It seems to be that such a way of analysing things is clearly tied to a philosophical perspective, which is positivism' (Foucault 1998: 250). Philosophers became the legislators of what is to be known and who we are. The result is that people are assessed, categorised and subject to a whole set of practices. Cultural differences are judged according to acting 'rationally' and dialogue assessed upon the participants' abilities to exercise 'reason'. Yet the power of reason is double-edged: it excludes on the basis of difference. Thus for Foucault we have become the subjects and objects of knowledge, 'as both that which must be conceived of and that which is to be known' (Foucault 1992[1970]: 345). Foucault looks upon this as 'an event in the order of knowledge' (1992[1970]: 345).

Foucault drew on the legacy of the Frankfurt School, but expunged of a metaphysics of presence and centred on how capitalism produces subjectivity: 'To take care of the self, to work on the self and on one's own life, means concerning oneself with the ways of doing and saying necessary to occupy the place allocated to us within the social division of labour' (Lazzarato 2014: 246). In his historical studies of medicine, sexuality and deviance,

Foucault was influenced not only by Nietzsche, but also by Gaston Bachelard (1884–1962) and Georges Canguilhem (1904–95). Here we find references to the subject being avoided in favour of studying the structures of knowledge which could not be separated from the operation of power: 'My objective has been to create a history of the different modes by which, in our culture, human beings are made subjects' (Foucault 1982a: 208). Thus in Foucault's essay on Kant's 'What is Enlightenment?' (*Was ist Aufklärung?*) he writes of conducting a 'critical ontology of ourselves' (1984a: 50) through a critique of what we think, say and do.

Foucault conducted his investigation around three questions. What are the relations we have to truth, through scientific knowledge, in which we are both subject and object? What are the relations we have to others through strategies and power relations? And 'what are the relationships between truth, power and self?' (Foucault 1988: 15). As described further in Box 5.1, his mode of inquiry is genealogical in form: 'it will not deduce from the form of what we are what it is impossible for us to do and to know; but it will separate out, from the contingency that has made us what we are, the possibility of no longer being, doing, or thinking what we are, do, or think' (1984a: 46). As a history of the present, social science requires that we are consciously aware of our place in and impact on the social scientific process. This is historical analysis that does not fall back on the metaphysics of presence, teleology, or the idea that the truth of the present takes us back into the past upon which we may then judge: 'Genealogy does not oppose itself to history as the lofty and profound gaze of the philosopher might compare to the molelike perspective of the scholar; on the contrary, it rejects the metahistorical deployment of ideal significations and indefinite teleologies. It opposes itself to the search for "origins"' (Foucault 1998: 370). If any critical ideal remains in this process, it lies in the possibility of being set free, but without any residual subject-centred reason free from power. The internal modes of the ordering of truth are examined in power-knowledge relations, but not in the name of a truth beyond those, and so it is argued the possibilities for transgression are opened up (Visker 1995).

We have seen in our journey a change of emphasis away from an analysis of representations towards an analytic – that is, the 'attempt to show on what grounds representation and analysis of representations are possible and to what extent they are legitimate' (Dreyfus and Rabinow 1982: 28). Herbert Dreyfus and Paul Rabinow saw that Foucault moves beyond structuralism and hermeneutics to an 'interpretive analytics', in which the genealogist 'recognizes that the deep hidden meanings, the unreachable heights of truth, the murky interiors of consciousness are all shams. Genealogy's coat of arms might read: Oppose depth, finality, and appeals to unity. Its banner: Mistrust identities in history; they are only masks, appeals to unity' (Dreyfus and Rabinow 1982: 107). This is based on Foucault's recognition that power/knowledge is bound together and that there can be no presupposition of their separation. Power exists in a state of 'agonism' with freedom, thereby making ideas of individuality a 'political' problem. Therefore it is subject to struggle and potential transformation: 'We are prisoners of certain conceptions about ourselves ... We have to liberate our own subjectivity, our relations to ourselves' (1989a: 298). The idea of 'governing' appears in terms of how the 'possible field of action of others' (Foucault 1982a: 221) is structured.

▬▬ Box 5.1 ▬▬▬▬▬▬▬▬▬▬▬▬▬▬▬▬▬▬▬▬▬▬▬▬▬▬▬▬▬▬▬

Social science as a history of the present

Foucault did not hold with grand theories or the possibility of explanatory frameworks that could capture any objective external reality. As a result, there is no single theory for which he can be credited, rather 'multiple Foucauldian theorizations, each one designed to address a definite phenomenon in the course of a specific inquiry' (Garland 2014: 366). Underpinning his works is a conception of the task of social scientists to write the 'history of the present'. A term first appearing in his (1977) work on the birth of modern prisons, Foucault grounded his work in a diagnosis of the current situation and looked back to the past to reveal and uncover conflicts and contexts: 'his aim was to reveal something important – but hidden – in our contemporary experience; something about our relation to technologies of power–knowledge that was more clearly visible in the prison setting than elsewhere' (Garland 2014: 368).

'What I'm trying to do', Foucault said, 'is to make a diagnostic of the present, to tell what we are today' (Foucault 2001: 634). This is where genealogy comes in as a method of using history to revalue values, writing in a field of power relations and political struggle (Roth 1981: 43). In taking contemporary issues and deconstructing them to understand how we reached this point, current practices which are taken for granted and hard to grasp are rendered more intelligible. For Fuggle et al. (2015), this approach retains much value in examining issues such as capitalism, police power, migration, deportation, social networks and biopolitics to name but a few.

There is a fine line between the academic work of writing histories of the present and journalism. Foucault occasionally presented himself as a journalist-philosopher, asserting in 1973 that 'what interests me is ... what is happening around us, what we are, what is going on in the world' (Raffnsøe et al. 2016: 1). In 1978 he worked as a journalist in Iran, as a special correspondent for *Corriere della Sera* and *Le Nouvel Observateur* (Afary and Anderson 2005). Yet judging Foucault as intellectual rather than journalist has meant his Iranian experiences have often been swept away or 'dismissed' for misreading and supporting a particular version of Islam (Binkley and Capetillo 2009). For Foucault the two roles were not dissimilar: the journalist, like the academic, cannot mirror reality but can only reflect different versions of the truth, with many angles and sometimes incompatible renderings of the facts. However, his interest as a journalist was in understanding not the deep reasons for the movement, but the manner in which it was lived and experienced in the minds of those involved. In both roles, he wanted to be inside the 'pit of science' from where it produces its effects (Afary and Anderson 2005).

The exercise of power presupposes a free subject: if there is no choice in actions, there is no power. A slave, therefore, is not in a power relationship, but one of physical constraint (Foucault 1982a). The opportunities for autonomy have potential within a historically located relation between self and the world. Once a vantage point from which to critique existing social relations in, for example, the name of a postulated ideal (autonomous self) is abandoned, what is left is an examination of those present modes of organising social relations in terms of their potential. Eschewing grand theoretical gestures, Foucault's approach is not a study of institutions, theories or ideologies, but regimes of practice, 'with the aim of grasping the conditions which make these acceptable at a given moment; the hypothesis being that these type of practices are not just governed by institutions, prescribed by ideologies, guided by pragmatic circumstances – whatever role these elements may actually play – but possess up to a point their own specific regularities, logic, strategy, self-evidence and "reason"' (Foucault 1991b: 75).

So what we find is 'an ethos, a philosophical life in which the critique of what we are is at one and the same time the historical analysis of the limits that are imposed on us and an experiment with the possibility of going beyond them' (Foucault 1984a: 50). There is no 'gesture of rejection' in this ethos as we found in the Frankfurt School. It moves beyond an 'outside–inside alternative' that 'consists of analyzing and reflecting upon limits' (Foucault 1984a: 45). What is the motivation? 'How can the growth of capabilities be disconnected from the intensification of power relations?' (1984a: 48). If the Kantian question was 'knowing what limits knowledge has to renounce transgressing' (1984a: 45), Foucault wanted to turn that into a more positive one: 'what is given to us as universal, necessary, obligatory, what place is occupied by whatever is singular, contingent, and the product of arbitrary constraints? The point, in brief, is to transform the critique conducted in the form of necessary limitation into a practical critique that takes the form of a possible transgression' (1984a: 45).

Consequences for social scientific practice

The most productive way to approach Foucault's work is not as a denial of truth, but an examination of the conditions for its emergence. Discourses select and are significant for what they omit, not just include. The consequences of selectivity, the appearance of particular statements and their 'conditions of existence', opens up a space for alternative modes of organising social relations and to ourselves cleansed of 'transcendental narcissism' (Foucault 1989b: 203). He rejects a social science which focuses on the search for origins through speaking in the name of objects beyond discourses, or idealised ideas of subjectivity. Validity and meaning must exist in some kind of relation for there to be a reflexive recognition of how the analyst and the objects of analysis may be implicated in co-production. Yet from the point of view of research practice, this does not mean adjudicating between the true and false, but considering instead our own relation to truth.

What we take from Foucault is the insight that critical social scientific knowledge, conceived of in post-Cartesian fashion, cannot embark on its practice on the presupposition of an essence to humanity. Further, that a call to reflexivity for both social scientific practitioners and persons in general is bound up with a disciplinary power. Social scientific critique cannot therefore begin from a normative point of view, but instead 'consists in seeing what kind of self-evidence (évidences), liberties, acquired and non-reflective modes of thought, the practices we accept rest on' (Foucault 1982b: 33). A desire for curiosity is met by texts that open up otherness to the reader. His hope, therefore, was that his 'books become true after they have been written – not before' (Foucault 1989a: 301).

■■ Box 5.2 ■■■■■■■■■■■■■■■■■■■■■■■■■■■■■■■

Governmentality and reflexive thought

Foucault's ideas of power and the subject have implications for how we see and analyse the modern state. Rather than focus on governments in terms of sovereignty and the exercise of power over territory, 'governmentality' is instead about the techniques and procedures for directing human behaviour, managing populations to make them more 'docile' and 'productive'. By focusing on the 'art of governing' or 'conduct of conduct' (Foucault 1984b: 314), attention is drawn away from the specific structures and processes of state agencies and towards practices and calculated strategies. This means analysing the 'discursive fields' in which the exercise of power is rationalised and the interventions embedded in programmes and techniques. Given his work on power and knowledge, governmentality is, for Foucault and like the critical theorists before him, a political project focused on social spaces and means of intervention. Governmentality has been used in relation to studies on changing state relations, for instance devolution in the UK, as a way to concentrate on the procedures, discourses and practices of governing (Raco 2003).

Whilst many focus on the negative sides of state power, new studies are emerging. Marilyn Taylor (2007) argues that governmentality shows how state power persists even when governing is devolved, and also how 'active subjects' can shape and influence new spaces into which they have been invited. This is why governmentality matters in our journey on reflexivity. Unlike studies of governance, the analytics of governmentality are more radical and see reflexive thought as being part of, not outside, structures of power, liberty and technology (Cotoi 2011). There is a concern for transformative action that 'by focussing on strategies from below which aim to resist governmental ambitions, this emphasises that subjects are reflexive and can accommodate, adapt, contest or resist top-down endeavours to govern them if they so wish' (McKee 2009: 20). This applies to our roles as citizens as much as social scientists in terms of the transformative strategies we may wish to adopt.

Foucault is not without his critics. In moving from epistemology to historicism, we seem to have no means to speak of progress and no grounds upon which to 'account for its own position of enunciation' (Žižek 2012: 332). The abandonment of freedom and truth as ideals leads us to a permanent imprisonment in power relations in which history simply supplants one set of configurations for another with no discernible means for judging their relative merits. Foucault did, however, say that where there was power there was resistance from which a new force may emerge, leading to studies of tactics and strategies in the process of change (May 1999b). Hence, as we suggest in Box 5.2, by seeing state power not as a set of obdurate institutions but as a set of practices, the reflexive subject can mobilise forms of knowledge to challenge existing ways of governing. The issue remains that we seem to be branded by disciplinary powers whilst seeking to resist them. Where is our ability to be reflexive and how does that relate to a capacity and capability to effect change (May with Perry 2011)? Our actions are thus generated by the very forces we seek to resist and we are constituted by them. However, what of our agency and the reasons we give for our action and how we are constituted as being accountable for those actions? Foucault is critiqued for bypassing these processes of subjectivisation in his earlier work, because in order to account for discipline and subordination it needs to be ignored (Žižek 2008a).

Whilst this is a clear critique of Foucault and one to which those sympathetic to his work have responded (see Hoy and McCarthy 1994), the issue of reason and transparency – to ourselves and others – remains an important dimension of who we are, what we can know, and thus what we can hope for. In resisting we also refuse and to that extent give reasons for our actions which are also part of the subject matter of the social sciences. What we find is an underestimation of 'the resilience of the self, neglecting the extent to which individuals are reflexively aware of the attempts made by others to shape their selves' (Cohen 1994: 176). At the same time, how is 'a critical ontology of ourselves' to be conducted without a reflexive space of consideration?

We can take a different path. This is one that Judith Butler (2011[1993]), in her studies on sex and gender, has chosen in examining the relations between social determinants and agency. For this she draws on the works of Slavok Žižek who, in discussing Foucault's idea of the subject in the relations between power and resistance, notes there is an excess he does not consider: 'the possibility of an effect escaping, outgrowing its cause, so that although it emerges as a form of resistance to power and is as such absolutely inherent to it, it can outgrow and explode it' (Žižek 2008a[1999]: 303). Power has an excess it cannot control – an 'obscene supplement which sustains its own operation' (2008a[1999]: 304). The route here is thus a different one towards an emphasis upon 'extimate causality' which gives a name to the process in which subjects are generated in a social field: 'the social operation that gives us social identities, properties, and relationships. In producing the social subject, extimate causality also leaves a remainder or indeterminacy, so that every subject bears some unspecifiable excess within the social field' (Rothenburg 2010: 10). With this in mind, we now turn our attention to existential analytics to further understand reflexivity in social life in general and social science in particular.

A REALPOLITIK OF REASON

Where is agency and the space for reflexive consideration of the conditions under and through which we live? What are the abilities, understandings and capabilities that social science attributes to people as part of their armour of representations? How do these representations have an effect upon how we see ourselves and the world of which we are a part? If we follow Foucault's approach and accept that things are true or false only within particular configurations of power-knowledge, we hit another issue in terms of social scientific analysis: what is left for critique? In terms of addressing the relations between theory and practice, experience and representation, and the consequences for a rigorous and reflexive social science, few equal the endeavours of Pierre Bourdieu.

Bias in research production

In examining the production of social scientific knowledge, it is clear that the academic field as a site of production, as Alfred Schutz recognised, constitutes a particular way of viewing the world. Pierre Bourdieu's call to reflexivity takes him beyond phenomenologically inspired accounts and those of Alvin Gouldner (1971, 1975). The reason is to be found in a need to understand the *'intellectualist bias'* in research production (Wacquant 1992: 39; original emphasis). When examining the mediation of lay and social scientific concepts, the focus has been upon 'the *social* origins and coordinates (class, gender, ethnicity, etc.) of the individual researcher' (Wacquant 1992: 39; original emphasis). These forms of psychological reductionism, that characterise organisations like universities, have no implications for institutions of knowledge production (May 2005; May and Perry 2013). It is the position of the researcher within the academic 'field', constituted as a set of objective relations with others, that requires examination (May with Perry 2011).

How researchers define themselves, in particular through their difference from and distance to others with whom they compete in the academic field, is a key element that brings together the disposition *and* position of the individual practitioner without a lapse into individualism. What is encompassed here is not knowledge as such, but a 'relation to knowledge' expressed through knowing how to construct an object of analysis in ways that are recognised by others in the field (Bourdieu 2004). How researchers retreat from and think about the social world requires examination, as this is built into concepts, methods of analysis and the practical manner in which research is conducted. This call to reflexivity 'extends beyond the experiencing subject to encompass the organizational and cognitive structure of the discipline' (Wacquant 1992: 40). Why? To *'produce more science, not less. A* situated, rather than objectivist reflexivity, is not designed to discourage scientific ambition but to help make it more realistic. By helping the progress of science and thus the growth of knowledge about the social world, *reflexivity makes possible a more responsible politics,* both inside and outside of academia' (Bourdieu in Bourdieu and Wacquant 1992: 194;

original emphasis). This speaks back to the concerns of Adorno and his colleagues that science was increasingly negatively implicated in systems and structures of oppression.

Here we find no credence for the 'usual somewhat fatuous discourse about "neutrality"' (Bourdieu 1993: 11) whereby interest and truth are seen as opposites. As Weber recognised, we need an interest in producing the truth in the first instance. There are parallels with the view that, for something to be objective, it must be justifiable in a manner that is independent of one individual, leading to an inter-subjective understanding through a culture of testability as a pre-condition of scientific status (Popper 1968[1959]). Habermas, following Peirce, argued the same point. Bourdieu recognises that there is a tension between the necessary interest aiming at the production of truth, and an excavation of the conditions that give rise to classificatory practices that frame ways of seeing the world. Whilst examining relations between power and knowledge is essential for reflexive practice, the task is often suspended by the scholastic point of view in what, following Husserl, is a 'neutralizing disposition' (Bourdieu 1998: 128). Indeed, a condition of entry into the academic field is often held to be an attitude in which the necessities of life are suspended in order to constitute curiosity and contemplation as an end in itself. A commitment to understand the relations between classificatory practices and social and economic conditions – key to which is recognising how practical urgency is constituted, along with its reasons and effects – may easily be suspended or forgotten by those for whom such a temporal emergency, and even an economic necessity, are bracketed.

This disconnection is part of a set of scholastic fallacies that fall into three domains: ethics, aesthetics and knowledge (Bourdieu 2000: Ch. 2). In the domain of knowledge we find a conflation of practical and theoretical reason (Bourdieu 1998). If Kant awoke from his 'dogmatic slumbers' (see Chapter 1), a process of awakening was now needed from 'scholastic slumbers' through epistemological questioning, not denunciation. The tools that Bourdieu deploys for understanding are turned back onto the ways in which they are constituted and represented. After all, an objective distance from necessity, what Weber called a 'stylization of life', enables a focus upon the modes of representation deployed in the social sciences via the gaze of the scholastic mode of thought that is used to demarcate the inside–outside of social scientific activity.

▬ Box 5.3 ▬

Reflexivity in the academy

In a recent special edition of *Ephemera* (2008: 273–4) in a discussion between Stephen Dunne, Stefano Harney, Martin Parker and Tony Tinker, several salient points emerged: the right-wing nature of most American business schools and the 'implicit denigration of all state and "social" interests that might stand opposed to the accumulation process'; how business schools position themselves as the voices of 'labour' or 'capital' (2008: 274); or the interrelationships between universities and the reproduction of capital. Business schools are dubbed the 'Trojan Schools' of modern capitalism, and there are limits to how critical management studies can productively engage and transform these wider forces. Little wonder that business schools and technological universities want states to invest in innovation and technology transfer to realise the promise of the knowledge-based economy (May and Perry 2017).

Are academics deploying their intellectual credentials to make political points, without acknowledging their standpoints? Owen Jones, columnist for the *Guardian* newspaper and broadcaster, thinks so. In *The Establishment* he charts the dimensions of this 'organic, dynamic system … which is bound by shared economic interests and common mentalities' (2014: xvii). He locates the guiding principles of the Establishment in 1947 as a group of 40 intellectuals met in the Swiss village of Mont Pellerin. What followed was a series of processes in which intellectuals, convinced by the power of their own ideologies, worked with politicians and established interests to set a new orthodoxy. Friedrich Hayek, Milton Friedman and Madsen Pirie were amongst those who moved from academia into think tanks designed to propagate their ideas about the world, including the Institute of Economic Affairs, the Centre for Policy Studies and the Adam Smith Institute (see Chapter 1).

Such think tanks popularise policies, aligned with media campaigns, and translate dogma into everyday language. On the left, similar organisations exist bridging the gap between academic and policy worlds – amongst them the Institute for Public Policy and Research, Demos and New Economic Foundations. Yet the victory, according to Jones, is for the right. Fellow *Guardian* writer Adita Chakrabortty sees this as the legacy of neoliberalism: 'fencing off the means of knowledge production, claiming it as theirs' (Jones 2014: 44). Jones holds that these 'outriders' are a serious part of the problem: 'their biased, loaded policy suggestions – which if introduced would sometimes directly benefit their sponsors – are frequently treated by journalists as objective and impartial … the outriders are a reservoir of intellectual material for defenders of the Britain they have helped to create' (2014: 45). This is often translated into the less polemically stated problem of 'policy-based evidence', which leads to the view that politics is 'so pathological that no decision is based on an appeal to scientific evidence if it gets in the way of politicians seeking election' (Cairney 2015: 3).

There is an issue here: those conditions of relative stability that provide a connection between disposition and position, enabling the scholastic gaze, are less often open to reflexive scrutiny. However, that is not a situation of unthinking complicity, but an analysis of degrees of integration (Bourdieu 2000: 160). Box 5.3 examines this issue in relation to business schools and the role of the academy. Bourdieu's critique goes straight to the heart of the academic establishment in his calls for reflexivity as part of a responsible politics. On the one hand we see how some have harnessed the power of ontological exclusion to explicitly and audibly link knowledge to position and power. In claiming a standpoint that is fundamental to claims to know the social world, positionality becomes the very basis for a privileged form of knowing in which values are not bracketed but celebrated. Yet what happens when such standpoints are not explicitly acknowledged? Does this mean they do not exist?

What we often find are investments among researchers that become objects of denial in celebrations of limited notions of autonomy, or because misrecognition is character-istic of a field informed by the search for, and conferring of, individual distinction. The combination of disposition and position is therefore double-edged because the advan-tage of distance has a cost for the insights generated into practical reason. These cultures of inquiry are 'characterized by the suspension and removal of economic necessity and by objective and subjective distance from practical urgencies, which is the basis of objec-tive and subjective distance from groups subjected to those determinisms' (Bourdieu 1986: 54). Distance and time produce the conditions that enable an unhastening of sci-ence whose calling is to 'give us the close-up, the slow motion replay and the still frame rather than the hellish image blitz of the MTV model of entertainment' (Pels 2003: 219). Yet this bracketing of time is double-edged because it also informs a scholastic illusion that is 'itself correlative with the tendency to transform the privation linked to exclusion from the world of practice into a cognitive privilege, with the myth of the "impartial spectator", or the "outsider" according to Simmel, who are exclusive beneficiaries of access to the point of view on points of view which opens perspectives on the game as a game' (Bourdieu 2000: 224).

Intellectual tools of inquiry

Bourdieu gives us tools of inquiry to examine these issues in modes of knowledge produc-tion and reception in order to open up spaces of possible transformation. His concept of the subject lies between forms of objectivism and subjectivism through the deployment of the Aristotelian idea of habitus – a 'socialized subjectivity' (Bourdieu in Bourdieu and Wacquant 1992: 126) where the re-enactment of history takes place in the dispositions that people acquire over time and bring into social situations. Habitus both generates and shapes practices, carrying with it not only a 'sense of one's place' but also a 'sense of the other's place' (Bourdieu 1990: 131). It is 'an open system of dispositions that is constantly subjected to experiences, and therefore constantly affected by them in a way that either reinforces or modifies its structures. It is durable but not eternal!' (Bourdieu in Bourdieu and Wacquant 1992: 133)

As Bourdieu acknowledges, his concept of action stands to that of Dewey (Bourdieu and Wacquant 1992: 122) and shares, along with Heidegger, Merleau-Ponty and Wittgenstein, a critique of the body and subject–object duality. Habitus 'enables an intelligible and nec-essary relation to be established between practices and a situation, the meanings of which is produced by the habitus through categories of perception and appreciation that are themselves produced by an observable social condition' (Bourdieu 1986: 101). Here the 'field' structures or conditions the habitus, whilst it also constitutes the field as a place wherein a person decides to invest their energy. Therefore, there is a two-way relation between the habitus and field: 'Social reality exists, so to speak, twice, in things and in minds, in fields and in habitus, outside and inside of agents' (Bourdieu in Bourdieu and Wacquant 1992: 127).

Fields are constituted by distributions of economic, social and cultural capital (Bourdieu 1986), which are mobilised in the power struggles which take place within them – for example, for recognition within scholastic fields. A concentration, for example, on economic capital has enabled a dominant version of economics to saturate explanations of human action according to self-interest and value in terms of money, thereby reproducing what is a historical invention of capitalism now accelerated by particular forms of globalisation (see Bourdieu 2008, 2010). Whilst the objective power relations will be internalised by people in the form of categories of perception, the form of struggles within fields will vary. What is at stake is the conservation or subversion of the structure of the capital within the field, without which it is 'impossible to account for the structure and functioning of the social world' (Bourdieu 1986: 241). Those inclined towards conserving its power relations engage in orthodoxy, whilst newcomers to the field are likely to engage in strategies of heresy, with disjunctures between field and habitus producing a 'Don Quixote effect' where practices appear 'ill-adapted because they are attuned to an earlier state of the objective conditions' (Bourdieu 1986: 109).

In the combination of these intellectual tools being turned back upon the mode of knowledge production we find a challenge to scientific practice through an examination of presuppositions built into the 'oxymoron of *epistemic doxa*' (Bourdieu 1998: 129; original emphasis). A 'genuine epistemology' is 'built on knowledge of the social conditions under which scientific schemata actually function' (Bourdieu in Bourdieu and Wacquant 1992: 178). Importantly, this means that reflexivity is no guarantee of autonomy because the latter 'does not come without the social conditions of autonomy; and these conditions cannot be obtained on an individual basis' (Bourdieu in Bourdieu and Wacquant 1992: 183). If we reduce scientific activity to reflect the pervasive individualism that saturates contemporary views of social relations, we fail to see how fields of production are not only competitive, but also co-operative in sharing information and knowledge. A resulting ambivalence thereby occurs between conflicting expectations of competition for excellence and co-operation. Nevertheless, this is not a 'collective finalism' characteristic of the functionalist approach of Merton (1976) to scientific activity, but the result of socially constituted dispositions informing degrees of disinterestedness in the scientific field.

This collapses the differences between scholastic and practical point of views by assuming that the theory–practice relation is removed through a description of the processes of comprehension. It collapses the real issues that lie between thinking and being and seeks to side-step inevitability: a conceptual scheme is imposed on practical actions through scientific work. These, however, are matters of the world, not the words of the analyst. As Karl Marx put it, 'Their resolution is by no means, therefore, the task only of the understanding, but is a *real* task of life, a task which *philosophy* was unable to accomplish precisely because it saw there a *purely* theoretical problem' (Marx 1963[1956]: 87;

original emphasis). To avoid 'the things of logic' becoming the 'logic of things' it is necessary to get behind strategies to the practical sense that is part of the feel for the game within fields. Bourdieu recognised this and did not confuse clarification with resolution: 'Because the truth of the social world is the object of struggles in the social world … the struggle for the truth of the social world is necessarily endless' (Bourdieu 2004: 115). A resulting 'realpolitik of reason' aims to work 'towards social conditions permitting rational dialogue' (Bourdieu 1999: 226).

Social scientific practitioners should not hide in the technocracy of method, but need to free themselves from presuppositions and the 'illusion that they do not have any, especially about themselves' (Bourdieu in Bourdieu and Wacquant 1992: 195). Thus to remain vibrant and relevant to its day, research must consider its forms of categorisation and representation and its place and purpose within social relations more generally. Without this it commits the fallacy of internalism that plagues so many calls to reflexivity – namely ways of seeing and modes of constructing objects as if they were bounded within particular communities, as opposed to being bound up with what is viewed and the conditions under which they are viewed as part of the social world in general. The idea of autonomous fields – frequently assumed within the presuppositions of scholastic doxa – is replaced by 'regulated liberty' in terms of the mediation of social relations with the realm of social scientific knowledge production: 'It is through the illusion of freedom from social determinants (an illusion which I have said a hundred times is the specific determination of intellectuals) that social determinations win the freedom to exercise their full power … Freedom is not something given: it is something you conquer – collectively' (Bourdieu, 1990: 15). Therefore a series of tendencies, not determinations, enables the reproduction of society that does not translate into a fate, but a likely outcome from which an individual may escape. This empirically based 'existential analytics' (Dreyfus and Rabinow 1993) does not give itself over to those theories of resistance that celebrate the inventiveness of agency, nor to those approaches which cannot account for changes in social conditions.

STANDPOINTS AND DIFFERENCE

We are faced with a dilemma in our estimation of actions aimed at betterment: if we are to understand and improve social science through an analysis of the conditions under and through which it is practised, then the means we use must be as good as we are able to make them. The ultimate test then becomes 'success in identifying the conditions of existence and of coming into being of less oppressive forms of social and intellectual community' (Lovell 2000: 44). An emphasis upon the fit of habitus to social contexts provides an alignment that explains continuity but not transformation. The role of reflexivity at the level of social science is clear, but less so in terms of the possibility of social change at the level of society. Here the absence of a sufficient account of social change has implications for the reflexivity of social scientific practice (Lash 1993; Adkins 2004).

As noted, there is a restricted conception of human action at work outside of the domains of exchange and instrumentality that is emphasised by a concentration on strategies within fields of action. Specifically, there are forms of action that are omitted from these lenses, which we highlight by considering the particular implications for the position of women in society.

Relations of ruling

The reluctance to extend 'reason' to women that characterises the history of philosophical and scientific thought is carried into the contemporary world. However, the opposing of reason to emotion, as if a neat and unproblematic demarcation line, misses the issues in its desire to repeat popular stereotypes. The arguments are not about supplanting one with the other, but about having a better understanding of ourselves, our knowledge, how we live together and the effects of our actions upon the environment. As Genevieve Lloyd puts at the end of her essay 'Man of Reason': 'The impoverishment of woman through the imposition of sexual stereotypes is obvious. Exclusion from reason has meant exclusion from power. The corresponding impoverishment of men is less obvious, for what they miss out on has been downgraded. What is needed for the Man of Reason is realization of his limitations as a *human* ideal, in the hope that men and women alike might come to enjoy a more human life, free of the sexual stereotypes that have evolved in his shadow' (1992: 127; original emphasis). In respect to the works of Michel Foucault and Pierre Bourdieu, the idea of reason, knowledge and the subject is the focus of critique and revision. Feminists have therefore found strengths in utilising their work, but also weaknesses when it comes to an understanding of identity, resistance, the body and social change (Adkins and Skeggs 2004; Butler 2011[1993]). Going against the voluntarist tendency that informs ideas of individual fashioning in the relations between reflexivity and detraditionalisation (see Beck et al. 1994; Heelas et al. 1996), feminist-inspired writers have highlighted limits to resistance through an analysis of the forms of domination over particular groups (McNay 2000; Skeggs 2004; Lawler 2014). Informing these approaches are two questions. The first concerns the matter of epistemology directed towards excavating: '[W]ho knows what about what and how is this knowledge legitimized'? The second revolves around the purpose of feminist theory itself: '[E]xploring the nature of women's experiences, with a view to explaining the mechanisms through which inequalities are generated and reproduced' (Maynard 1998: 124).

With these questions orientating feminist social sciences, the idea of the universal standard through which to judge all knowledge is placed in question. To this, of course, there are several reactions. First, to deny these forms of critique or to ignore them in the hope they disappear. As Sandra Harding (2006) puts it, we may find a preference here for a form of 'weak objectivity' in order to maintain a value-neutrality. Second, there is the embrace of relativism and subjectivism. A third approach is to see the ascendancy in science as linked to the struggles that occurred in the emergence of modernity. Here we find a relation between the development of science and ideologies of domination (see, for example, Rose 1993; Gibson-Graham 1996; Haraway 1997; Keller Fox 2010). One approach would view feminist struggle as 'a fundamental part of gaining knowledge, including knowledge about and through science' (Harding 1991: 72). Such an approach would recognise how the concepts and practices of the sciences are part of cultural contexts and so knowledge is not beyond them, whilst also focusing upon 'the importance of strengthening both the existing ideal and procedures for achieving objectivity' (Harding 2006: 147). Quite simply, science may be a social product but 'particular scientific conclusions may be more or less credible and trustworthy' (Oakley 2000: 303).

In grappling with these issues, such writings are central to the investigation of reflexivity in general and scientific practice in particular. We find an examination between subject and object which does not derive from the supposed position of disinterest, but that interest arises from 'being engaged'. Deploying Marx, Nancy Hartsock writes of the relations between abstract masculinity and a feminist standpoint: 'The construction of the self in opposition to another who threatens one's very being reverberates throughout the construction of both class, society and the masculinist world view and results in a deep going and hierarchical dualism' (Hartsock 1987: 169). What is placed in question is the idea of bias in terms of possessing 'interests'. At one level this is undertaken through a general comparison of the differences between men and women – an 'abstract masculinity' compared to the 'connectedness and continuities' between women living in everyday life.

As we saw in the development of phenomenology and pragmatism, there is a tendency for scientific abstraction to gloss over experience in everyday life: for example, the unseen and yet fundamental efforts involved in emotional labour, relational work with significant and generalised others, the politics of reproduction and 'feminist commoning' (see Larrabee 1993; Hochschild 2003; Tyler 2013). A silence on the investigation of these issues leads to questions about how partial understandings of the social world are constructed and passed off as universal truths. As Donna Haraway puts it, there is no 'dodging' of the world-making practices of knowledge that results from taking this critique seriously: 'All that critical reflexivity, diffraction, situated knowledges, modest interventions, or strong objectivity "dodge" is the double-faced, self-identical god of transcendent cultures of no culture, on the one hand, and of subjects and objects exempt from the permanent finitude of engaged interpretation, on the other' (Haraway 1997: 37).

Drawing upon those such as Schutz, Garfinkel and Marx, Dorothy Smith takes the absence of women's experiences in social scientific accounts as symptomatic of 'relations of ruling' 'that coordinate people's activities across and beyond local sites of everyday experience' (Smith 2002: 45). The creation of a sphere in which women can make links between experiences and the images and ideas to make sense of them is thus limited. This sphere of reflection can be created by employing the ontological exclusion of women in the service of heightening scientific insights. As Lloyd noted in the *Man of Reason*, women are not seen as possessing 'an autonomous source of knowledge, experience, relevance and imagination' (Smith 1988: 51). The methodological starting point is that of women's standpoint which is '[d]esigned to establish a subject position from which to begin research – a site that is open to anyone – it furnishes an alternative starting point to the objectified subject of knowledge of social scientific discourse. From women's standpoint, we can make visible the extraordinary complex of the RULING RELATIONS, with its power to locate consciousness and set us up as subjects as if we were indeed disembodied' (Smith 2005: 228; original emphasis).

Ontological exclusions

Whilst negative in terms of positions within society, exclusion from dominant societal processes can be positively deployed in research practice to give a 'scientific advantage to those who can make use of the differences' (Harding 1991: 120). What emerges is a 'strong objectivity' in which thinking from women's lives uncovers processes and structures that – from a male point of view – appear natural. With the focus upon macro tendencies what is then permitted is 'a more robust notion of reflexivity than is currently available in the sociology of knowledge or the philosophy of science' (Harding 1991: 149). What are the problematic relations between experience and representation via social scientific work that are brought together through an objective vantage point from women's lives as the 'other'? Conventional epistemology speaks of knowledge as a free-floating voice. Instead this approach examines the significance of the gap between the points of view of oppressed groups and the dominant conceptual schemes that gloss over these experiences in the name of a 'weak' objectivity. A resulting 'standpoint', unlike a perspective, requires *both* science and politics to achieve (Harding 1991: footnote: 276; original emphasis). Knowledge, therefore, is a product of human activities in which the social and rational are not seen as dichotomies (Longino 2002).

Given this recognition, what of the relations between facts and values and their implications for the practices of the social sciences? We have seen how value can inform what science is done, but should not interfere with its process. Equally, there are those who have argued that interest is apparent in its very practices, and thus question any integrity born of autonomy rendering science as one cultural practice among many (Barnes 1974). However, a different argument can be made in drawing a distinction between constitutive and contextual values. The former are those values that underpin 'rules determining what constitutes acceptable scientific practice or scientific method'. The latter 'belong to the social and cultural environment in which science is done' (Longino 1990: 4). These exist in a dynamic interaction that is actually required by the process and practice of scientific inquiry. Contextual values can draw upon constitutive ones: for example, in an age where information saturation is evident, populations still looks to science for critical insight and that can be mobilised in the protection of integrity from dominant interests. Equally, constitutive interests express fluidity in the sense of being open to modification in the light of more general changes.

A social account of objectivity avoids claims to relativism through seeing within constitutive values a protection against scientific inquiry being nothing more than subjective preferences. Whilst there are differences between Longino's views and those of Habermas, particularly in terms of his acceptance of a positivistic view of the physical sciences, the inter-subjective realm of scientific inquiry is central to a rejection of individualism and recognition of the importance of social and cultural contexts for its practice. This works to both protect and challenge scientific claims: 'the development of knowledge is a necessarily social rather than individual activity, and it is the social character of scientific knowledge that both protects it from and renders it vulnerable to social and political interests and values' (Longino 1990: 12). In this respect we have seen how claims to scientific autonomy are often based upon the separation of facts and values as acts of purifying ambiguity in the name of defending scientific activity and certainty. However, to regard this as a strictly epistemological matter rules out what is an inevitable feature of scientific activity: its social context. In this way in the research process 'validity is not just based on rigour, standards, responsibility and recognition of situatedness and partiality, but also on the connections that are made in the relationships established' (Skeggs 1997: 34).

During the process of social investigation it is necessary to take these insights on board and translate them into research practice. A reflexive concern does not focus upon the self for this is to individualise a social process and commit the fallacy of transparency: 'What we need to do is to return to reflexivity as practice and process as a matter of resources and positioning; not as a property of the self' (Skeggs 2002: 369). Such a relational approach takes on board the power relations in the research process and how processes of value extraction occur across race, gender and class: 'For me the ability to use the time of others in whatever form (e.g. via the service economy, caring labour, entitlement to attention, etc.) is what is significant to making and maintaining the class relation. As ethnographers of class have long shown, the ability to access and use other people in the making of one's life is a class relation of exploitation' (Skeggs 2015: 217).

The process of research itself is not regarded as being valid by virtue of being constituted by the reflexive attitude of the investigator's point of view. Research is a dialogic process whereby the views of research participants are incorporated into the findings (Cook and Fonow 1990). Rooting actual experiences within institutional relations brings to light similarities, but also demonstrates disjunctures between experiences that require analytic attention, as opposed to being glossed over in favour of the bounded certainties of scientism. These are the lived realities of the world. A process of 'explication' arises in which relevance derives from the subject's 'lived actualities', and not from 'an abstract space with relevances determined by notions such as the cumulation of a body of scientific knowledge ... The discovery of an objectively existing social process is thus, through its capacity to generate bases of experience, seen *from such bases of experience*. The aim is to disclose the social process from within as it is lived' (Smith 1988: 176–7; original emphasis). The analysis takes the ambivalence that arises from seeking to answer the questions 'who am I?' and 'how do others see me?' An absence of connectivity due to occupying contradictory social locations (inside and outside) is then turned into an analytic advantage.

The issue of judgement remains. Wealth and power divide women as much as men, so does this evade, as oppose to seek to resolve, issues associated with the relations between research and everyday life? Situatedness can end up as a celebration of difference through subjectivism that refers to a knowledge that is atomised and so without relational connection. That may, of course, be celebrated! However, it is an examination of the causes of such differences that connect them. This, in turn, contributes to an 'intellectual participatory democracy' into which the results of research are fed and discussed: 'To enact or operationalize the directive of strong objectivity is to value the Other's perspective and to pass over in thought into the social condition that creates it – not in order to stay there, to "go native" or merge the self with the Other, but in order to look back at the self in all its cultural particularity from a more distant, critical, objectifying location' (Harding 1991: 151). So we find the need to recognise and investigate, rather than deny, the relations between subject and object and an avoidance of adherence to a 'truth ideal'. Such ideals mask attempts by powerful groups to legitimise how we interact with nature and organise our social relations (Harding 2006).

Overall this is held to be a common project that involves a critical reflexivity through paying attention to history in the collective constitution of women as 'other'. A dialogic approach to scientific activity then acts as a check upon the privileging of social scientific accounts according to one standpoint as an assumed 'universal'. The aim is to create a forum through which the lost voices of women may be recovered in terms of making links between women's experiences in a more public rather than private forum. In the process women's reflexivity within everyday experiences is revealed, rather than concealed in the partial perspectives of 'scientific' findings.

The emphasis on the epistemological advantages of ontological exclusion is a novel move and not one limited to the experiences of women. We noted in Chapter 1 that our history of the ideas of thought was largely influenced by white European males. This was, in part, a consequence of the differences between oral and non-verbal ways of knowing and the Western traditions of codifying scientific and philosophical enquiry into text. If history is written by the victors, then the history of social science has also been written by those in the most powerful and privileged positions. That this has come to shape what counts as knowledge, our rationalities and methods for knowing the social world is beyond contestation, as outlined in Box 5.4. It moves from the apparent certainties of early modernity to a vantage point from which to view the dominant processes that shape our lives. To speak in the name 'of' women requires some unifying factors. This may be, for instance, the identification of a common group of powerful men as rulers. However, it may be ventured that the very category 'woman' should be the subject of questioning. Thus Judith Butler writes of performativity in relation to both gender and sex as different from performance, for there is no presupposition of a standpoint rooted in ontology. Taking performative speech acts – those that bring something into being as a result of being named – plus the insights of those such as Foucault, Bourdieu, Lacan, Derrida and Žižek, it is discourse that brings into being the subject, not the subject producing discourse. In this way performativity becomes *'that aspect of discourse that has the capacity to produce what it names'* (Butler 1994: 33; original emphasis).

━━ **Box 5.4** ━━━━━━━━━━━━━━━━━━━━━━━━━━━━━━━━━

Challenging the canon

Increasingly scholars are challenging the philosophical canon, through paying attention to absent and invisible voices and laying the foundations for a more reflexive social science that understands the diversity of its foundations (Witt 1996). Park (2013), for instance, explores the development of an exclusionary canon of philosophy in the decades of the late eighteenth and early nineteenth centuries to challenge the genealogy of philosophy that starts with the Greeks. Park argues that European scholars deliberately undertook a successful campaign to exclude Africa and Asia from the history of philosophy. Similarly, Mills (1997) notes that philosophy is one of the whitest of the humanities. Critical race theory investigates the extent to which social science can achieve racial emancipation and anti-subordination; racism is engrained and only a standpoint which explicitly tackles power and the subjugation of the subject can address this. At the same time, standpoint theory has its limits as those subjected to double exclusions – such as African-American women – face different challenges in constituting their identities in one group or another (Collins 1998).

Historical philosophical and contemporary social exclusions are mutually reinforcing as knowledge produced by groups without intellectual standing can be dismissed as irrelevant. For Mills what is needed is a Racial Contract (1997: 4): 'a conceptual bridge between … on the one hand, the world of mainstream (i.e. white) ethics and political philosophy, preoccupied with discussions of justice and rights in the abstract, on the other hand, the world of Native American, African American and Third and Fourth World political thought, historically focused on issues of conquest, imperialism, colonialism, white settlement, land rights, race and racism, slavery, jim crow, reparations, apartheid, cultural authenticity, national identity, indigenismo, Afrocentrism etc.' This is a political as well as a moral and epistemological endeavour.

───

Celebrations of difference as a process through which subjects make gains in self-consciousness in relationship to 'others' may easily become problematic. Jacques Derrida alerted us to the metaphysical desire to constitute the essence of identity through the exclusion of the 'other' as embodying a negative that enforces the positive attributes of identity. Stabilisations are not natural and are based upon that which is unstable and it is because of this that politics and ethics are possible (Derrida 1996). Interests can then turn to the ways in which the 'other' is denied the capacity to constitute an identity in terms of current forces of social change and those forces can contain contradictory elements. For instance, American families have been seen as the 'shock absorbers' of a stalled gender revolution. Ideas of labour, at home and work, are part of a 'cultural cooling' of change where men are resistant. Equally another opposite force is exerting its influence: 'It isn't that men are changing too slowly, but that, without quite realizing it, women are also changing in the opposite direction – in the sense of assimilating to old-time male rules – too fast. Instead of humanizing men, we are capitalizing women. If the concept of the stalled revolution raises the question of how to be equal, the concept of the commercial spirit of intimate life raises the question: Equal *on what terms?*' (Hochschild 2003: 29; original emphasis).

The implications for social scientific practice see a tendency towards privileging the local, specific and discrete, over issues concerned with articulation and contextualisation (Fraser in Benhabib et al. 1995). This discursive idea of agency leads to the very issues which standpoint feminism sought to examine. Echoing an issue with Foucault and Bourdieu's approaches, how do you enable power for marginalised groups through taking advantage of the surplus that is generated in the process of subject formation? The role of reflexivity in discursive approaches of this type is not adequately examined. Insufficient attention has been given to how feminist practice illuminates the relationship between politics and science and that between social science, cultural context and its potential consequences for subsequent actions and transformation. In respect to this approach in Butler's work, 'Time and again she gets tripped up by an inadequate conception of the source and role of signification in subject formation, relying continually on a belief that somehow, the excess attending signification can be eradicated. In this persistent gesture, Butler reveals that she does not understand the subject itself as a site of excess' (Rothenburg 2010: 107). In addition, to locate sexuality within the objectivist emphasis upon language places agency into sexuality: 'While sexuality is a significant part of identity, a perspective on embodied being in context reveals that it is of fluctuating importance in the flow of existence where individuals are situated as citizens, workers, mothers, consumers, etc.' (McNay 2008: 171).

SUMMARY: REFLEXIVE LIMITS

Michel Foucault reminds us that if the quest for certainty remains sealed within scientific practice, it is doomed to fail for that tells us little about the issues of the world. What is reproduced is nothing more than a cognitive platform that people in an alienated world should simply appreciate and recognise. In pursuing historical studies of knowledge practices he reminds of the constitutive role of the social sciences. Discourses constitute how we obtain reference on the world and remind us of how that is bound up with the conditions which enable that gaze to take place. He provided us with an understanding of the social production of knowledge and the effects of the knowledge produced by the human sciences for the control and submission of populations. A critical ethos must be seen as a necessary, but not sufficient condition, to guard against 'power as evil'. This appears as a process without end. The potential for critical theory, considered genealogically, is its ability not only to 'reveal reality', but also to 'deconstruct necessity' (Hoy 1998).

What is at stake is not only our domination by others but also how we dominate our-selves, and here we find ambivalence between immanent and transcendent critique. Perhaps Foucault had this in mind when he spoke of reaching consensus as not being a regulatory principle in his work but a 'critical principle' (Foucault 1984a). What he could not provide us with is how that might be taken forward in a reflexive relation that seeks to attend to its practices through an awareness of its modes of representation. What we can take is a cautionary awareness in which we project ourselves against the complacencies of the present. Without some sense of the 'good', however, this has a price. We can therefore say that 'in rescuing us from the supposed illusion that the issues of the deep self are some-how inescapable, what is Foucault laying open for us, if not a truth which frees us for self-making?' (Taylor 1986: 99).

Pierre Bourdieu recognised that the 'philosopher-king' as the bearer of absolute knowl-edge should be uncrowned (Bourdieu 1990: 33). Once dethroned, however, we are not then immersed in a reflexive free for all. Deconstruction in the name of endless reflexivity is not the end but reconstruction. Politically engaged and committed as he was, Jacques Derrida noted that deconstruction did not readily translate into political programmes (Bernstein 1992: Ch. 7). Bourdieu turned reflexivity into the production of a better social science which meant the systematic attempt to grasp both the objective and subjective features of the world. Through numerous studies he demonstrated how the world is reproduced through a rigorous focus upon the practice of the social sciences. His studies of the fields of art, education, media and everyday life exposed dearly held beliefs within each. He turned his attention to the role of intellectuals in culture where commitment easily gives over to the seduction of 'success' in the media. Because of the forces of globalisation and their destructive tendencies, intellectuals 'can no longer be just a voice of critical con-science, seeking to assert with the political world the truth and values that prevail in his or her universe. He or she must also bring a genuine specific competence into the service of the causes he or she wants to defend' (Bourdieu 2010: 258).

If Bourdieu provided one of the best insights into the need for reflexivity in scientific practice, issues remained in terms of agency and reflexivity. As a check against self-referential indulgence and scholastic slumber, whilst engaging with the social world, we need a dynamic that recognises not only differences but also limitations, and does so in the spirit of contributing to human betterment. Social scientific practice informed by feminism sees the connection between politics and scientific practice not as a weakness but a strength. Here we added to a long list of writers who, whilst abandoning the idea of transcendental truth, turned their attention to a critique of sciences without resorting to a relativist social constructionism. In her studies on democracy and science, Sandra Harding notes that whilst the marginalised require a language with which to engage with contemporary forms of exploitation, 'it is equally important to insist that the dominant groups find a more widely beneficial substitute for their rhetoric about the truth ideal' (Harding 2006: 144). Being positioned and positioning oneself in a scientific field may often be accompanied by an unreflexive attitude that reproduces a view of reality as if there were no other account available that has any legitimacy. Such arrogance can be accompanied by a deficit model of the audience – a hypodermic practice in the public understanding of science whereby the public are assumed to be deficient in understanding (May 2005).

Whilst acts of categorisation and representation need to be carefully considered in scientific practice, they are routine in social life. They range from the mundane to the trans-local dynamics of capitalism that constitute commodities as desirable and add to forms of consumption that are indifferent to the contexts and consequences of their production. There is no shortage of those who are willing to undertake this endeavour on the basis of power, ignorance and prejudice. This means that spaces of possibility are not only being closed down in the face of contemporary forces but also opened up. Here knowledge and imagination both play a role. The former should speak, but in such a way that there is recognition it cannot be exhausted, whilst the other carries within it the seeds of that which has not yet been brought into being. One is potentially irresponsible in its saturation of the possible through scientism, whilst the other can be irresponsible in its denial of the real in a leap from the actual. One concerns comprehensibility about context and the other its expulsion to unleash the realm of the possible. Social science has a role to play in this process as translator and this requires reflexive spaces for deliberation to inform transformation. Such spaces are, however, in scarce supply. In the twenty-first century, the relationship between science, technology and socio-economic progress receives much emphasis. Whilst some writers critically examined the consequences of these dynamics and the changing relationship between knowledge and society, governments and industry embraced a particular vision of science as the motor of economic growth, with consequences for the practice of the social sciences.

6

THE DYNAMICS OF SCIENCE IN SOCIETY

CHAPTER CONTENTS

Socrates has left us to make sense of the puzzling sentence: I know that I know nothing. The fatal irony into which scientific-technical society plunges us is, as a consequence of its perfection, much more radical: we do not know what it is we don't know – but from this dangers arise, which threaten mankind!

(Beck 2006: 329)

INTRODUCTION

If the contemporary era is characterised by anything, it is the speed, intensity and complexity of change. The reasons for this state of affairs have been attributed to advances in information technology, globalisation and capitalism, and this new epoch brings with it fragmentation, disaggregation and feelings of a loss of control, along with a turn to the apparent certainties of fundamentalist beliefs. Towards the end of the twentieth century, writers began to consider how these vast changes in society were having considerable implications for recasting the relationship between science and society, driven by science and technology in the context of first industrial and then post-industrialisation. In our journey so far we have already seen how Cartesian thought has been challenged by the romanticists, pragmatists, critical theorists and post-war social theorists. In this chapter we continue to question the idea of a disinterested scientific practice by considering the changing relationship between science and society. As we shall see, authors have increasingly rejected binary categories such as science/society, application/justification and research/practice. This chapter addresses such issues and examines the transformations of such boundaries and the implications for social science.

First, we consider the changing nature of the relationship between science and society. We draw on the works of Sheila Jasanoff, Zygmunt Bauman (1925–2017), Bruno Latour, Ulrich Beck (1944–2015), Scott Lash and Anthony Giddens. We then turn to examine the consequences for the boundaries between justification and application, drawing on the ideas set forward by those such as Gibbons et al. (1994), and Funtowicz and Ravetz (1993). We consider the changing values attributed to social scientific work in terms of its funding, methods and status. Finally, we examine the implications of these pressures in terms of the boundaries between research and practice, via a reflection on the contemporary emphasis on co-production and the implications for forms of endogenous and referential reflexivity. Our aim, as it has been throughout the book, is not to rehearse the full works of these writers, but to draw on them to improve our understanding of reflexivity as a condition of survival, functioning and a transformational prerequisite in the reshaping of modern societies.

CO-PRODUCING SOCIETY

In our history of reflexivity we have considered a wide array of debates concerning the relationship between ourselves, our approaches and ways of knowing and researching the world. Under the influence of huge social and technological change from the 1960s and 1970s onwards, a new interdisciplinary field of study, called Science and Technology Studies, began to develop. In the context of concern about the relationship between science, technology and social progress in the post-World War II Cold War era, writers emphasised the ways in which endogenous and then exogenous factors – within and outwith academic fields of enquiry – were changing the contexts and cultures of knowledge production. Thomas Kuhn's (1962) study *The Structure of Scientific Revolutions* is seen as a classic in positioning science as the product of socially conditioned investigations. Even prior to this, the roots of the field of STS has been traced to C.P. Snow's identification of 'two cultures' in society, one comprising scientists and the other humanists (Cutcliffe 2001). Some have traced parallels between developments in Britain and Germany in the context of critiques on the social construction of science (Collins and Pedersen 2013).

The contextualisation of science and society

Increasing complexity, uncertainty and dialogue between science and society has led to the 'contextualisation' of a more socially accountable science which itself requires a different reflexive relation to work on the part of the researcher. For some, the social distribution of expertise and the fragmentation of established linkages between expertise and institutional structures have been fundamental in informing degrees of reflexivity (Nowotny et al. 2001). The result is not only shifting boundaries between the public and science, but also intellectual property and public and private forms of knowledge (Dreyfuss et al. 2001; Harvey and McMeekin 2007). For Sheila Jasanoff (2004) this gives rise to a new 'idiom of co-production', namely the proposition that the ways in which we know and represent the world (both nature and society) are inseparable from the ways we choose to live in it: 'Scientific knowledge is not a transcendent mirror of reality. It both embeds and is embedded in social practices, identities, norms, conventions, discourses, instruments and institutions' (2004: 3). Drawing on Latour's earlier work, Jasanoff's co-production is an *idiom* rather than a theory, a way of interpreting and accounting for complex phenomena that can be applied to how knowledge-making has been incorporated into processes of state making, and how in turn the practices of governance influence the making and use of knowledge. To this extent, knowledge becomes the object of study itself as it is 'crystallizing in certain ontological states – organisational, material, embodied' (2004: 3).

If impermanence and undecidability are features of the contemporary landscape, then social science should be judged according to its ability to provide the means to enable people to forge their lives in better ways. In this 'endless labour of reinterpretation' (Bauman 2007: 315) there are many competitors and these are not simply, for example, from the worlds of art, film and literature. What we now find are large corporations collecting enormous amount of data about our habits, lifestyles and preferences. Despite the evident concerns of the authorities towards the 'Bible of capitalism', by the end of 2012 China alone had 377,800 advertising agencies, employing 2.18 million people with revenues of $75.52 billion (Puppin 2014).

It is not only advertising but also technology that is shaping our sense of self and others. The latter, evident in smart technology, is hailed as the twenty-first-century manifestation of that same quest for certainty as a 'solution' to our 'problems'. Enormous amounts of data can be mined, we are connected, and a 'utopia of openness' is hailed for the future. Yet this can not only open up reflexive relations, but also shut them down in terms of their implications for constituting boundaries. After all '[t]echnologies actively shape our notion of the self; they even define how and what we think about it. They shape the contours of what we believe to be negotiable and non-negotiable; they define the structure and tempo of our self-experimentation' (Morozov 2013: 344). As we expect more from technology, we may come to expect less of each other (Turkle 2012)! In this sense the power of technology cannot be underestimated, and as we march forward allusions to the past are regarded as millstones around the neck of those who only see wonderful futures.

Whilst markets had been fashioned by the work of states (Polanyi 2001[1944]; Graeber 2011), we now have global flows of goods and services (Castells 2010). Societies of consumers have been formed in which problems are shared, but the means of their resolution is privatised. This leads to a paradox: 'left to the resolve of individuals, thereby charging them with the impossible task (note that, once enforced and unavoidable, tasks turn into duty) of handling individually, on their own, challenges that are socially produced (and only socially resolvable). The result is something akin to buying family shelters in order to cope with an imminent nuclear war and to divert its impact from oneself' (Bauman 2014: 124). The concern is commodification manifested in the seduction of consumption for the pursuit of status. In the face of this our destinies appear 'ready to be wiped clean in order to admit new images, and boasting a life-long guarantee only thanks to that wondrous ability of endless self-effacing' (Bauman 1997: 25).

Zygmunt Bauman takes the attempt to eradicate ambivalence and its consequences as the topic of his inquiries, which leads him to the view that '[w]hat is left outside of the confines of rational discourse is the very issue that stands a chance of making the discourse rational and perhaps even practically effective: the *political* issue of democratic control over technology and expertise, their purposes and their desirable limits – the issue of politics as self-management and collectively made choices' (1991: 276; original emphasis). Following Michel Foucault, Bauman argues that two kinds of critique are available to us: a general analytic of truth and an ontology of the present. Once relieved of a method of production/ interpretation, both the artist and viewer/listener engage in a process of meaning production which, in bringing together questions of truth and grounding of reality, opens up possibilities 'free from the tyranny of consensus' (Bauman 1997: 111).

Bauman approvingly quotes Foucault: 'A critique is not a matter of saying that things are not right as they are. It is a matter of pointing out on what kinds of assumptions, what kinds of familiar, unchallenged, unconsidered modes of thought the practices that we accept rest ...' (1997: 111). This is not taken to be easy in terms of the need to mediate meaning between communities, 'given the incurable split of the human world into a plethora of fully or partially autonomous, institutionally entrenched traditions and meaning factories; and given the undeniable need of mutual communication and understanding between them' (Bauman 1989: 197). Bauman takes issue with a science conceived of in terms of its own self-belief and hermetically sealed off from the world it seeks to comprehend, as if the limits imposed by the 'garrison commanders' cannot be transgressed. The spirit is clear from his earlier writings: 'The price the theory which subjects itself to the test of authentication pays for pulling down the barrier dividing the "experimenter" and his "objects", for dissolving the difference in status between them, is likely to be considered exorbitant by a science concerned more with certainty than with the significance of its results' (Bauman 1976: 109).

As social and technological problems have become larger, so the search for certainty has become more challenging for social scientists faced with complexity and interdependence. In efforts to manage this complexity we have already seen how boundaries have been constituted to deal with and avoid the encounter with ambivalence. For Bruno Latour, a nature/culture divide pervades us and we should put aside the state of nature: 'The world is young, the sciences are recent, history has barely begun, and as for ecology, it is barely in its infancy. Why should we have finished exploring the institutions of public life?' (Latour 2004a: 228). Latour (1993) takes the non-human elements in the world to be on a par with the human through a network approach in which the domains of nature, society and language become integrated and subject to a process of 'hybridisation'. What is avoided is the subject–object duality in which humans not only stand at the centre of the universe, but through which the objective is also approached as exteriorised and the subject interiorised.

If the quest for certainty moved us from an understanding of 'argumentation' in Renaissance humanism towards a concern with 'proof', critique needs to attend to matters of concern (Latour 2004b). Matters of concern are about not just discrete fields of endeavour that support the aspirations of scientism, but also those things that have become part of the everyday practices of life. Those changes that informed Descartes' time and informed the search for certainty now inform the constitution of the contemporary world. Whereas there was a belief that a rationally organised world of scientism would produce outcomes that could be universalised, we now see an increasing disenchantment that requires a process of 'perpetual reorientation' (Bauman 2014: 54).

The search for certainty and the impossibility of its attainment rears its head once more Yet changes in the relationship between science and society have removed that goal even more clearly from vision. A more reflexive social science concerns the replacement of certainty with the relations between knowledge, uncertainty and choice (Morgan 1983a). This means a 'new discursive culture of perception, communication and collective attempts to define and resolve an unprecedented problem turned into a public and political issue' (Strydom 2002: 5). What is needed is a broader understanding of 'the more pervasive cognitive dimension that embraces acts of recognition and knowledge, processes of the generation of knowledge and the micro, meso and macro cognitive structures shaping, forming and containing knowledge from the outset and throughout' (Strydom 2002: 148). For Piet Strydom, the work of Habermas is central to this development (see also Strydom 2000). We can witness this in Habermas's remarks on Dewey: 'The question for certainty is the obverse side of a consciousness of risk which is aware of the fact that enduring "adaptive" behavioural patterns can develop only through productive coping with disappointments and the progressive mastering of problems. What sets human being apart as active beings is precisely this problem-solving behaviour' (Habermas 2006: 134–5).

Risk and reflexive modernisation

As societies become more complex and interconnected in the context of forces of globalisation and technological development, so the possibility of attaining certain knowledge recedes. At the same time, the effects of these changes are seen as negative: an increasing encroachment of instrumental rationality into the lifeworld with a resulting diminution in freedom; dehumanisation and the shifting emphasis from a sphere of reflexive understanding to the calculation of particular means to secure predetermined ends (Ritzer 2015). For those who have sought to explain the crises endemic to contemporary capitalism, this is characteristic of dialectic relations between helplessness and omnipotence when societies are 'dominated by the wage form of labor and commodity form of need satisfaction' (O'Connor 1987: 167).

In turning towards science to seek certainty, we find a body of knowledge open to continual revision. The idea of a 'risk society' (Beck 1992) is central here, mixing with recognition that forces have been unleashed whose control depends upon a global effort (Giddens 2009; Koch 2012). Ulrich Beck was a German sociologist influenced by Habermas who worked with British sociologists Anthony Giddens and Scott Lash. *Risk Society*, first published in German in 1986, was the first of many works examining the relationship between structures and agency in the era of 'reflexive modernisation' (Beck et al. 1994). There is so much to know and so little possibility of doing so: 'Where is the line between prudent concern and crippling fear and hysteria? And who defines it? Scientists, whose findings often contradict each other, who change their minds so fundamentally, that what was judged "safe" to swallow today, may be a "cancer risk" in two years' time? Can we believe the politicians and the mass media, when the former declare there are no risks, while the latter dramatize the risks in order to maintain circulation and viewing figures? Let me end with an ironic confession of non-knowledge. I know that I, too, simply do not know' (Beck 2006: 345). The idea of a risk society, discussed in Box 6.1, is one in which ecological disasters mix with an increasing circulation of knowledge and a micro-ethics of responsibility that heightens uncertainty. Such conditions increase the need for reflexivity about the strengths and limitations of our knowledge claims.

Risks and opportunities created by post-industrial society and the extent of human intervention in all areas of life lead away from loyalty to institutions and structures towards the grounding of meaning and identity in the self. In the context of late modernity, Giddens sees that the 'self becomes *a reflexive project*' (Giddens 1991: 32; original emphasis). Self-identity is not a given but must 'be routinely created and sustained in the reflexive activities of the individual' (1991: 52). This means a focus on biographical narrative and aligns with an apolitical individualism in the face of heightened risk and complexity. It is a coping mechanism as both society and the self are in flux, such that 'the altered self has to be explored and constructed as part of a reflexive process of connecting personal and social change' (1991: 33).

━━━ Box 6.1 ━━━━━━━━━━━━━━━━━━━━━━━━━━━━━━━━━━━━

Climate change and the risk society

Climate change is a perfect example of the risk society, in Ulrich Beck's eyes as 'the more emphatically the existence of the world risk society is denied, the more easily it can become a reality. The ignorance of the globalization of risk increases the globalization of risk' (Beck 2006: 330). The risk society focuses on conflicts of accountability over how the consequences of risk – as the anticipation of crisis or disaster – can be attributed, controlled and legitimated. The Intergovernmental Panel on Climate Change (www.ipcc.ch/) have examined multiple sources of evidence and concluded that the balance of evidence supports the impact of humans on the changing environment, the issue being not whether the climate will change but how much. Despite this, climate science is one of ripest and contested examples of the changing relationship between science and society: 'climate science cuts against the grain of common sense and undermines existing social and ethical commitments' (Jasanoff 2010: 233). For Jasanoff the issue is that the processes through which knowledge stabilises into accepted bodies of knowledge interpenetrate with how society stabilises itself, through four sites of co-production – the making of identities, institutions, discourses and representations. Citizens are 'acculturated' into settled ways of making and debating public knowledge and this reflects a number of 'civic epistemologies'. It also means that scientific studies that may be accepted as evidence in one country may fail to make their mark in another. Environmental knowledge, for instance, achieves 'robustness through continual interaction – or conversation – between fact-finding and meaning-making' (Jasanoff 2010: 248).

'Climategate' is one example of these issues. In the weeks before the 2009 Intergovernmental Panel on Climate Change emails were hacked from the University of East Anglia's Climatic Research Unit. These emails were subsequently strategically and tactically deployed to bring climate science into disrepute. Whilst subsequent independent evaluations found no evidence of wrongdoing on the part of the scientists, the debate was mobilised to achieve fear and distrust in science. This was supported by particular factions of the media which claimed that this was the 'worst scientific scandal of the generation' and that 'scientists shouldn't get away with it' (*Telegraph Online*, 2009).

This is a clear indication of how society's views on science are shaped by those with access to channels of communication, and that there are complex processes by which science, regardless of its modes of production, comes to be stabilised and accepted

(Continued)

(Continued)

as valid. In the wake of Climategate, the Tyndall Centre, a partnership across eight UK universities working on sustainable responses to climate change, published a report on the issues of expert legitimacy in working with complex scientific and social issues (Nordhagen et al. 2012). It concluded that a reflexive examination of the relationship between the body of knowledge, the expert and the institution they belong to would be critical in establishing credibility.

Reflexivity concerns society itself: 'Let us call the autonomous, undesired and unseen, transition from industrial to risk society *reflexivity* (to differentiate it from and contrast it with reflection). Then "reflexive modernisation" means self-confrontation with the effects of the risk society that cannot be dealt with and assimilated in the system of industrial society' (Beck in Beck et al. 1994: 6; original emphasis). The social and natural worlds are 'infused with reflexive human knowledge' (Beck et al. 1994: vii). The reflexive modernisation thesis states that as modernity unfolds alongside an increasing knowledge of the social conditions and situations in which we find ourselves, there is an increasing optimism concerning improvements in the human condition. A reflexivity concerning modernity, on the other hand, may lead equally to a more pessimistic account in which the world appears as a juggernaut out of control for there is no implied connectivity between circumstances, their understanding and transformation. It is not necessary for the social scientist to exercise a choice in relation to either of these perspectives. However, these issues will inform the predispositions or background assumptions of practitioners, and to that extent are of core interest.

The processes and forces of reflexive modernisation give rise to differential amounts of embedding and disembedding in the practices of the social sciences. Social scientific knowledge is part of this process and knowledge is viewed in terms of a greater normalisation within everyday practice. It does not operate in a revelatory manner, but is co-opted into the constitution of relations. From the point of view of knowledge reception we then find that '"[o]penness to criticism" among social scientists inevitably implies "openness to utilization" on the part of others' (Giddens 1989: 290). With the force of globalisation, decisions affecting daily life stretch away, in time and space, from the immediate environment. Coupled with processes of decentring of the self, everyday life becomes 'detraditionalized and individualised but also *palpably globalized*' (Beck and Beck-Gernsheim 2002: 151; original emphasis). The overall result is a 'disembedding of mechanisms': 'Few people anywhere in the world can any longer be unaware of the fact that their local activities are influenced, and sometimes even determined, by remote events and agencies' (Giddens in Beck et al. 1994: 57).

Increasing uncertainty is manifest in a turn from tradition to expertise in which the latter, in comparison to lay knowledge, implies an imbalance in a given field of action in which we can find expertise interacting with 'growing institutional reflexivity, such that there are regular processes of loss and re-appropriation of everyday skills and knowledge' (Giddens 1996: 38–9). Scientific knowledge may be deployed as a justificatory mechanism for de-skilling the workplace, or it may be challenged in terms of its implications within the domain of the political as the exercise of rights. In neither case is scientific knowledge necessarily the problem, but as the boundaries move so too can the relations between justification and application.

'NEW' MODES OF KNOWLEDGE PRODUCTION

The relations between knowledge, economy and society matter in terms of wealth creation, social inclusion and public understanding or expertise. Knowledge has become the subject of policy aspirations across a range of fields. The result is a challenge to boundaries as captured in the idea of 'soft capitalism' (Thrift 2005). The role of the state to protect curiosity-driven research as a cultural obligation has given way to a greater emphasis on meeting the needs of industry and deploying knowledge for economic gain (Ruivo 1994; Gibbons 2001). In the current era of 'knowledge capitalism' (Burton-Jones 2001) innovation becomes the driving concern. Recognition of science's capacity for innovation leads to a wish to exploit this systematically in order to achieve various socio-economic goals. If knowledge, whether directly or through an alteration in its enacted environment, is seen as a tool in the management or resolution of economic and social issues, then 'relevance' and 'usefulness' assume increased importance. This in turn structures what knowledge should be produced and how it might be judged.

Justification and application

Knowledge production, it is argued, has moved out of disciplinary silos in universities and into new societal contexts. Sites of problem formulation and negotiation of solutions are said to move from their institutional domains in government, industry or universities into wider society in a process of 'contextualisation' (Nowotny et al. 2001), linked to the 'social robustness of knowledge' and the fragmentation and dispersion of expertise outside of traditional structures and institutions. It is argued this has resulted in a greater focus on both interdisciplinarity and applied research, necessitating user involvement in the process of knowledge production. Knowledge in the context of application implies closer connections between different institutions and actors in the knowledge production system, and requires universities to 'reach out' and co-operate with industry and government to a far greater extent than before (see also Etzkowitz and Leydesdorff 2000; Harloe and Perry 2004). Such changes are located in wider shifts in social organisation which characterise the globalised and knowledge-based world, notably the increasing prevalence of the 'network' in a plethora of social, political, economic and technological domains (Graham and Marvin 2001; Castells 2010).

Changeable dynamics between justification and application are regarded as characteristic of transformations within a broader framework of societal change. Indeed it may be argued that if we are interested in power then we should turn to an examination of the structures of justification that inform our social and political relations (Forst 2014b). Previously bounded scientific work, as a condition of production, is now in question as the conditions of its justification in terms of the consequences of its application are open to public scrutiny. This has also meant more scientists taking on an intermediary role between funders, publics and institutions in order to enable a continuation of degrees of relative autonomy for scientific work (May with Perry 2011). Gibbons et al. (1994) note that a key feature of the new knowledge economy is the emergence of a 'Mode 2' of knowledge production. 'Mode 1' science is generated within disciplinary contexts, problems are set and solved by means that are controlled by the specific disciplinary communities themselves. By contrast, 'Mode 2' research is created in broader, transdisciplinary contexts. It is carried out in a 'context of application' and the previous distinctions between 'pure' and 'applied' research are increasingly transgressed: fundamental problems are investigated in the course of 'applied' research programmes and the possibilities of application are increasingly shaping programmes of 'pure research'.

Post-normal science is another way of framing these issues, developed by Silvio Funtowicz and Jerome Ravetz (1993), which mirrors this need for new modes of knowledge production where there is uncertainty, disputation, urgency and high stakes. We cannot know the future, scientific work is contested, and topics such as climate change or immunisation programmes have high decision-stakes. As such, justification and application require an 'extended peer community': 'Natural systems are recognized as dynamic and complex; those involving interactions with humanity are "emergent", including properties of reflection and contradiction. The science appropriate to this new condition will be based on the assumptions of unpredictability, incomplete control and a plurality of legitimate perspectives' (1993: 739).

Concern is turning not only towards the positive but also the negative transformational effects of scientific application: 'the fear that we know too much and are about to assume the role of God ... increasingly replaces the concern that we are to a large degree poorly informed' (Stehr 2004: xi). Here it is not so much science itself that is under scrutiny but its application. We can no longer 'taste the delicious savour of "useless knowledge"' (Russell 2004[1935]: 25), and have moved from a situation of lamenting a deficiency of relevance of scientific knowledge towards a 'surplus of effects' (Stehr 2004). Turning towards a concern with the relevance, contestability and effects of knowledge requires a greater degree of preparedness to enter into the domain of referential reflexivity, and with that into less bounded spheres of action than traditionally found in academic communities (May with Perry 2011).

Justification within bounded communities, where values are attributed to different knowledges and activities on the basis of assumed internal norms and practices, can mean that concerns with application are absent, accidental or delegated to some intermediary responsible for 'knowledge transfer'. An over-concern with relevance can collapse those boundaries as application becomes justification, with consequences for the independence of research (Quiddington 2010). Further, those who move unwittingly into the terrain of relevance through application, without due concern for the content and context in which knowledge is produced, end up in a state of capitulation to the assumption that knowledge is a one-way street to be judged according to its context of application. As we have argued throughout this book, whilst knowledge is mixed with other factors in our lives, its context-revising force and the efforts needed to make it intelligible are then bracketed in a triumph of instrumentalism.

■■ Box 6.2 ■■■■■■■■■■■■■■■■■■■■■■■■■■■■■■■

Cities and the promise of knowledge

Scholars have critiqued the supposed exceptional qualities of laboratories by examining the importance of the everyday contexts of knowledge production in shaping how research is performed (Latour and Woolgar 1979; Knorr-Cetina 1981). Attention has then turned to the need to 'take in questions outside the laboratory' so as not to fall back into an 'internalist' vision of science (Latour 1985: 141). In the twenty-first century these questions outside the laboratory are increasingly of an spatial nature (May and Perry 2016). The expectation is that that knowledge will lead to economic, social, cultural, educational, health and environmental improvements – sometimes, it appears, all by itself! Cities seek these outcomes with recipes for growth whose origins and perpetuation lie not just in the practices of consultancies, but also in academia (O'Mara 2005; Perry 2010). What we see are expectations which tend to ignore contexts of translation in favour of the value placed on the content of ideas (May and Perry 2017).

More recently the rise of urban laboratories and 'living labs' is merging with ideas of experimentation (Evans and Karvonen 2014; Karvonen and van Heur 2014). This can be interpreted in different ways. Are urban laboratories seeking to replicate the processes of the physical sciences to clothe themselves in scientific credibility in the context of risk and uncertainty? Or are these more radical innovations in the social organisation of social science? One danger is that experimentation may deny the importance of context, ignoring history and place-based dynamics (May and Perry 2016). This also speaks back to the dynamics between justification and application.

When conducting comparative work on science and regionalisation in the UK, Spain, Germany and France (Perry and May 2007; Perry 2012), one of us interviewed an eminent scientist who was well known for their work. We waited for some time in a large office at the top of a building that had been financed by the regional authority. Upon entering the office, the person threw a pile of papers on the desk and declared 'You wish to interview me about

(Continued)

(Continued)

regional science? I have no interest in this topic. This will not take long.' Undaunted, we continued through a more circuitous route to try and discover the links between financial support of the authority and the laboratory processes. After one and a half hours and despite initial protestations, context mattered to what they did and brought with it the need to demonstrate relevance to the regional authorities who contributed to its possibility.

As relevance or impact criteria grow in importance, the disjuncture between content and context also becomes more problematic. Context increasingly informs not only what work is funded, but also how it is performed and the conditions in which value judgements about its ultimate worth are made. Questions which define the boundaries of work are not only directed at what research, but also at how, with whom and where? Problems are set and solved in the context of application, and widely understood as being outside the university, not only in industry, but within broader social and political arenas. Indeed, context operates at multiple levels. Although often interpreted through an interpersonal dynamic or at the micro-level, as indicated through laboratory-based studies, contemporary politico-economic pressures necessitate a broader understanding of context in, for example, institutional and spatial terms. In the knowledge-based economy, knowledge is attributed with value and seen as a source of competitive advantage (Bryson et al. 2000: 1). City officials in various countries have demonstrated a difference in the issues they face, but a similarity in aspirations to search for symbolic and material advantage which includes marketing themselves as flourishing places for investment by global capital (Perry and May 2015). Such efforts are oriented around the ideas of knowledge corridors, clusters, capitals and valleys, as outlined in Box 6.2.

If the form of critique upon which social scientific analysis of these trends and their consequences relies upon frameworks of understanding that do not have a purchase on matters of concern, it can bypass what is important in the name of conceptual clarity at an endogenous level within the community of inquiry itself. The result would be endless publications in journals read by few and yet held in esteem by the epistemic community, along with conferences where they speak to each other as if that guaranteed they had something of importance to say about the world. Those same outcomes can be achieved through a habitual choice of method as if that were sufficient for analysis and forgets how it can produce its own reality (Law 2004).

We have here a similar outcome for the practice of social scientific understandings that seeks to understand the world through engagement via the application of methodological rigour: degrees of ambivalence. Justification may be readily invoked in different ways in order to reduce this outcome. A community of scholars may agree, consciously or otherwise, to apply a particular method and a similar community may come together to celebrate the work of a particular school of thought or scholar. In both cases this may occur without concern for the justification–application continuum. Surely, however, we might argue that justification is also a matter of interpretation? If we are to better understand the place of social research in society, then we need to see how and under what circumstances an interpretation is appropriated by those whom it concerns. Equally, we need to consider how such interpretations are mediated, or not, by others in positions of power whose selectivity has an effect on its understanding and dissemination in the public realm.

The value and role of social science

There is a clear distinction in the writings above between those that are concerned with what *is* happening to the boundaries between science and society and those that are seeking to *make* changes to the boundaries to realise particular goals. As the boundaries between justification and application become more permeable and contested, we see alterations in what society expects of knowledge and its purpose (Perry and May 2006). Different values are attributed to the social sciences in terms of their marketisation and commodification, the value of meaning or of numbers, and their role in supporting the 'real' work of science and technological discovery via dealing with issues of risk and public engagement.

The largest system ever invented through which value is attributed to things is the market. Its ascendancy to its present state is not a natural process, but one enabled by a set of practices born in the eighteenth and nineteenth centuries (Polanyi 2001). It is to such historical research we need to turn in order to counter the trend that may be detected in the type of economics that hovers at the end of arrogant and insulated scientism – often epitomised by the idea that it deals with the realities of how the economy works, whilst others can idly ponder about such matters as the 'good life'. Such blinkered slicing of the social into neat, digestible pieces of endogenous reproduction continues against the backdrop of the exercise of corporate power that rests upon the desire for a monopoly position (Crouch 2011). Whilst there are issues to be taken on board in applying Polanyi's ideas (Dale 2010; Hann and Hart 2011), the power of the market to attribute value to things cannot be underestimated in terms of its influence over our lives along with the contribution of social media to turn private affect into that which becomes publicly comparable and measurable (Arvidsson 2012).

The economy increasingly deploys cultural means through which to reproduce itself and that requires new ways of understanding its consequences. Roy Bhaskar (1975) writes of the 'epistemic fallacy' in Western philosophy: we should not confuse our knowledge of reality with reality itself. Yet, as the Frankfurt researchers analysed, is it the very manipulation of that reality through the capitalist market place that turns meaning and value into calculation. As the epistemic becomes commodified, we cannot assume that the bounded practices of social sciences are then not for sale: the new spirit of capitalism, embodied in the idea of the information and knowledge society, shows its ability to not only absorb critique, but also furnish a need for models through which to market goods, services and places. This can easily become social science in the service of a particular politics (May 2015).

With globalisation in mind, there has been much discussion of the 'death of distance' or the 'end of geography' (Morgan 2001) as the internationalisation of markets, economies, societies and environments signals the breaking down of the boundaries of time and space. Whilst contextual factors still play their role (Sassen 2011), we see an increasing relation here and elsewhere in the constitution of the social with the relations between affect and economic value. It is the value placed in science and innovation to secure economic growth that has been situated at the heart of global competitiveness. Such instrumentality is found in language that includes 'drivers', 'opportunities', 'pillars', 'initiatives' and 'solutions' (see, for example, Dresner 2001) and an emphasis on physical development in terms of 'hubs', 'incubators' and 'science parks' (Youtie and Shapira 2008). When combined with technology we find these 'Invented Edens' where 'the techno-city represents an experiment in integrating modern technology into the world of ideal life' (Kargon and Mollela 2008: 12). These developments are the product of new forms of international power relations which are characterised as representing a new doxa: 'Like the Catholic *doxa* of the Middle Ages, the new neoliberal *pensée unique* seemed to provide solutions for all kinds of social and ecological issues. Often neutralised in academic terms and amplified by associated intellectuals within and outside the mainstream media, these solutions are relentlessly preached – not least to students who will constitute the elites of the future' (Koch 2012: 190; original emphasis).

In the clash between increasing globalisation and the boundaries constituted by peer review, we may detect a connection between *relevant* and *relative* knowledge which is seen to be of less value and more contestable than knowledge produced through traditional modes. This perception stems from the range of criteria that might be taken to constitute relevance, whether the strategic military interests of states, the economic interests of commerce, the political interests of parties or the social interests of community groups. The view that relevance implies the involvement of different interests and as such a 'contamination' of research integrity is commonly held. What emerges in the process of peer-review, for example, is not a disembedded set of justifications formulated through the invoking of universal reason, but a set of pragmatic constraints and rules that regulate actions (Lamont 2009).

When we turn to the social sciences in order to understand these contemporary issues in a mix of duration, intensity, frequency and causes and consequences, it is sometimes held that quantification is concerned with justification, whilst qualitative research is about discovery in context. The differences between quantitative and qualitative approaches are often seen in terms of establishing validity through number and generating and capturing meaning. Quantitative research is often viewed as being able to 'prove', whilst qualitative research acts as a kind of under-labourer in the name of uncovering areas which can then be subject to quantification. In the politics of implementation, qualitative research can be seen to orientate in the name of discovery, whilst quantitative methods control in the name of destiny. Yet the dichotomy which is produced between the two approaches obscures more than it clarifies, with those deploying qualitative methods alluding to its contextual authenticity and those utilising statistical approaches invoking validity and generalisation.

We can hide from complexity and uncertainty in the comfort of numbers, as if the latter offered some place of shelter from dealing with the limits of our knowledge claims. Alan Bryman (1998) notes how both quantitative and qualitative accounts resort to justification in terms of the control of variables, albeit through employing different means to achieve that end. Methods use different 'distancing techniques' in terms of active and passive modes of reporting. Quantitative methods are seen to produce more objective results, yet control/management of data metaphors prevails in all kinds of texts (Bryman 1998). A critical approach to statistics becomes ever more valuable in terms of construction and use, as trends over time are captured and large corporations increasingly deploy these to make market calculations concerning patterns of behaviour and spending. If a bias in their use counts for anything, for Nate Silver (2013) it is the belief that we can predict in ways we simply cannot. As he notes in his conclusion, the years of the new millennium have been rough with many disasters, and in the face of that '[m]ay we arise from the ashes of these beaten but not bowed, a little more modest about our forecasting abilities, and a little less likely to repeat our mistakes' (Silver 2013: 454).

More broadly, we see a division of labour between social scientific and physical scientific research in terms of justification and application. Making a distinction between 'political epistemology' and an epistemology that is concerned with a knowledge and description of scientific practice leads to a characterisation of the latter as 'respectable', whereas the former seeks to 'humiliate politics' (Latour 2004a). This is because its goal is not to '*describe* the sciences, contrary to what its etymology might suggest, but to *short-circuit* any and all questioning as to the nature of the complex bonds between the sciences and societies, through the invocation of Science as the only salvation from the prison of the social world' (2004a: 13; original emphasis). From this point of view, social scientific concerns have been with the application of scientific work to the world itself, although the history of social studies of sciences tells us that there are also those who have deconstructed the official accounts that surround laboratory practices (see, for example, Gieryn 1999; Knorr-Cetina 1999; Fuller 2000; Bloor 2011; Norris 2014).

Multiple assumptions persist. Science is seen as difficult, hard and therefore an expert activity; social science, in providing understanding, can be seen as soft and able to be performed by many. Science remains the preserve of scientists, whether within university or industrial laboratory settings, while social scientific sites of knowledge production are being undermined by a plethora of new knowledge consultancies that proclaim to offer understanding and analysis, but frequently do little but provide that which is already known, or confirm existing prejudice. Science is often seen as expensive and time-consuming, whilst social science is assumed to be much cheaper and able to be performed at speed. The media have a key role in influencing the perceived status of different work within the cultural consciousness. Despite a strong unified message from different disciplines that there are no easy answers to contemporary dilemmas, the big issues tend to be couched in scientific, black and white terms. Science is portrayed as both remedy and cause, whilst it is the shocking, unusual or controversial that courts attention, rather than contributions to understanding or meaning. Given the normative orientations which take 'Big Science' as the standard against which other forms of enquiry are judged (Fuller 2000), social science can be relegated to the position of second-class citizen. Reflexivity is seen to be central to those working within the social sciences, but is too often overlooked, though sorely needed, by those working in all disciplines. 'Bad science' leads whole disciplines into disrepute, as outlined in Box 6.3.

The debate on relevance in the social sciences has been couched in very particular terms. Two positions seem to predominate. First, social research acts as a form of consciousness in the provision of ethics to the 'real' work of scientific and technological discovery. Second, it is a tool to enhance the effectiveness of dialogue with the public about (rather than public understanding of) science via new forms of engagement. Yet it is an end-game additionality, rather than a transformation of practices, that dominates. Social research becomes recognised for its validation of existing epistemological hierarchies, or easing the passage of the application of particular forms of knowledge. It becomes a 'troublemaker' if it calls into question 'a scientific hagiography which scientists often take part in and which they need in order to believe in what they do' (Bourdieu 1993: 9). Social scientists should 'take a hard look at their present structures and try to bring their revised intellectual perceptions of a useful division of labour into line with the organisational framework they necessarily construct' (Wallerstein 1996: 96). As Pierre Bourdieu reminds us, however, there are difficulties in positions that contradict received wisdom as it leaves one open to charges of 'ideological bias' or 'political axe-grinding'. The result is that the social sciences must work harder to provide 'infinitely more proof than is asked of the "spokesmen" of common sense' (Bourdieu 1993: 11).

▬ Box 6.3 ▬

Big Science, Bad Science and reflexivity

The journey in this book has concentrated on the social sciences but reflexivity is a set of dispositions which needs to underpin all areas of science. This is because the application of science to so many areas of life is now so great that questions are increasingly being asked about its justification. Engineering, physics, chemistry and biology have such vast applications with variable regulations and degrees of openness about links to the military, industry or government. When issues hit the public consciousness, 'civic dislocation' emerges (Jasanoff 2010: 243): 'When techno scientific systems radically fail to fit their contexts of use, the consequences may be disruptive, even tragic.' 'Mad Cow Disease', the Measles, Mumps and Rubella vaccine (MMR), GM crops (Bonneuil et al. 2008), nuclear technologies (Wynne 1992) and fracking for shale gas are all examples of this.

In many of these cases, following the co-production idiom, it is the representation and portrayal of these issues in the media and in politics that are as much to blame as the processes of knowledge production themselves. In other cases, there is a remarkable and disturbing silence about the relationship between justification and application, even where actual 'harm' is being done. In his book on *Bad Pharma* (2012) Ben Goldacre puts forth a scathing and robust analysis of how the interests of drug companies are systematically invested in ensuring that science conducted within laboratories – within and outside universities – will lead to favourable results *for them*. Missing trial data, not allowing access to data, poor regulation, distorted evidence and partial publication in academic journals are leading to bodies of evidence which, at their end point, undermine patient health and safety. Whilst some academic researchers are complicit in this scandal, others are unaware of, or unable to act against, the interests of sponsors or journals. These examples of 'bad science' (www.badscience.net) distract attention from well-conducted, rigorous scientific and social studies that are routinely undertaken in universities and laboratories around the world. This is exacerbated by media which are inclined to exaggerate and ignore evidence and nuance in their search for the 'big story', side-stepping genuine scandals in favour of invented ones. It is for such reasons that scientific work across the disciplines is so much more closely scrutinised, thereby requiring reflexivity throughout the knowledge process.

Attempts to harness scientific knowledge may negatively impact on the quality of that knowledge and hence undermine its inherent value, producing a dangerous normative disconnection between application and production: 'normative solutions to problems of epistemic legitimacy may appear authoritarian if exclusive attention is paid to articulating the ends of knowledge production, thereby implying that virtually any means is justified in the process of achieving those ends' (Fuller 2004: 46). For Pels (2003: 2–3), the uniqueness of science lies in its 'lack of haste, its relative stress-freeness, or its socially sanctioned withdrawal from the swift pace of everyday life and alternative professional cultures'. Consequently, he argues for 'the preservation of a place of quiet, stillness and unhastened reflection, which must be incessantly negotiated for and demarcated against the speedy cultures of the "outside" world' (2003: 2–3).

This distinctiveness has largely been forgotten. Intellectual critique can be attributed with a partial role in this respect. Pels (2003: 1) blames accounts of science that have reduced it to the 'level of an ordinary enterprise that is just as idiosyncratic, localised, interest-ridden and "political" as other forms of endeavour'. De la Mothe (2001: 7) also refers to the growing social relativism of scientific knowledge as a 'reaction to modern knowledge … in part the result of the academic Left, particularly in France and the United States, deconstructing knowledge and applying post-modern norms'. Focus has been directed towards the blurring of boundaries, the scientification of politics and politicisation of science (Hellstrom and Jacob 2000) and the difficulties in identifying any borders between science and non-science (Gieryn 1999). Some social scientists have stressed how boundaries are collapsing between politics/society/culture/science without mounting any coherent defence of intellectual distinctiveness. What this means is that it is perfectly possible to have a situation where science and expertise is highly valued and central to political and social life, in the ways postulated by Turner (2003) and Knorr Cetina (1999), alongside a decline in the status of the university and academic authority.

CO-PRODUCING RESEARCH

In *States of Knowledge*, Jasanoff (2004) considers whether co-production 'loops back' and is reorganising the way we think about the relations of knowledge, power and culture: 'are there signs that co-production – itself a constitutive, historically situated, cognitive frame – is having this kind of influence in the world? Is it only an analyst's category or is it also playing a role, in however limited a fashion, as an actor's category and, if the latter, then for which types of actors?' (2004: 281). The *coproducing society* proposition concerns changes in the world and as such provides an analysis of how the relationship between science and society is changing under the confluence of pressures in the twenty-first century. It has given rise to a related idiom: *coproducing research*. This is driven as much by endogenous as exogenous factors, and in its stronger variants embodies not only descriptive but also prescriptive and normative orientations. In this we see an alignment with Kant's three questions we set out in Chapter 3: What can I know? What ought I to do? What may I hope?

The co-production imperative

What we have called a 'co-production imperative' has multiple histories and trajectories. Most recently, co-production has become a call for action in the redesign of public policies and services, involving implementing and delivery services in equal relationships between different stakeholders in the process (Boyle and Harris 2009; Durose and Richardson 2015). Forerunners of the co-production imperative can be seen in multiple studies from health-related disciplines, based on the longstanding practices of nurses, midwives and health practitioners. Elinor Ostrom's (1996) work is often seen as seminal, drawing on two cases in Brazil and in Nigeria related to the relative encouragement/discouragement of citizen engagement in urban infrastructure and primary education. Diana Mitlin's works on civil society capacity building have pointed to how co-production is increasingly not only about service delivery, but also chosen as a strategy for the urban poor to consolidate their local organisational base and negotiate with the state (Mitlin 2008). Other studies have focused on inclusive sanitation and co-production as an empowerment strategy for low income, marginalised groups (Banana et al. 2015) and on literacy practices in households (Pahl 2014). Vanessa Watson (2014) examines the co-production of goods and services in her work on the global South and notes that co-production can be state- or society-initiated. In all this we can see evidence of the looping back that Jasanoff suggests, as boundaries are seen not only to be collapsing, but also actively reshaped in order to allow multiple voices and forms of expertise into the policy process. Co-production is seen as a 'woolly word', but one which has traction and roots in designing and delivering better public services (Osborne et al. 2016).

Whilst we have seen a longstanding concern with the relationship between thought and action, theory and practice, science and society, throughout this book, the discourse of co-production has now explicitly extended its reach into social scientific research. To Watson's bi-partite distinction, Polk and Kain (2015) add a further dimension – that of 'research-initiated' co-production. On the one hand, this can be viewed as the latest manifestation of a long lineage in participatory research (Facer and Enright 2016), drawing on a rich vein of action research and co-operative inquiry (Greenwood and Levin 1998; Reason and Bradbury 2001). A less favourable interpretation is that the co-production imperative is the result of the extension of the narrow instrumentalisation of research and the 'impact agenda' into the social sciences and arts and humanities, reaching in and through processes of knowledge. The result is an increasing attempt to regulate, manage, control and direct science in a new form of 'knowledge politics', with resultant implications not only for social scientific knowledge but also for the university itself (Stehr 1994; May with Perry 2011). So what space does this leave for reflection among multiple expectations (May and Perry 2006)?

■■■ Box 6.4 ■■■

Wicked problems and strategic messes

Urban sustainability is an increasingly urgent policy challenge, with 54% of the world's population living in cities. Cities benefit from density, agglomeration and proximity – characteristics which simultaneously create (often highly localised) problems including pollution and stress (Swyngedouw 2009). One key task for urban growth coalitions has been developing strategic solutions to urban sustainability problems, a quintessential epistemic mess (Bulkeley and Betsill 2005), whose causes and consequences are embedded within multiple layers of urban society. The governance of sustainable cities represents a 'wicked' issue whose solution is necessarily trans-disciplinary, requiring multiple stakeholders' knowledge, skills and expertise (Polk 2015). Addressing urban sustainability problems requires capacity to integrate and manage a huge range of intersecting forms of global and local knowledge in order to develop appropriate policy responses, instruments and interventions (Moser 2013).

The term 'wicked problem' was coined by Rittel and Webber in 1973 in their examination of planning problems, in which they concluded that contemporary intelligence was insufficient to the complex task of planning across multiple domains, given the pluralities of interests and objectives involved. Whilst science is about 'taming', planning problems are getting wilder and more 'wicked' (1973: 160). Wicked problems have a number of characteristics,

(Continued)

(Continued)

including the absence of clear definitions and any sense of what is true/false or good/bad. Climate change is said to be a 'super wicked problem' (Levin et al. 2012) insofar as it is also characterised by intense urgency, those addressing the problem also causing it, weak or non-existent central authority, and policy responses which irrationally discount the future. In this we see Funtowitz and Ravetz's post-normal science rear its head. In a similar vein, others have written about 'messes' – a term used by Russell Ackoff to characterise systems of problems which need to be addressed: 'the dynamic situations that consist of complex systems of changing problems that interact with each other … Managers do not solve problems they manage messes' (Ackoff 1979: 90–100). Complex problems have little consensus on how to solve them, and often take place in contested and negotiated policy arenas.

A number of strategies have been addressed for dealing with these wicked problems and strategic messes. Roberts (2000), for instance, notes the relative merits of authoritative, competitive and collaborative strategies depending on the levels of conflict present, the distribution of power among stakeholders, and the degree to which power is contested. Yet we can also see that co-production is a potential strategy for dealing with wicked problems and strategic messes, and is distinctive in taking the question of expertise seriously. It fundamentally requires a reflexive disposition in bringing together endogenous and referential concerns.

The drivers here come from the alignment of perspectives between endogenous and exogenous concerns. First, it is argued that in the context of risk and reflexive modernisation and the increasing complexity of society, global challenges are such that they cannot be addressed by any single discipline. They are 'wicked' or 'strategic messes' requiring different processes and practices of knowledge production (see Box 6.4). Epistemic boundaries work against, not for, the production of social scientific knowledge which must combine with other forms of expertise to be relevant in the world. This is reinforced by an endogenous drive that the most interesting questions are at the intersections between disciplinary boundaries. Inter- or transdiciplinary knowledge production is needed to combine knowledge and make new areas of inquiry. Second, under conditions of uncertainty and contestability of knowledge claims, not only the authority but also the sufficiency of expertise is questioned – whose knowledge matters and whose knowledge counts? This draws attention to ways of knowing and forms of expertise that are traditionally excluded from the knowledge production process. Third, then, co-production is heralded as a more ethical or even democratic way to produce research. Drawing on the traditions of participatory action research, many welcome co-production as part of a more open and democratic process of knowledge production (Brock and McGee 2002; Durose et al. 2011).

In the process, the deficits of a process in which impact is narrowly instrumentalised around a disembedded idea of economic value are addressed. Policy-makers often commit the 'fallacy of context-free knowledge production' (May 2005: 207) – that is, they fail to acknowledge what is important about the ways and places in which science is produced. Similarly, governmental priorities for harnessing the value of research during the 2000s have focused on science, technology and economic growth via science parks and invoking general models of collaboration, and far less on the roles of the social sciences, arts and humanities or relationships with communities. In addressing both context and community, the co-production imperative is positioned clearly in the traditions of those whose works we have considered in this book, drawing attention to the need to socially situate our knowledge claims in relation to ourselves and our reciprocal relations with others. Context matters and there is no single approach or method that can capture the diversity of approaches to co-production.

Endogenous and referential reflexivity

Co-production in research might be seen as the collapse of the final boundary – between research and practice: 'co-production of knowledge requires that contributions from specific disciplines and social actors are not privileged over what other disciplines and social actors contribute' (Pohl et al. 2010: 217). Across multiple definitions there is a general consensus that co-production means valuing different kinds of expertise in the research process from the definition of questions through to the analysis and representation of findings. End stage impact, 'knowledge transfer' and dissemination are dethroned in favour of an interactive, reflexive, learning and dialogic process of research which dismisses the juxtaposition between a 'knowing subject to a supposedly ignorant one' (2010: 17). Accounts are largely positive and optimistic about both the quality and impact of co-production. Our emphasis on excellence and relevance as mutually compatible and achievable goals of a mature and reflexive social science (Perry and May 2006; May with Perry 2011) has been more recently echoed in the insistence that, through co-production, both 'social relevance' and 'scientific reliability' (Polk and Kain 2015) or 'intellectual insight' and 'wider public benefit' (Campbell and Vanderhoven 2016) are possible. Most studies report positive effects and experiences (Facer and Enright 2016) and focus on trust, reciprocity and commitment as factors in building successful relationships.

The claim being evaluated through pilot studies (Campbell and Vanderhoven 2016) or large-scale international programmes (Mistra Urban Futures 2016b) is that co-production leads to 'better' knowledge that is more immediately useful and usable in practice. Yet studies equally report challenges and issues relating to the institutional power and strength of the university, funding constraints and continued hierarchies which impact on the degrees of equality within participants in projects. Co-production offers no quick fix or panacea to address silences, exclusions and inclusions within different research spaces and places. Power is fundamental – on the one hand, producing imbalances wrought by the bureaucratic weight of the university, on the other, raising the spectre of co-optation and silencing critique, to ensure that research does not capitulate to the 'technocratic demand for evidence' (Durose and Richardson 2015). Challenges emerge throughout the research process, from design to implementation and the communication of results. Some have noted a negative qualitative shift in this research journey in the move from conception to analysis and writing up which accelerates the process of de-participation and exclusion (Bain and Payne 2016). What is sought to be avoided is a 'symptomatic social science' (May 2015: 411), a 'process of cooptation to which we are all subject that should be open to analysis'. Academic careers are made on the back of reproducing conventional wisdom with neologisms which are attributed with insight by those who benefit from them.

Co-production is said to be qualitatively different from other research experiences. The reasons are said to relate to the arguments we have revisited in this book – the collapse of the subject/object dichotomy, the embrace of 'interest' as fundamental to the conduct and value of the research, the positioning of the research in the context of application. Co-production is not new. What is distinctive is how co-production in the twenty-first century has been mobilised as a backlash against a narrow, economic-driven impact agenda, working as a call to action for a more engaged social science. It is becoming a receptacle into which all aspirations and hopes for a better social science are currently being poured. Yet critical analysis of its promise, politics and possibilities can only be achieved by interrogating its methodological and ethical dimensions, underpinned by a reflexive ethos and disposition. Indeed, co-production centres the need, now more than ever, for a reflexive social scientific practice. To consider the dynamics that inform reflexivity and their implications for scientific practice, we can divide it into two interrelated dimensions that constitute a whole: endogenous and referential reflexivity (May 1998, 1999a; May with Perry 2011).

Endogenous reflexivity refers to the ways in which contexts, understandings and accounts relate to practices. There are specific expectations, often latent and unarticulated, that are made up of the practices and forms of knowledge that are deployed in particular fields of endeavour: for example, to invoke ideas of value-neutrality to justify practices enables an existential distance to be maintained from the consequences of research work and those who are part of its investigations (Gouldner 1971). Endogenous reflexive practice thus refers to how we practise in our social and cultural milieus, including academic disciplines, crafts and professional and epistemic communities as a whole. Referential reflexivity, on the other hand, takes place where accounts of action meet contexts of reception that seek to render them intelligible via a meeting of points of view. The power to ignore or act upon these is variable among and between different groups, and that informs the extent to which production and reception are differentiated, conjoined or collapsed into domains of activity and spheres of communication. Both dimensions are informed by our previous discussions in which the relations between representation, reflexivity, transparency, individualism and reason have been subject to extensive critique.

At the level of social scientific practice to consider endogenous reflexivity alone does not allow us to see how this is constitutive of social relations. The Frankfurt School alerted us to this, as did writers such as Michel Foucault – albeit with a Nietzschean twist. Without this dimension of understanding, a one-way hermeneutic is replicated whereby social science is separated from social life as if it were hermetically sealed from varying interpretations and power relations, or, to express it another way, content, context and consequence are divorced in considerations. Endogenous reflexivity is not just a reflection of everyday life, but takes that experience on board through a focus on practice. A movement from endogenous to referential reflexivity may be characterised as one possessing the potential to move from reflexivity *within* actions to reflexivity *upon* actions, enabling connections to be made between individuals and the social conditions of which they are a part.

Knowledge is a core component of our understanding and an ingredient that informs the possibility of change. Into the understanding of the relations between knowledge and action, we should add the power of denial, as well as that of 'excess', embodied actions and the inevitability of retrospection in processes of comprehension. Excess here refers to the subject and their relation to others in the sense that we know ourselves only through others. As we seek to understand ourselves through others they, in turn, only know themselves through us! This produces something that is always incomplete but inevitable. Along with the recognition of embodied actions that are not transparent to us, this is an obstacle to the idea of a transparent knowledge of ourselves and also a necessary ingredient for that to occur (Rothenburg 2010). As Henrietta Moore puts it at the end of an essay on the genealogy of the anthropological subject and the process of individual identifications with subject positions, 'No one, not even the most creative and interactive person/self, has complete knowledge of themselves or of others' (Moore 2007: 41).

The meanings of our actions are not given to us *a priori* and so social scientific understandings become the institutionalised and systematic components of a knowledge that whilst never complete, exhibits 'epistemic gain' (Taylor 1992). What is captured by this idea is that we do not move towards an absolute truth, but can find better ways to understand ourselves – through our relations with others, in terms of the social contexts that we inhabit, and how and why they relate to our dispositions, actions and aspirations: 'The concepts of identity, singularity and uniqueness are logically tied up with the embodiment of a human being as a thing among things in a world laid out in space and time' (Harré 1998: 72). In this way we can understand how and why knowledge has outcomes that both reproduce and transform existing relations. Within this space social scientific knowledge is interpreted, forged, acted upon, incorporated, ignored and denied. We will return to these issues in our final two chapters.

SUMMARY: REFLEXIVITY CENTRED

The revolution that Descartes brought to our understandings was to place experience within the realm of science, whereas prior to that time experience tended to belong to common sense and science to its manifestation in an active individual: 'In its search for certainty, modern science abolishes this separation and makes experience the locus – the "method"; that is, the pathway – of knowledge' (Agamben 2007: 22). It was not a case of how the subject came to comprehend and explain the object, but the relation between the one and the many that preoccupied prior attempts to grasp the human condition. Whereas the divine captured that which we did not know, it was science, given time, which would render all we did not know finally explicable. It became the single repository of all experience that was to be admissible and judged as knowledge and encapsulated in the scientific subject. In this we see a clear distinction assumed to exist between science and society.

In the late twentieth and twenty-first centuries scholars turned to examine how the boundaries between science/society, justification/application and research/practice have become ever more blurred or even dissolved. Debates have focused on how processes of social change, in which science and technology mix with cultural transformations and ever-increasing concerns over the future, leave little apparent immunity for science – there is no place from which to claim a privileged objectivity, no voice from nowhere, even within the laboratory. The search for certainty is abandoned and replaced by increasing recognition of the limits to our knowledge claims about the social world. Science is seen to be moving closer to society in a process of 'contextualisation', creating social spaces – the 'agora' (Nowotny et al. 2001) – where the justification, production and application of knowledge are contested by multiple stakeholders.

As Sandra Harding puts it in her study of the relations between science and social inequality, the forms of science that were once envisaged to promote democracy in the past need rethinking. New ways of producing scientific knowledge are appearing and the knowledge politics they are producing calls into question established modes of scientific production. That is not necessarily always a good thing for it depends on the causes of those forces and their consequences. What we now see is that '[t]he rise of new social values, interests, and the relations they direct requires inquiry practices and principles that can support and in turn be supported by these new forms of, we hope, democratic social relations. Our methodological and epistemological choices are always also ethical and political choices' (Harding 2006: 156).

Even if a particular quest for certainty has failed, does not social science need to do more than add to a cognitive platform for individuals in an alienated world? Is its practice also not concerned with the generation and maintenance of its authority? What then matters is the extent to which findings and ideas are seen as legitimate and allocated time for deliberation in the public realm. This, in turn, depends on the quality of democracy that is available to all citizens. However, we are left with a central reflexive issue with boundaries that remains of importance to the legitimacy and integrity of knowledge production. In the face of contemporary forces, we cannot escape a practice that requires 'a balanced blend of self-confidence and demureness. It also takes a kind of courage: interpreting human experience is not something I would recommend to weathercocks' (Bauman 2014: 131). In order not to become weathercocks, we need reflexive communities of inquiry sensitive to contemporary concerns and prepared to speak out when powerful forces seek to mould our practices in their image.

So where does this leave the social scientist? To take all the insights and debates in this book in one direction could lead to paralysis. Yet to embrace these issues and concerns as part of a mature and reflexive social science leads us in an altogether more hopeful direction. A set of practices are needed that do not seek resolution or certainty, but understanding and clarification about the social world – fully cognisant of the limits of those claims. In the last two chapters, we draw on our own experiences of seeking to deal with these issues and then discuss the implications for the practices of a reflexive social science.

7

REFLEXIVE PRACTICE

The lived world can never be exhaustively described or enumerated. It is always more and other than anything that can be said, written, or pictured of it. Any kind of storytelling selects from the raw material, shapes it, and creates discursive order.

(Dorothy Smith 2002: 23)

INTRODUCTION

It will be apparent by now that reflexivity is not a method. It is a critical ethos and set of dispositions which enable the researcher to reflect on the basis for their claims to know the social world, via an understanding of the relations between the content of knowledge, the context in which it is produced and the consequences that arise from its practice (May with Perry 2011). Reflexive thinking does not seek closure and cannot be confined to one element of the research process, bracketed or appended; it is an iterative and continuous characteristic of good social scientific practice. Reflexivity is a necessary ingredient in systematic approaches to the production of social scientific knowledge. Attentiveness is also needed to the adoption of appropriate methods, as well as their interpretation, translation and representation.

How can the insights covered in this book be translated into practice? What are the implications for tackling thinking–being–doing relations? This chapter addresses these issues by emphasising the move beyond individualism to the conditions, contexts and cultures that inform social scientific work. Rooting actual experiences within institutional relations not only brings to light the similarities in experiences, it also demonstrates the disjunctures that need analytic attention to forge better understandings, as opposed to being glossed over in favour of formulaic neatness. Active and practical efforts are needed to create spaces to enable research to improve and refine its insights and hence understandings of the world. The search for a more mature, open and reflexive social science is a struggle, and this in turn makes circumstances better for alternative modes of knowledge production to emerge, which are more aware of their limits and confident of their claims.

In this penultimate chapter we draw on our own experiences to illustrate the need for and limits of reflexive practice in relation to the changing contexts and cultures of knowledge production in the twenty-first century. First, we focus on the work of making a context in which critical-engaged urban research is possible and the challenges of creating institutional shelter within a university setting in the UK higher education sector. Second, we move to consider key experiences of working within this context and the difficulties in snatching time for reflexive analysis under pressures for income generation and institutional survival. Finally, we move away from the idea of creating reflexive cultures within universities to questions of reflexive research design, reflected in our systematic approach to embrace the strengths and limits of the 'participatory turn' in the co-production of knowledge (Facer and Enright 2016).

There is a chronology to this account of our practices, which we have told with the pronoun 'we'. Of course we played different roles over time relevant to our positions and experiences. However this, we both maintain, is a collective story formed through the importance of disappointment (Craib 1994) and sense of achievement. Many other characters were on the stage with us and each played their part in the developments we describe and to whom we have degrees of loyalty and friendship. This is not a confessional tale.

Rather, our point is to share general insights and specific examples from our experiences to illuminate broader dynamics about the interrelationships between disposition, belonging and position, and the cultures and contexts in which social science takes place.

THE WORK OF MAKING CONTEXT

For the best part of the last fifteen years we constituted and worked in a research centre called 'SURF' – the Centre for Sustainable Urban and Regional Futures – which was established in 2000 at the University of Salford, Manchester, UK. With an ethos of producing academically excellent and policy relevant research, it has occupied different positions in its history on the continuum between research centre, think-tank and consultancy. Since that time we have worked on a number of research projects, funded by academic research councils, European framework programmes, governmental organisations, charitable or research foundations and business organisations (see Table 7.1). A mixed economy of research was required to run the Centre based upon research council funding and more local sources with a target income of half a million pounds per year. By financial criteria, it was a success.

The original aim for the Centre was underpinned by a desire to create the possibility for an 'intensive intellectual and affective fusion' (Bourdieu 2007: 19). Early on all members of staff were asked to present and discuss their biographies, motivations, interests and passions for their work. Such efforts were variably received and acted upon across the team. Yet for those with a disposition to do so, these initial explorations – continued through away-days and supervisions and a concern with generating a supportive culture – provided a basis upon which collaborations could be built, and the various attachments, uncertainties and insecurities of academic life could be shared, navigated and, where possible, acted upon. Through our upbringings, histories and biographies, we each brought with us multiple 'ghosts' (Doucet 2008). Collectively manifesting and exploring these was a critical element in creating a culture in which reflexivity could be a relational and collaborative rather than self-referential and individualised exercise. Yet achieving the ideal of a reflexive intellectual space was a constant struggle, in the context of the need for institutional survival, financial reproduction, the increasing expectations linked to the political economy of research in the UK, and issues of institutional politics and positioning.

The macro-political economy of research

The commitment to undertake excellent and relevant work from within a university setting placed the Centre at the frontline of changing boundaries between science and society. Ideas of relevance, impact, interdisciplinarity, collaborative working, the need to publish in recognised journals and be outward-facing, mixed with systemic organisational turbulence and restructuring brought about as a result of changes in the UK higher education

Table 7.1 A mixed economy of research

Project	Dates	Type of project	SURF role	Partners
'Making Science History': The Regionalization of Science Policy	2002–2003	Academic; UK national research council	Independent researchers	None
Knowledge Capital: From Concept to Action	2003	Consultancy	Contracted researchers for the Contact Partnership of Greater Manchester Universities	None
Building Science Regions in the European Research Area: Governance in the Territorial Agora	2004–2007	Academic; UK national research council	Independent researchers	University of Newcastle
Government Office North West (GONW): From Translation to Transformation	2006–2007	Collaborative process and organisational development	Researchers as facilitators contracted by GONW	None
Renewable Energy Acceptance and Tools (CREATE Acceptance)	2006–2008	European Framework project	Independent researchers	European partners
The Embedded University in the Science Economy: Capacities, Contexts and Expectations	2006	Academic Research Network Grant	Setting academic agendas	University of Manchester; University of Newcastle
The Greater Manchester Urban Knowledge Arena	2006–2007	Consultancy	Contracted researchers for the Contact Partnership of Greater Manchester Universities	University of Manchester; Manchester Metropolitan University

Project	Dates	Type of project	SURF role	Partners
Realizing the Potential of Science Cities: Evidence, Practice and Transferable Lessons	2006–2007	Consultancy	Contracted researchers for Science Cities Policy Development Consortium	None
Manchester Innovation Ecosystem Analysis	2007	Consultancy	Contracted as independent expert by Manchester Enterprises	None
Business and the Knowledge-Based Region	2007–2008	Academic Research Council Impact Grant	Engaged researchers; facilitating knowledge exchange with business	British Business Chambers
Changing Behaviour in Energy Demand	2008–2010	European Framework program	Independent researchers	European partners plus Manchester Knowledge Capital
Urban Knowledge for Shaping Critical Infrastructure: New Models for City Regions	2008–2009	ESRC Business Placements Fellows Scheme	Placement in global consultancy firm, Arup	Arup
Northern Way Research Program on Innovation and Symposium	2009–2010	Discussion and debate series	Independent expert	University of Newcastle
Formative Evaluation of Manchester Innovation Investment Fund	2008–2010	Consultancy	Formative evaluators; critical friend	University of Manchester, Regeneris consultants

landscape. Behind these contradictory expectations sat the dynamics between the justification for research within a bounded community of scholars via processes of peer review, and the application of research in terms of its dissemination and interpretation by different groups. In this game of numbers (see Box 7.1), we saw both demands for a more socially accountable science, but also an increased detachment from socially excluded communities through the clamour for an institutional elitism that concentrated resources in particular sites of research production. We also saw changes in the configuration of urban environments as they sought to position themselves in the knowledge economy (Perry and May 2017) with resulting consequences for the context in which we worked and how the content of what we produced was recognised – or ignored.

■ Box 7.1 ■■

Evaluating research

In the UK higher education sector, research exercises have traditionally been conducted which take metrics – such as citations, outlets for publications, number of postgraduate students, research income and indicators of esteem and impact – and turn them into scores that produce hierarchies between similar disciplinary units of assessment in different institutions. This has implications for subsequent funding. Judgements by a panel of selected peers are combined with metrics that inform practices of measurement and value. Taking the 2008 Research Assessment Exercise as their case, Aidan Kelly and Roger Burrows (2012) compared the deliberations of the sociology panel with a simple three-variable linear regression model comprising the number of outputs, per capita research income from research councils, and the percentage of articles published in the top quartile of the more 'influential' journals. Whilst admitting a 'performative play' at work in their comparisons, these 'shadow metrics' produced similar rankings to that achieved by a long and complex qualitative process of judgement of value.

What we are dealing with here is not an unfamiliar story and it is apparent across disciplines and communities of practice. Along with the authors of the study, we might speculate as to the direction between these qualitative judgements and metrics. Indeed, the metrics themselves may be derived from an original judgement of quality as the journals with a higher 'impact' have already been assessed as being of more value than those lower down in the Article Influence Score (AIS). We may also be dealing with the effects of environmental factors that inform tacit judgements, such as already existing hierarchies of esteem enshrined in elite academies where it is assumed the best work will be conducted. That, of course, would be a more controversial inference among those who have spent a great deal of time seeking to avoid such self-fulfilling prophecies. Their data cannot confirm these inferences for certain. What we can conclude is that 'a reflexive engagement with some of this data can still usefully make explicit some of the parameters of enactment within which we operate within the contemporary academy' (Kelly and Burrows 2012: 148). These are the 'frames' or 'concepts' deployed to mediate our explanations and understandings. This is not confined to one discipline and is a characteristic across the spectrum from the physical and social sciences to the humanities. It is also a feature of practices in social life which filter visions in order that we can see in the first place. How and why should always be subject to critical reflexive scrutiny.

Over time we increasingly encountered a neoliberal zeal to reshape urban contexts in the name of competitiveness, manifest in the pursuit of spatial attractiveness to obtain investment from mobile capital looking for an opportunity. In the search for sources of funding we undertook work which fed into this idea of 'international competitiveness' as a central plank of urban policies, with indices of international comparison between cities a driving force for city politics and officials. These trends were part of a logic of supra-nationalisation where the flow of capital, goods, people and images has been intensifying (Castells 2010) in a process that appeared to be increasingly unconstrained by national boundaries. As a result we witnessed a tendency towards the devolution of responsibilities from national to sub-national levels (Brenner 2004), a growing recognition of the importance of cities to regional and national economies (Sassen 2011), and the intensification of cities as the sites of responses to those forces, including from climate change (Koch 2012) and resistance to capitalism (Harvey 2012). All of these factors framed the relations that existed between cities and knowledge and hence the work we undertook (May and Perry 2017).

As the financial crash of 2008 sent shockwaves throughout the world, we saw a general disdain for welfare for the most vulnerable being turned on its head in favour of providing welfare for the most powerful. We could only agree with David Graeber's assessment: 'Neoliberalism was the system that managed to convince everyone in the world that financial elites were the only people capable of managing or measuring the value of anything, even as in order to do so, it ended up promulgating an economic culture so irresponsible that it allowed those elites to bring the entire financial architecture of the global economy tumbling on top of them because of their utter inability to assess the value even of their own financial instruments' (Graeber 2011: 112). All of this took place at a time when economic, social and political boundaries were being recast, along with differentiated national responses to global forces.

Context and content are not, of course, divorced from one another. Those persons cited above are writers who have critically examined the causes and consequences of globalisation for cities and their populations. Equally, there are the armies of the representatives of globalisation, including academics, who were to limit the political in the name of an apparently unproblematic idea of the 'economy' (Cameron and Palan 2004; Mirowski 2014). It seemed that matters of choice and value evaporated in the naturalisation of global competition. Our work was not immune from the same pressures that cities have found themselves under. We found that knowledge was viewed as a panacea to specific economic problems, with a strong instrumental and strategic role, and UK universities became subject to the same pressures. There were pockets of resistance, but many enthusiastically embraced the new realities, including those who had previously welcomed the apparent fluidity of a 'post-capitalist' world. Academic work can be critical of these developments; at the same time, new forms of capitalism are often able to absorb and neutralise their effects and capital concentrated in a few hands can easily take flight in looking for new opportunities (Chiapello 2014; Harvey 2014).

Universities in the UK underwent significant changes that included charging tuition fees whose amounts increased significantly over time. Once again, this reflected the same gamble being played in the name of money and markets (McGettigan 2013). We turned our attention to these matters and ran workshops, obtained grants to study their causes and consequences, and sought networks of resistance and alternatives. We were concerned that social science was becoming less a practice in the service of illumination for a greater common good, and more a tool in the reproduction of a particular idea of the 'economy'. Knowledge was to produce competitive advantage. It was to be harnessed, codified, managed and stored with a translation into direct economic advantage being paramount, along with the ability to measure, define and demonstrate success in knowledge hierarchies through metrics and league tables of innovative output in the struggle for money and symbolic advantage (Perry 2010; May and Perry 2013; Perry and May 2015). As we so often found in our practice, to question those processes was to constitute oneself as one who does not understand the self-evidence of 'necessity' (May 2001; Baker and May 2002). To explain this we were led to explore some uneasy parallels within universities themselves (May and Perry 2013).

Institutional constraints

For us, a critical challenge for contemporary urbanism was first to understand how to develop the knowledge, capacity and capability for public agencies, business and multiple users in city-regions to systemically re-engineer their built environments, urban infrastructures and social fabric. To this end, cities around the world were focused on developing city visions for 2030 and beyond, and our work became more and more judged according to its ability to reflect those trends. In response our view was that, in order to explain processes of sustainable urban development, integrated perspectives were needed combining diverse knowledge and skills, alongside an analysis of the differential and uneven effects of changes on different communities. This meant concentrating more on deconstructing and reconstructing pathways towards greater economic, social and environmental justice (Brenner 2012).

Our turn towards collaborative work with communities in place of elites was also accompanied by shrinkage of the spaces for deliberation in the face of what were the constructed necessities of the economic. We maintained that spaces of communication for the production of critical knowledge needed to be constituted over time through changes in dispositions and mentalities, new cultures, processes and ways of working; they could not be magically brought into being through the kind of quick-fix thinking that often accompanies technology as a panacea to those problems. Instead, what we witnessed were proprietary behaviours and academics bearing their models as solutions, displacing attempts to obtain more common ownership of the city. We recognised the friction between liberation and the institutions that over-determined the urban in order to justify their existences. We were dealing with disaggregation and increasingly specialised divisions of labour. In our studies for universities on their socio-economic contribution to their localities, we found disciplinary fragmentation despite allusions to interdisciplinary working, an absence of governance frameworks beyond elites and a failure to learn from the past (May and Perry 2006; Strober 2010).

In these contexts our reflexive awareness and intellectual commitments informed a wish to resist closure around our means of production as if this would render immunity from these forces, at the same time as seeking to resist the negative elements of their consequences. After all, 'The same forces we see at work in our field sites shape the science underlying the policies we critique, as well as the counter-science we sometimes use to oppose them. We can no longer afford to ignore their interconnections in either our intellectual or political practice' (Lave 2012: 32). Yet the institutional conditions which enabled such a position to be maintained were tenuous and fragile. In the absence of closure, institutional recognition and shelter were necessary to create a space of relative autonomy in which critical engaged urban research, informed by a set of reflexive practices, could develop. Recognising the need for relative spaces of shelter within universities is neither irresponsible nor indulgent, rather a necessary condition for the production of reflexive social science that can not only critically interrogate current pathways but also contribute to their transformation.

The epistemic permeability of the boundary around our Centre was important otherwise we would be simply reactive to the latest trends. Equally, we had income targets to meet. We had undertaken a great deal of work with policy elites, and in addressing the above issues we wrestled with the relations between immanent and transcendent critique. We also wrestled with income generation in terms of just how far to go in the relations between engagement with and capitulation to external expectations, when effects cannot simply be known in advance. Our experience of working intensely with policy-makers was supplemented by extensive work not only in the UK, but also internationally on science, governance, urban sustainability, regions and the future of universities. Research council funding enabled a greater distance, relatively speaking, from these often short-term contracts in which research reports were expected in ever-increasing short timeframes. Yet recalling Ryle's comments on the relations between theoretical and practical reason, and placing those against Žižek's (2009) observations, we seemed to see a reversal whereby we were saturated by an ideological view that could only see the 'economic' as if it were somehow separate from the social and cultural spheres. It seemed at times as if the fantasy of this view was the reality for those decision-makers with whom we worked in the urban field as particular policies cascaded down from government. There were also variable responses in the Centre and within the university sector to these trends. Critique was often conducted in a distance from the interactions with city officials and politicians which formed the very basis of much of our contracted work.

The possibility of realising critique and engagement, excellence and relevance, was mediated by the institutional positioning of the Centre within the university context over time. The Centre was facilitated, in the first eleven years, by being a cross-faculty unit with staff located within different university departments. The total number of staff did not exceed eleven at any point because those running the Centre did not wish to become full-time managers but to remain engaged in research. We worked with many different partners in universities nationally and internationally, but also with consultants. This led to differences within the Centre in terms of its overall purpose, and also the motivations that individuals had in terms of their career aspirations and values. Yet what were our limits to absorbing these trends? We made a deliberate choice not to become a limited company, or take the offers of other universities to buy the Centre. We wanted to remain employees of the university. We wanted to believe that it was possible to balance the relations between excellence and relevance within the 'devilish dichotomies' that informed our work (Perry and May 2010). So we turned our attention to the spatial nature of knowledge, the role of universities and cultures in its production, and the inclusion of communities in the process of research who are often excluded from dominant interests. It was that which increasingly informed the content of the research we undertook. We also made this possible by building up reserves of income which enabled writing to take place without a belief that that was an end in itself. What writing provided was a process of clarification without the assumption of resolution for the issues in the world itself. That cushion, however, was to be removed in time.

In 2011 the Centre was relocated by the university from being a cross-faculty research which could reach across different disciplines, to being placed within a single school. At the same time the institution was seeking to manage reduced budgets, introduce tuition fees, and meet demands for industry engagement and user relevance. What followed was merging and restructuring, burgeoning expectations and the development of processes to 'ready' ourselves for the Research Evaluation Framework. Although university managers had always professed an interest in maintaining and supporting the Centre (hardly a wonder given the income it generated!), there was little enthusiasm to understand the conditions which made it successful. Bit by bit the relative institutional shelter diminished as the levers for influence and spaces for discretion were eroded. With this the possibility of maintaining spaces for reflection receded. Our experiences of doing the institutional boundary work between science/society, justification/application and research/practice, as set out in Chapter 6, had been difficult enough whilst a degree of relative institutional shelter had been provided by our income and position in the university; without this, however, the transaction costs of making a context became overwhelming. Between 2011 and 2016 the conditions facilitating any 'intellectual fusion' or realisation of excellence and relevance diminished. The Centre's infrastructure was altered and some staff moved to other institutions.

THE CONTEXT OF MAKING WORK

The limits and possibilities for reflexive practice are shaped by different contextual factors. Not only characters and commitments, but also the cultures in which people work shape the 'multiple reflexivities' they exhibit (see Lynch 2000; Mruck and Mey 2007). In our case, the context – in relation to the Centre, the university, its urban and regional environments, funding regimes and policy frameworks for research – also shaped the 'degrees of reflexivity' exhibited over the passage of time (Mauthner and Doucet 2003). Reflexive dispositions were mediated through variable positions and career trajectories, shared and individual relationships to the Centre, the institution and each other, and the values that informed what we did. We held onto the possibility that the goals of intellectual vibrancy and societal relevance were not mutually incompatible. At the same time, how we approached research topics, the nature of the work, the methods deployed and the outputs desired and expected from varying groups have differed over time. Here we give two examples amongst many which illustrate reflexivity in the context of doing research work. The first relates to a UK research council-funded project and the second to a piece of contract work. This distinction is important in accounting for how differential funding pressures and pre-determined client expectations influence the relative space and time for reflexive practice.

Endogenous and referential reflexivity in practice

In 2002 we successfully applied for funding to the UK Economic and Social Research Council's (ESRC) Science in Society programme for a one-year pilot study. The research aimed to build an understanding of the dynamic interaction between existing scientific practice and regional needs, in particular to assess how far the articulation of regional needs in the UK had reshaped the governance, processes and outcomes of national science policy. According to the criteria deployed by referees, the project was graded 'Outstanding' and led to a successful large grant under the second round of the Programme (2004–2007). Expanding the scale and scope of the project to include case studies in France, Germany and Spain, the work took the study of regional science policy into a comparative context and focused on different approaches for building science regions in the European Research Area. This project also gained an 'Outstanding' grading.

Neither project was conceived to embody an iterative or reflexive approach. A linear methodology was envisaged from research question through to fieldwork, followed by a discrete period of data analysis and representation. Within the terms of the project, reflexivity was neither planned nor anticipated as a prerequisite of funding or assessment. Nonetheless, given our commitment to the context and culture of the Centre, research practices emerged which facilitated reflexivity within the project and a move from endogenous to more referential concerns. Project meetings and supervisions provided critical spaces for reflexive practice (see also Elliott et al. 2011). These facilitated reflection on the design, conduct and results of the interviewing process as it unfolded, as well as constituted spaces for a collective discussion of emerging themes and issues of validity, representativeness and authenticity. Whilst we did not follow a single method, such as listening guides or multiple voice analysis (Mauthner and Doucet 1998, 2003; Gilligan et al. 2005), project spaces enabled the data to be re-evaluated continuously through listening from different points of view, multiple readings, or comparing field notes and observations with transcriptions of key interviews.

The process enabled us to analyse dynamics and asymmetries of power – not, in this case, by giving over power to research subjects as equals or co-constructors, but by acknowledging the inherent interests at play in presenting particular versions of events (England 1994). These were not people from disadvantaged communities or marginalised groups. Furthermore, the vast majority of interviewees were older, male and in positions of seniority in higher education, with much to lose from an unfavourable account of their actions and decisions. A reflexive approach to data analysis was critical in highlighting the limitations of the data and the basis upon which claims could be made. Whilst we had some privileged access to key decision-makers and documents, it became apparent that we could not expect our study, given the resources available, to penetrate the political spheres of influence shaping policy-making processes. These reflections strongly influenced the aims and objectives of the second round project which took us beyond a one-year timeframe. The emphasis here was more deliberately on illuminating the construction and mobilisation of discourses around scientific excellence and territorial relevance. Prior intellectual interests were critical in reshaping and refining the research to examine not only regulative and structural accounts, but also the normative and cognitive frames which created particular conditions in which contemporary developments around the innovative region or city were being formed.

In seeking to create a 'safer space' for critical reflection and engagement within the Centre, we were able to submit the relationship between the Science in Society project and our own institutional position to scrutiny. Whilst the methodology for the project remained relatively traditional and linear, the culture of the Centre forged a context for us to examine how our roles as academics informed the analysis of our data. Our research was increasingly looking at the mechanisms through which universities were engaging with 'their' localities, the hierarchies which emerged, and the values attributed to and assumed by different organisations and forms of knowledge. Combined with other projects we were undertaking for the Greater Manchester Universities and Manchester: Knowledge Capital, we were forced to examine how our position informed our critique of research-excellent universities and the capturing of regional development agendas by a narrow and elitist search for global excellence.

The role of academics and university managers, often known to us, was subject to internal critique through the project and broader context. Collective and iterative discussions of interview material, encompassing discussions of the dynamics, body language, content and space of the interview, enabled us to see how our own positions were being invoked and used in particular ways to legitimise existing justifications, or constitute alternative discourses. With such statements as 'you know how it is, as academics, we all play these games', uncomfortable questions were often dismissed as naive, whilst interviewees simultaneously sought to co-opt us and invite us into the collective idea of regional relevance and practices that often carried on regardless (Perry 2007, 2012).

These sets of reflections created an ambivalence and hesitancy about forms of writing, the prioritisation of different narratives, modes and forums of representation and audiences (May and Perry 2006; Perry and May 2006, 2007; May 2011a). The process of writing as an act of analysis was critical in this respect. Faced with complex sets of circumstances, we developed different forms of representation – to funders, participants, stakeholders, policy-makers, academics, etc. We produced versions of final reports for different groups, along with policy briefings and academic articles, and collectively discussed presentations and key messages for audiences. Anticipation and a desire to protect the integrity of our work were key facets of a reflexive approach. In this respect we were bolstered by having continuously 'tested' the validity of our analysis and the reception of work through presentations to those involved, informal workshops and formal seminars.

In these projects a reflexive approach to data analysis enabled not only checks on bias, but also the movement from endogenous to referential concerns. This took place through the culture of the Centre rather than planned in-project methods. Data analysis could not be seen as clearly bounded within a single phase, as ongoing project meetings, workshops, presentations and forms of representation over time created different spaces for reflexive analysis. Reflexivity allowed a process of deepening awareness of the production of valid and reliable data, strengthening a commitment to the value of this awareness and generating a willingness to be open to 'hostile information' (Gouldner 1971: 494).

Reflexive snatches

Our second example relates to work we were commissioned to undertake through a formative evaluation of the Manchester Innovation Investment Fund (IIF), supported by the National Endowment for Science, Technology and the Arts, the North West Development Agency and Manchester City Council. The aim of the Fund was to bring about a step-change in the innovation capacity in the city-region through the injection of circa £9,000,000. Our role, alongside the University of Manchester's Institute of Innovation Research, was to act not as consultants but as 'critical friends', providing real-time feedback and lessons that could inform subsequent actions rather than produce an end of project summative evaluation. The mode of working was developed at our instigation – indeed, we wrote the brief – drawing on our critique of academic engagement and linear models of knowledge transfer. Our aspiration, shared by one of the key organisations involved, was to bring endogenous and referential concerns, excellence and relevance together in a novel approach to inform practice – not as a by-product or end-product, but as an intended collaborative outcome. This can be seen as embodying a frustration with existing academic practices and a desire for a more critical and emancipatory form of research (see McCabe and Holmes 2009).

These concerns were reflected in the terms of reference for the evaluation with the emphasis upon learning and representation at a programmatic level. The intention was for direct access to materials, and the methods deployed were observation of meetings and events, documentary analysis, and interviews with funders, participants and stakeholders, as well as questionnaires and focus groups. We produced work package reports designed to inform the process with the intention that these might 'red-kite' any issues unfolding, and thus provide the possibility of a realignment or adjustment of priorities, processes and the trajectory of the IIF. The work was planned over three years with the intention that we would then synthesise the formative learning into a summative report.

Reflexive spaces for participants were actively planned as part of the data collection and analysis process. Having explored the motivations, desires and perspectives of the funders and managers privately through interviews, they were then brought into a collective forum in which they could reflect on and within actions. Through analysing and comparing the transcriptions of the interviews and the focus groups, alongside a self-completion, open-ended questionnaire, we were able to see how individuals performed different roles publicly and privately and the extent of capacities to reflect and share their assumptions, uncertainties and concerns as a precursor to effective learning. At the time, these forums were credited by participants as being extremely helpful in generating a common under-standing and exploring the purpose of organisational and individual motivations and contexts that otherwise would not have been gained. A temporary sense of belonging together in a collective endeavour emerged.

As the political and governance context for the Fund altered over time, the degrees of reflexivity that the funders and managers were able to exhibit – in the spirit of real-time learning and evaluation – reached a limit. Our interview data revealed a mix of positive and negative messages for the managers in terms of structures, experiences, processes and impacts. These were met with variable reactions, from acknowledgement and legitimation through to dismissal and refutation, not only according to the nature of the statement (informally, through verbal asides, through interview spaces or in public forums) but also according to the point of time in the process. It was particularly noticeable how the dispo-sitions of funders and managers to engage in reflexive learning changed in line with their positions and organisational expectations in the context of the financial recession.

What this highlights is the relational nature of reflexivity and the interactive nature of endogenous and referential dimensions. Reflexive spaces were planned as the basis for learning within in-project spaces – yet the limits to the reflexivity of others increased the need for reflexivity on our part at the very time when our own organisational culture was under pressure and not due to financial issues. We were working on different projects, whilst trying to defend our governance model which had worked well for ten years and responding to the needs of funders and clients. We were also struggling with our own motivations and sense of belonging in a changing academic context and with meeting the expectations placed upon us in different spheres. The result of these contexts and cultures, despite our proclivities, was to reduce systematic reflexive spaces to ad hoc 'reflexive snatches', grabbed when servers failed and email was blissfully suspended, or on the telephone in the odd moments when we needed a break from discussions on the survival of a positive organisational culture.

The emphasis was on the representation of the work, given the sensitivities of the funders, our own involvement in the research and our commitments to those we had interviewed to ensure that their voices were clearly heard. Again, the process of report writing was essential to the process of analysis as we sought to navigate the thin and uncomfortable line between academic credibility and capitulation to the need for easily digestible and positive stories of success that would justify the investments made. To establish the legitimacy of the reports according to our concerns with accurate representation and the ethics surrounding data collection, we sought to give space to the voices of others to allow for the material to speak, by including interview quotes alongside extracts from public meetings, minutes and workshops. We sought to deconstruct and reconstruct ways forward for the Fund to enable different perspectives to be recognised and reconciled within practices. Such writing was challenging whilst we were also minded that 'responsi ble, reflexive text announces its politics and ceaselessly interrogates the realities it invokes while folding the teller's story into the multi-voiced history that is written ... no interpretation is privileged' (Denzin 1997: 225).

For the funders, representation took priority over learning; reputations were on the line for all involved. After all 'who benefits from our representations? Are our representations valid? Do they matter?' (Pillow 2003: 175–6). The feedback and review process on the final submitted report was extremely revealing. At the point of representation and with the prospect of the report being made publicly available, our work took centre stage. The report became a lens through which the funders saw themselves and simultaneously acted as a mechanism through which differences were seen. We received four different, contradictory 'word, line, paragraph and page' amendments with no guidance on how to mediate between them. Our position became untenable and unwinnable. Ultimately, our report was described as 'so accurate it would never see the light of day'. We were informed that we needed to provide solutions, as if the differences of opinion between those involved were irrelevant. The contract came to an end with a consultant being employed to undertake the work of representation and produce 'best practice' case studies for other cities.

We were left with a series of ethical dilemmas and choices relating to the spirit in which we had undertaken the work and our responsibilities to the funder, our commitments to participants, and our standing with academic and policy/practitioner circles. Distance and time away from the project were needed before we could systematically consider these issues, particularly as there were multiple battles to secure the boundaries and reproduction of the Centre. It took eighteen months before we had the space and time and felt able to return to the work. Acknowledging how painful we had found the process, we then created new spaces to reflect on the work, in part through removing ourselves from our environment and presenting at conferences on the process of the work. This ongoing reflexive re-analysis of our roles and the relationship between creativity and critique in urban governance and policy processes acted not only as 'confession, catharsis and cure' (Pillow 2003), but also to inform our current practices.

The project illustrated multiple reflexivities in data analysis. Following Anderson (1998) we undertook a dialectical process consisting of analysing our own constructs and those of research participants, research data, an awareness of our ideological biases, and the historical, contextual and structural forces that conditioned the study. Reflexivity was employed as a deliberate tool to produce transformative outcomes and learning amongst fund managers, to enhance the validity and integrity of the work, to inform choices about representation/ analysis, as a mechanism of support and understanding, and finally as a rescue package for the work in an ironic retreat into endogenous circles. It also highlighted how the relationship between academic research and engaged work was not straightforward nor linear and the complexities of seeking to work in partnership with multiple organisations in the urban space (May and Perry 2011b).

REFLEXIVE RESEARCH DESIGN

In the above examples two elements are worth emphasising. First, there is no such thing as a *method for reflexivity*. The issue, as we outline in Box 7.2, is instead whether existing methods are or are not deployed reflexively. This is an essential point: no method can be a guarantee of reflexivity – it is not what method you choose but how you to choose to approach it and the issues you are seeking to understand and explain. Second, the projects themselves were not reflexive by design but were undertaken in a Centre which maintained a commitment to reflexive practice to the extent it could preserve sufficient levels of institutional shelter against the cultural changes occurring in higher education (see Furedi 2017). Taking these experiences forward, both positive and negative, we have retained a belief that the effort required to create, maintain and draw value from reflexive spaces for different participants in the research process is worthwhile.

Informed by our experiences and writings, we have increasingly sought to embed reflexivity within all stages of the research process from conceptualisation through to analysis, representation and evaluation (Knoblauch 2004). In our work since 2011, as the transaction costs to maintain the boundaries of the Centre intensified, so we sought to engage in greater reflexive research design within projects themselves, in search of programmatic shelters outside institutional pressures. Again we draw on two examples: first the proactive deployment of reflexivity in the formation of interdisciplinary epistemic communities and communities of practice, and second the creation of spaces where all participants could be encouraged to think about their dispositions, positions and sense of belonging in a meeting between endogenous and referential concerns.

■ Box 7.2 ■

Deploying methods reflexively

We have noted that there is no such thing as a reflexive method; rather methods can be deployed reflexively. Writing is a common approach to aid reflexivity in the research process, as can be seen through our own experiences, whether in diaries, letters, essays or working with transcripts. For Diane Watt (2007) writing notes iteratively throughout the research process is one approach which allows researchers to discover things they did not know were there. Writing connects episodic moments of reflection in areas of home-schooling, midwifery, health and social care, community engagement, race, sexuality, climate change and in policy/practitioner engagements. Similarly, Williams (1990: 255) considers her use of reflexivity as a form of additional fieldwork: 'My notes constitute the field, and my attempt to understand them is in a very real sense fieldwork.' For others reflexivity infuses the research process only when researchers explicitly 'think differently' in rejecting the categories/language that is available. Elizabeth St Pierre focuses on the importance of paying attention to 'transgressive data ... or data that escaped language' as a means of being aware in the field (1997: 177–9). In all cases the danger is that such writings turn too far into confessional, indulgent or 'narcissistic' endeavours (Denzin 1997). As Patai (1994: 64) puts it, she has no time for a series of academic fads in the crisis of representation when 'babies still have to be cared for, shelter sought, meals prepared and eaten'.

Reflexivity is different from reflection. Whereas the latter involves looking back on past experiences in order to capture learning, the former constitutes a process of meta-learning – not only reflection *in* but *on* action. Reflection entails 'in-the-moment reflective episodes', whereas reflexivity is 'a conscious cognitive process whereby knowledge and theory are applied to make sense of remembered reflective episodes' (Dallos and Stedmon 2009b: 4). At the same time the idea is that processes of reflexivity also lead to self-change and are transformative at the level of the individual. Within such distinctions is the idea that it is not even possible to be reflexive during a study and such perspective and distance can only be born over time rather than in the immediate context of the field (Hobbs and May 1993).

Authors have sought to add nuance to the different ways in which reflexivity can be applied to the processes of research. Denzin (1997) identifies five different types of reflexivity: methodological, intertextual, standpoint, queer and feminist. Ryan (2005) focuses on dimensions of reflexivity which are either focused on introspection, deconstructing praxis, considering presuppositions, theories and methods, and beliefs and assumptions. Making sense of these options, some offer 'maps' for five variants of reflexivity – introspection, intersubjective reflection, mutual collaboration, social critique and discursive deconstruction (Finlay 2002). Clearly there are multiple choices – what matters for the researcher is considering how a reflexive application of methods and tools can lead to more honest and mature practices.

Inter-referential reflexivity

An increasing emphasis on funding mechanisms that encourage inter-disciplinary, cross-institutional and multi-annual projects for the receipt of larger sums of research money became apparent. Mirroring developments elsewhere around the concentration of resources, linked to expectations of excellent academic work with high impact, groups of academics have increasingly needed to form alliances in order to successfully apply for Research Council funding. Whilst this may happen independent of Research Councils, processes – such as research 'sandpits' – have been designed with the intention of forging new collaborations between academics who may have never previously met, but may work together on multi-annual projects based on a single moment of contact.

Context and culture, disposition, position and belonging all shape the content of research in terms of its legitimacy, quality and potential impact. We sought to develop a reflexive process within such projects as a precursor for effective team working. In so doing we drew on work such as Gilbert and Sliep's (2009: 468) call for 'inter-relational reflexivity', which includes 'a concern for moral agency and the negotiation of account-ability and responsibility for action, as social action requires a joint deconstruction of power in the voices and relationships operating between the stakeholders within a per-formative space'. From Hosking and Pluut (2010: 59) the relational approach highlights the need for 'regular reflexive dialogues as part of, and directed at, the research process [to] heighten the local use value of research for all participants and ... facilitate new possible realities and relations'.

At the outset of a large research project, *Cultural Intermediation*, funded by a jointly funded Research Council UK programme called 'Connected Communities', we instigated a process of bilateral exchanges to facilitate the sharing of orientations, motivations and expectations between team members as a foundation for interdisciplinary knowledge production (see also Mruck and Mey 2007). In the very process of bid development in 2011, we carried out individual interviews with team members, shared examples of previous work, and had bilateral exchanges with a write-up of issues. This enabled a sense of orientation and history was able to be brought into the new collaboration. The project itself focused on how different processes and mechanisms could connect or disconnect margin-alised communities from participation in and benefitting from the creative urban economy. A central plank of this work was the allocation of £100,000 for local people to determine cultural priorities and activities for themselves in two inner city areas recognised as suffering from multiple indices of deprivation. Underpinning these aspirations within the research design was a commitment to collaborative reflexive analysis.

The process started with a series of interviews with the academic team to reflect on their motivations for research and to explore individual differences and collective orientations. These echoed what we subsequently came to recognise – that there were important differences between the team. Facer and Enright (2016: 46–7) identify motivations for engaging in co-produced work for communities; for instance, differentiating between the academic entrepreneur and the advocates for a new knowledge landscape, drawing on Becher and

Trowler's (1989) identification of academic 'tribes'. Early on we encountered strong differences in approach between cultures within social sciences and the arts and humanities. This had also been apparent in the peer review process which, despite the funding of the programme across Research Councils, suggested some suspicion that this was social science research masquerading as arts and humanities.

In the project, differential levels of 'epistemic permeability' in the endogenous realm (May with Perry 2011) proved as intractable and disadvantageous to the creation of spaces for reflexivity as inter-referential differences between those within and outside the academy. Attributed value to the idea of 'artistic practice' and experiences gained outside the university were often alluded to as a means of denigrating 'academic work', without understanding the conditions of its production or potential of its impact. Furthermore, as the speed of application deadlines passed, to be replaced with the urgency of new demands within the sector, the business of surviving in higher education took its toll on the aspirations of the project. The constantly shifting backdrop of institutional politics, restructuring, staff mobility, the Research Excellence Framework (2014), redundancy, the precarity of contract researchers, the stresses and mental health problems endemic in the higher education sector – all impacted on the creation of a genuinely new epistemic community brought into being through the project.

Practitioners were invited into their own parallel reflexive space through a diary-keeping exercise (Perry et al. 2015). Diaries are a common method deployed to aid reflexive analysis, along with fieldwork notes and aide memoires. Participants in this process commented positively on the spaces for reflexivity that had been created and the implications for their professional and personal identities. Spaces for reflection in the project were also effectively designed for non-academic participants as part of the community engagement process which led to positive reports of group identity and cohesiveness within communities of practice (Symons and Perry 2016). We always made sure that food was provided to create a sense of conviviality around such spaces (Parham 2015). Celebration was an important element in recognising and valuing the expertise and experience from community participants.

As the external demands of the project increased, so internal coherence within the academic team became harder to maintain, particularly in the context of split-site working across two cities in the UK. Navigating and negotiating the interests of stakeholders, adhering to good practice and ethical conduct in working with community groups, and working with and around tensions and cultural dynamics meant that efforts were inevitably oriented towards external management as opposed to internal reflexive analysis. During the most intensive fieldwork periods, there was less time for the creation of a single epistemic community bound by common interests and an inter-disciplinary orientation. Our energies and minds were turned outwards not inwards. As this intensity diminished we turned again to writing as a reflexive process. We designed a workshop in July 2015 as a supportive forum in which to discuss the relationship between expectations, practice, results and institutional contexts. This was aided by an exercise in which we asked participants to write a letter to an imagined confidant (see Box 7.3).

In the project a reflexive research design was readily conceived, based on our previous experiences, but less easily implemented. For practitioners and community participants a reflexive research design was realised in the creation of multiple spaces and moments of encounter. For the academic team the energies required to manage complex multi-partner relationships whilst delivering high impact work in communities led to an overly outward focus, whilst the demands of the business of higher education left their own scars.

▬ Box 7.3 ▬▬▬▬▬▬▬▬▬▬▬▬▬▬▬▬▬▬

Writing and reflexivity

Academic participants were asked to write a letter to present their experiences to a colleague who wanted more information about the project and to whom they had a strong commitment. With an expectation of reciprocal honesty, the letters addressed the reasons for the work being funded, individual contributions, measures of and criteria for success, reflections on methods and techniques, outcomes for the work and contributions to a field of knowledge.

The exercise was differentially received, as has been our experience in all such fora – yet even for those whose initial reactions were that this was 'just more bullshit', the experience of writing to an imagined other proved valuable. Some people's letters focused on the content of the project only, but most revealed a set of honest concerns, issues, hopes and aspirations about the promise and reality of doing this kind of work. The letters expressed a shared scepticism about funding processes and institutional politics, particularly given the context of debates which had surrounded the initiation of the Research Council programme as a whole. They also reflected the differential positions between research leaders and those in a 'cognitive precariat' represented in functional and intellectual divisions of labour. How to 'deliver without disappointment' was echoed in the desire not to 'parachute in' and avoid the pitfalls of an exploitative social science. Certain methods were found to aid processes of inter-referential reflexivity between academic participants and community stakeholders, such as walking interviews and iterative approaches of 'pushing back' and refining research processes.

We reflected on how projects such as these can be 'unsettling' for practitioners and academics alike: not everyone is comfortable with a light being shone on their practices. The unsettling of existing certainties – the lifting of the rug to reveal actual practices – challenges assumptions, and this required more commitment to each other and to working through inter-referential concerns than had originally been planned. Both the art of listening and the science of representation were invoked. A central challenge – and one that continues to challenge engaged social science – was the question of measuring impact. How can you capture a qualitative shift in someone's confidence? How is this valued against metrics that are based on quantity of outputs and indices of success that value certain kinds of evidence but dismiss others as anecdotal? Reflections on the institutional power and privilege of the university led to multiple discussions on the relationship between content, context, culture and consequences (May with Perry 2011).

This raises a very real issue of whether and how shared epistemic cultures can be created which take endogenous and referential concerns into account in real time when you are immersed in contexts and processes. From the 'swampy lowlands' (Schön 1983) to the lofty plains of academia, the lesson is that reflexive research design is central to work with communities, but all the more difficult to implement. This raises clear ethical issues as well as highlights that as the demands of project management, the realpolitik of international collaborations and institutional turmoil in the UK increase, the potential gap between a reflexive design and its practical realisation widens.

Safer spaces

An alternative example to the one above takes the question of reflexive research design as encompassing not only particular methods but also the governance of research projects. This reflects our ideas, elaborated in Chapter 8, about active intermediation based on the need for processes to constitute social arenas for the discussion and contestation of knowledge for and in cities and their regions. Our vision was to create safer spaces that were inclusive, imagined and brought into being by the collective actions of multiple partners rather than the forging of institutional mechanisms within the university (May 2011b; May with Perry 2011). International funders, working through a consultant, then approached SURF to produce a report on how a research centre could be organised on the basis of coproduction.

The result was our participation in setting up and delivering a new international centre in Sweden with partners from different countries, committed to co-producing sustainable cities. Mistra Urban Futures is an international centre funded by the Swedish Foundation for Strategic Environmental Research (MISTRA), the Swedish International Development Cooperation Agency (SIDA), and seven regional and local consortium partners. Mistra Urban Futures operates through five local interaction platforms (LIPs), two in Sweden and one each in Kenya, South Africa and the United Kingdom. Hosted by Chalmers University in Gothenburg, Mistra Urban Futures is based on the belief that the 'co-production of knowledge is a winning concept for achieving sustainable urban futures and creating fair, green and dense cities', through an innovative structure which brings local partners together in consortia to develop shared approaches to sustainability in city-regions with local relevance and global applicability (Mistra Urban Futures 2016, www.mistraurbanfutures.org/en).

SURF led the development of the Greater Manchester Local Interaction Platform (GMLIP) for the first phase of Mistra Urban Futures between 2010 and 2015. The GMLIP programme focused on how addressing urban sustainability challenges in the city-region required different forms of knowledge and skills. At the time regional governance structures were being dismantled and local authority budgets reduced in the context of austerity and public sector reform. The development of GMLIP therefore needed to be approached step-by-step, sensitive to changing political, economic and social issues. In 2012 a large pilot study *Mapping the Urban Knowledge Arena* brought together numerous stakeholders, identified issues and developed co-production projects (Perry et al. 2012). In 2013 a *Greater*

Manchester Partners (GMP) group was formed, bringing together the leads of key flagship projects, designed to bridge between academia and practice, and local partners were brought into the consortium. Initially projects were carried out bilaterally with each partner in association with SURF. But by 2014 GMLIP began to submit collaborative bids, and in 2015 successfully secured funding from the UK Research Councils for its first joint project involving all key actors. This aligned with a new and dynamic context as Greater Manchester became the first city-region outside London to sign a devolution agreement with central government.

Drawing on our experiences a number of different methods were reflexively deployed. A cross-section of politicians, civil servants, business and voluntary sector representatives, community organisations and activists were commissioned to write about their vision for a sustainable city. In response to a series of prompts, participants were invited to discuss and examine the reasons and motivations for their work and the choices they made in their writing in a formal and recorded interview. Conversations followed about the content of their work and issues arising in the interview space, allowing them time to review and, if they desired, revise their essay. The formal *Perspectives* were published on an online sustainability web portal, Platform (www.ontheplatform.org.uk). Elsewhere in the programme of work, interviews were deployed as co-constructed reflexive spaces. For example, a narrative practice-based reflection on an urban socio-ecological experiment in Salford, Greater Manchester, was produced through a series of ten interviews over a three-year period to situate learning processes from a practice-based standpoint (Cook and Brown 1999; Brown and Duguid 2001).

Interviews took the form of open conversations, recorded and transcribed to co-produce this subsequent narrative (Gherardi 2000; Polk 2015). Importantly, they represented a dialogic process of reflection, rather than a retrospective outside-in analysis. An outcome, a co-written chapter in an edited book, is a story of lived experience, but one negotiated between interviewer and interviewee to capture complex, multi-layered and nuanced understandings of the case and presented as a multi-vocal text (Perry et al. 2016). This process of treating interview transcripts as the shared basis for jointly owned and authored texts was mirrored elsewhere in the programme, in which moving from oral reflection to written data analysis enabled both endogenous and referential reflexivity. Although partners in Cape Town deployed different methods, the process of co-writing as a means of reflexive analysis between academics and practitioners was also valuable in a different context (Patel et al. 2015).

More significantly, the project as a whole systematised a series of internal, bilateral and external spaces for reflection into a process for considering the relationship between values and learning in urban environments. Learning, emancipation and transformation are facilitated through reflexive spaces in which individuals and groups can come to see themselves and their actions in different ways (Fay 1987). Even programme meetings became opportunities for decision-makers to consider the challenges they were facing, constituting safer spaces to think through practices and pre-conceptions. This constituted a strong challenge to linear ideas of knowledge transfer and the quantifiable impact; what mattered was the qualitative experience, based on trust, reciprocity and honesty. Echoing previous experiences, we found that the active boundary work necessary on the part of the academic to maintain and protect safer spaces was intense, with huge transaction costs. Such experiences resonated with those in all of the other LIPs (Mistra Urban Futures 2016). We maintained that the conditions for meaningful spaces of communication between urban groups could be created through actively mediating between different interests within innovative forms of social organisation. This entails a process of active intermediation which is a subject in our final chapter.

SUMMARY: REFLEXIVE MESSES

In this chapter we have examined core elements of a reflexive practice. Through examples from our experiences, a movement to more 'inter-subjective' concerns has been traced as the contexts, cultures and conditions for knowledge production transform under contemporary pressures (Beck in Beck and Beck-Gernsheim, 2002: 212). As modes of knowledge production are changing with researchers involved in collaborative knowledge generation, it is not only the multi-dimensional reflexivity of the researcher that comes into play, but also that of all knowledge producers in the process – and of how they interrelate. In our fragmented, fast-speed, time-poor, high-pressured societies, where policy proceeds at a startling pace in the absence of learning, collective spaces for reflection are needed even more. As epistemic permeability questions the boundaries between and within disciplines, institutions and the social world, the challenge is to design ways for collectively producing knowledge in a reflexive ethos, without collapsing into individualised therapy, whilst maintaining concern to contribute to the possibilities of transformation of the world in which we work and belong.

In our account it is clear that the history and development of the research centre itself and the relationship between the content, culture and contexts for innovative, excellent and relevant work have increasingly shaped the substantive subject matter for work. The examples we selected were 'messy' and did not 'seek a comfortable, transcendent end-point' (Pillow 2003: 193), but confronted the realities of doing engaged research. We recognised that multiple aspects are at play in terms of the dynamics between individuals, the work and the broader contexts and cultures in the urban sphere which influence how joint knowledge production, exchange and learning might take place in cities. In this it became evident that we do not subscribe to the view that reflexivity is just for those 'who stay up nights worrying about representation ... as a form of "methodological self-absorption"' (Patai 1994: 64, 69). Rather, by being 'vigilant about our practices' (Spivak 1984: 184), we can produce better research.

A reflexive approach to social science navigates between the paths of complacent arrogance and situated derision, deconstruction and reconstruction, and engagement and distance.

This means being concerned with how to acknowledge different viewpoints, ways of knowing and knowledge (lay/expert), without undermining the sites of knowledge production that enable a scientific gaze, nor giving over to the lure of 'scholastic slumbers' (Bourdieu, 2000). In addition, how researchers define themselves, in particular through their difference from and distance to others in the field of knowledge production, is a core element that brings together the disposition *and* position of the individual.

We are dealing with a continual process of seeking to understand what social inquiry sees, the manner in which it is constructed and its place within social relations more generally. The emphasis is upon practice and not the rhetorical flourishes to which we are all susceptible when it comes to justifying our actions, nor the abstract individualism that performs a simple separation between character, context and content. It is not easy and requires the development of supportive cultures of inquiry where we find a willingness to learn, assist others and understand limits and potentials. Whilst our experiences provide ample opportunity to remain sceptical as to the success of such a strategy, we maintain an aspiration in our work: to contribute to the possibility of knowledge having transformative outcomes that improve collective capacities to create more just and sustainable futures.

8

REFLEXIVITY REALISED

We could say that the excess produced by the extimate cause of subjectivity is both the obstacle to our knowing our meaning as social beings and the necessary ingredient of the social field within which we obtain the only meaning that we will ever have, however uncertain.
(Molly Anne Rothenburg 2010: 10)

INTRODUCTION

Our investigations have been far-ranging and indicative of a journey seeking to understand the place and role of reflexivity in social research. We have toured through ideas about the relationships between thought and action; rationalism, empiricism and romanticism; thinking, Being and Doing; language and the constitution of the social world; the multiple selves that we inhabit and exhibit; theoretical, practical and critical reason; power, politics and prejudice; science and society; justification and application; and the context and cultures of doing engaged work. In the process the cast of writers whose works we have examined has been extensive. We have found that reflexivity requires active engagement with these ideas in practice – an ability to account for them in the production of social scientific research and to debate them in defending the strengths and limits of claims to knowing the world, and importantly, supportive cultures of inquiry. In our uncertain and contested societies, no search for certainty can result in total knowledge. Furthermore, we cannot expect that tensions and ambiguities can be simply resolved in our domains of practice, but they can be subject to clarification as a condition of better understanding.

Social scientific findings are contestable in terms of their descriptions, depictions and procedural implications. Actions are forged in different contexts and produce consequences that require new interpretations. This is a cycle in which the social sciences gain their vitality to understand the characteristics and struggles of an age. In practising social scientific work, knowing limits as a condition of learning and regarding modesty as a positive attribute, both make sense because there are conditions beyond the control of agents. From our investigation, we conclude that a framework for reflexive thought begins by considering oscillations between the dimensions of endogenous and referential reflexivity and which inhere within social life itself.

In this final chapter and to illuminate this dynamic we first consider *belonging* through returning to questions of the self that we have examined throughout the book. In our understanding we need to know 'who' someone is and 'how' others view them. Second, to understand how this occurs requires an explanation of the conditions in which actions occur. Along with sufficient self-esteem, coherence and understanding, a study of *positioning* is of core consideration in terms of the capability to take action. Finally, the ability to conduct and construct research and the degrees to which it may or may not resonate with social life is informed by this relationship. What this means is resisting the position of the social scientist as legislator of knowledge and engaging with different viewpoints to illuminate contemporary dynamics in the spirit of *transformation*. This requires recasting the role of social scientists to focus on *active intermediation* as a set of reflexive practices concerning the boundaries of research and to produce a more mature and open social science.

WHO AM I?

When it comes to the understanding of the subject, let us add another question to those we have posed thus far: 'Who am I?' Without a consideration of this aspect of social life, ideas of the subject (and let us not forget, this includes those of us who produce explanations and understandings of the social world as social scientists) produce antiseptic accounts which do not resonate with everyday experiences – and 'resonate', not 'reflect', for we have seen that there is greater understanding to be found, but no final kernel of transparency to discover. 'Who am I?' concerns having a 'point of view'. It is about the singularity of experience constituted in the knowledge that this is generated in the dialectical relations between sameness and selfhood (Ricoeur 1994). Here we find our paradox: if we have resorted to the idea of a solitary ego we have found it wanting and have been led to the conclusion that 'the self that seeks is the self that is sought' (Harré 1998: 12). To enable us to see the singularity of experience, Paul Ricoeur's (1913–2005) approach constitutes a basis for social science to resonate with the experiences of everyday life, measured against the constraints and opportunities available for people to realise their potentials, limits, and also their experiences of abjection, exclusion and violence.

Embracing multiple selves

As we have seen, language informs the ability to monitor one's own actions and links to how one is positioned. As phenomenology, symbolic interactionism and ethnomethodology illustrated, we have the ability 'to give discursive accounts of and commentaries upon what we perceive, how we act and what we remember' (Harré 1998: 12). This is not a move to eradicate ambivalence at the level of social scientific method through a focus upon language use. Rather, what is at play, following Merleau-Ponty, is emotional inter-subjectivity. As the sociologist and group psychoanalyst Ian Craib put it, 'First we feel, and then later we learn to speak about our feelings' (1998: 174).

At the level of the individual the following elements are said to constitute reflexivity: coherence, vitality, depth and maturity. Coherence refers to a narrative dimension in which it is possible to sum up the changes that have taken place during a lifetime. Vitality concerns fulfilment in terms of progression towards who one wishes to become. Depth refers to the ability to have an understanding of the constitutive elements that make up an identity, and maturity to the ability to come to terms with the facts of the world without compromising coherence and vitality (Ferrara 1998: 80–107).

▬ Box 8.1 ▬▬▬▬▬▬▬▬▬▬▬▬▬▬▬▬▬▬▬▬▬▬▬▬▬▬▬▬▬▬▬▬▬▬

Blogademia

Our multiple selves are reflected in the conscious and unconscious creation of diverse personal and professional identities. Under conditions of reflexive modernisation, the project of routinely creating and maintaining the self (Giddens 1991) applies increasingly to the world of academia. Here reputations are forged through intellectual endeavour in which the cultivation of a professional identity is intimately bound up with the project of self-making.

(Continued)

(Continued)

There are multiple factors which influence the forging of academic identity: for instance, the primacy of the discipline (Henkel 2005) or the degrees of congruence with the 'prevailing discourse of corporate managerialism' (Winter 2009: 121). For Parker and Jary (1995: 328) the term 'professional' is a 'valued self-identity that implies both commitment and skill'. There are various directions that this increasing concern with academic self-making can take. On the one hand, 'academic capitalism' (Slaughter and Leslie 1997) is leading to the rise of new academic entrepreneurs for whom positioning and marketing of the self are part of the clamour for recognition and career progression. On the other hand, there are those such as Michael Burawoy who are more concerned with the critical and public face of social science. Burawoy's (2004) intellectual division of labour differentiates between a policy social science that produces instrumental knowledge for a professional audience, and a public one which produces reflexive knowledge for a critical audience. For him, the challenge is to engage with multiple publics in multiple ways.

New media increasingly play a role in the creation and maintenance of the academic self and in both the instrumental and altruistic presentations of the self. Kirkup (2010) provides an analysis of academic blogging as a new way of constructing identity, seeing this as a form of 'performative writing'. She outlines the emergence of 'multiphrenic' identities (Gergan 2000) which are 'created out of a variety of narratives, but performed and presented through a variety of media' (Kirkup 2010: xx). She credits Saper (2006) as being the first to coin the term 'blogademia' for this trend. Her own study reveals the complexity of motivations for those engaged in blogging, seeing both the entrepreneurial creation of the self as a commodity, and 'a genre through which academics perform their scholarly identity, engage in knowledge production, and become public intellectuals, at least on the internet' (Kirkup 2010).

Motivations to inform and share knowledge, as well as position oneself in search of prestige, are equally involved in the blogosphere. Similar studies are increasingly being undertaken with other technologies: for example, seeing Twitter as a tool for performing academic identity (Fransman 2013) or an informal learning space (McPherson et al. 2015), and the rise of academic research networking sites, such as Academia.edu and Researchgate. These personal network structures may reflect an expression of identity as public displays of connection, or relational self-portraits (Donath and Boyd 2004; Hogan and Wellman 2014; Jordan 2016).

Correcting a sense of self as manifest in simple continuity over time, we saw the disjuncture that Pierre Bourdieu (1986) calls the 'Don Quixote' effect. When there are sudden changes in fields, agents have difficulty in adjusting and become disoriented in terms of their own identity and roles. Yet we also need to avoid collapsing the self into a socially determined context. Our journey, after all, has witnessed an 'epistemic exaltation' of the self in Cartesian formulations and its 'humiliation' in the hands of Nietzsche. Ricoeur's approach, on the other hand, employs 'attestation' to denote the kind of certainty that is appropriate at this level: 'Whereas doxic belief is implied in the grammar "I believe-that", attestation belongs to the grammar of "I believe-in"' (Ricoeur 1994: 21). Clearly, this can lead to a resort to the kind of guarantees reminiscent of the Cartesian problematic. Nevertheless, it is the very contingency of the questioning itself that prevents such a resort by providing vulnerability through a 'permanent threat of suspicion'.

We need to balance suspicion as a permanent threat against what is taken-for-granted and believed in during the course of our lives. Self-annihilation is thus balanced against 'credence' expressed in the relationship between attestation and testimony. In terms of reliable attestation, we move into the realm of trust as a social component of our lives together: 'attestation is fundamentally attestation *of* self ... attestation can be defined as the *assurance of being oneself acting and suffering*. This assurance remains the ultimate recourse against all suspicion; even if it is always in some sense received from another, it still remains *self*-attestation. It is self-attestation that, at every level – linguistic, praxic, narrative, and prescriptive – will preserve the question "who?" from being replaced by the question "what?" or "why?" (Ricoeur 1994: 22–3; original emphasis).

The important point is that the asking of 'who' questions does not necessitate resort to a unity of self – and nor does the idea of a fragility of self give rise to a collapse into celebrations of contingency and multiplicity. A sense of selfhood (Ricoeur refers to it as 'ipseity') derives from where we are located and the events of which we are a part. It concerns the articulation of our sense of self, in time: 'My field of awareness, though centred in a singularity, is a complex structure of relations to my environment, past present and future ... To be one and the same person my point of view must be continuous relative to an all-encompassing material framework, including the world of other embodied beings' (Harré 1998: 91).

Role distance, sameness and selfhood

In our lives misalignment or alignment occurs between points of view, attributes, actions and context. One may wish to belong, but attributes and/or points of view are in disjuncture to the norms that inform social acceptance, and we see this in the dimensions of race, class and gender and sexuality. Having a point of view on 'who' one is relates to what one 'does', how actions are performed, and how others value our contribution and opinions. These are the sum of impressions that others have of us in terms of our changing patterns of dispositions and attributes. These local and variable presentations of the self are 'drawn from a culturally available repertoire' (Harré 1998: 87). Although there may be an ontological complicity at work, as Pierre Bourdieu notes in his studies, we find oscillations and ambivalences between a point of view, a set of attributes, and how the enacted social environment accords or does not accord with a sense of belonging in being accepted or rejected. When we spoke of endogenous reflexivity it comprises the senses between personal and self-identity which is derived through our interactions with others.

Erving Goffman's (1984[1959]) idea of 'role distance' neatly captures this process. The norms of a role may be given within a social setting, but the manner of its performance is variable: 'The manner in which the role is performed will allow for some "expression" of personal identity, of matters that can be attributed to something that is more embracing and enduring than the current role performance and even the role itself, something, in short, that is characteristic not of the role, but of the person' (Goffman 1974: 573). As a result of this variability, 'One can never expect complete freedom between individual and role and never complete constraint' (1974: 269). In this way, we can characterise selfhood as a dynamic produced between the questions 'Who am I?', 'What attributes do I possess?' and 'How do others see me?'

We have seen how those such as Jacques Derrida and Michel Foucault have argued that a sense of self as 'essence' is constituted by the exclusion of a negative. What we find in their work as a result is an emphasis on the inevitability of undecidability to guard against finality, or in Foucault's case, not wishing to be for consensus but standing against situations of non-consensus. The idea of self being presented here is neither static nor infinitely variable. Our singularity is made up through the invocation of others via a gallery of character inter-actions, typifications and expectations. In terms of their space–time content, these run from familiarity through acquaintance due to proximity, to descriptions via inference. Our acts of self-identification require discursive resources which we draw from our environment: '*The assessment of the maxim of one's intention, as these embody moral principles, requires understand-ing the narrative history of the self who is the actor; this understanding discloses both self-knowledge and knowledge of oneself as viewed by others*' (Benhabib 1992: 129; original emphasis).

Here we find a dialectic at work between sameness and selfhood. Paul Ricoeur's identity theory has five essential dimensions – language, history, time, space and body. Identity comprises two elements: one which changes and is unstable called *ipse* or 'selfhood'; another which is stable and unchanging, called *idem* or 'sameness'. Selfhood changes over time as the self actively affects and constructs a history and present. This equates to Ricoeur's idea of 'character'. Sameness relates to the characteristics that allow recognition of the self over time, either because it is one and the same thing (numerical sameness through, for example, numerated identity as used by corporations and governments), it has the same characteris-tics (qualitative sameness through attribution to our actions), or it is the same temporally even if it looks different (uninterrupted continuity). This equates to the idea of 'self con-stancy'. Of course, the keeping, or not, of a promise, as someone who is trustworthy, may produce a disjuncture between selfhood and social identity (see Box 8.2).

▬ Box 8.2 ▬

I promise

Narrative identity is the capacity of being oneself and maintaining a relationship to others in the world. However, 'with the question of permanence in time ... the confrontation between our two versions of identity becomes a genuine problem for the first time' (Ricoeur 1994: 116).

Ricoeur drew on the idea of a promise to illustrate this problem. Etymologically *promise* is derived from the Latin *pro*, meaning forward and *mittere*, meaning to send. It relates to a guarantee made in the present by one person to another that a particular action or commitment will be performed *by that same person* in the future. To this extent, a promise is a pledge or vow that holds its value only to the extent it is based on the character and selfhood of utterer. The self that promises must be the same self that will deliver on the promise, hence upholding selfhood, or as Ricoeur would put it 'holding firm'. To this extent, a promise is only distinguishable from a lie in terms of the intent to remain constant to oneself in carrying it out (see also Box 3.2). When promises are broken, we undermine our confidence in our own utterances and our ability to follow through on something we committed to, with negative implications for our self-identity.

An example illustrates this well. A promise, in political terms, is synonymous with a pledge, or a set of pledges commonly grouped as a 'manifesto'. Not to hold firm to these pledges leads to charges of misleading the public, being elected on false grounds, or even – if motives are then placed in doubt – of lying. Nick Clegg, then leader of the Liberal Democratic Party in the UK, got into problems in 2012 when he went back on his election promise not to support the introduction of tuition fees in higher education. He had worked tirelessly to cultivate an external image and gain the trust of the public, and his ultimate U-turn damaged his managed identity. This is why he was so keen not to defend his actions, but his motives, lest he be accused of lying in the first place: 'It was a pledge made with the best of intentions – but we should not have made a promise we were not absolutely sure we could deliver. I shouldn't have committed to a policy that was so expensive when there was no money around. Not least when the most likely way we would end up in government was in coalition with Labour or the Conservatives who were both committed to put fees up' (Nick Clegg in the *Guardian*, 20 September 2012).

The public judges politicians who break promises. However, for Schlesinger the issues are more complex. In his 2008 study of promises in the political sphere, he questions whether the one who holds to a promise despite changed circumstances is idealistic and principled or rigid? For him, keeping a promise is not always 'a defining act of moral maturity' (Schlesinger 2008: xii). Clegg may well have been pleased to hear such an assessment.

Now we have the issue of time to consider. Here we find both 'calendar' and 'internal' time which can be considered through the 'ability to integrate an account of the self within the context of a larger temporal framework' (Rasmussen 1996a: 17). Self-monitoring activity is amenable to understanding through narrative accounts where the self is socially located and may also become dislocated. This enables us, as we discussed in Habermas's work, to not simply allow inter-subjectivity to absorb subjectivity (Joas 1998) and captures what Hannah Arendt termed our 'twofold character of equality and distinction' (1998[1958]: 175). Character, culture and material conditions do come together, and Nancy Fraser and Axel Honneth illuminate those relations in their writings, but it does not follow they collapse into each other. That much is evident from the individual moral judgements and acts of political courage which we find littered throughout history – what Ricoeur refers to as 'holding firm'. These struggles for recognition concern the creation of spaces for having a voice, and are linked with 'the politics of moral geography and, as in all delicate environments, when the weather changes for some, sooner or later it changes for all who inhabit the territory' (Lemert 1997: 129).

There is a sense of self that refers to 'an ever-shifting set of attributes that characterizes a person at any one time' (Harré 1998: 5). It is not the same as the 'self' as a point of view, but an expression of a 'person with attributes' in the form: 'proper name + object name' to 'characterize oneself as the owner of an object, an attribute' (Harré 1998: 28). Here we find a sense of self-esteem and self-definition being fundamentally connected to an enacted environment for the realisation or frustration of agency. As Erving Goffman's observations illustrate, there is a gap here and it opens up a space of ambivalence from which endogenous reflexivity emerges. To further understand this, consideration must be given over to the impressions others have of these shifting set of attributes, as well as a referential component in relation to how and why positioning plays its role in social life.

HOW DO I RELATE TO OTHERS?

In terms of answering the question of 'who', we need to refer to the object side of our experiences to develop an understanding that takes into account the conditions of our actions: 'This detour through the "what" and the "how" before returning to the "who", seems to me explicitly required by the reflexive character of the self, which, in the moment of self-designation, recognizes *itself*' (Ricoeur 2005: 93; original emphasis). Social scientific accounts need to take account of those oscillations between personal and social identity via self-attestation that leads to the first moment of endogenous reflexivity. Nevertheless, to make referential reflexivity possible within everyday life, we require a sense of self that refers to questions of 'what' attributes are possessed, 'how' those attributes are viewed by others and 'why' this relates to positioning.

To understand this we must move into the world of action: 'There is no world without a self who finds itself in it and acts in it; there is no self without a world that is practicable in some fashion' (Ricoeur 1994: 311). We now add to the 'who' and 'how', the 'what' and 'why'. The study of what Pierre Bourdieu called 'fields' enables an examination of the relations into which individuals enter and are then positioned in particular ways and with what consequences. As Foucault also said of 'statements', we should analyse those positions that are occupied by an individual if they are 'to be the subject of it' (1989b[1969]: 96). As we have said, identity is not solely constituted by positioning for reflexive space would then evaporate, but the conditions in which we act inform our identities and capabilities in different ways.

Being positioned

A great deal of contemporary rhetoric revolves around 'choice'. What this does is to sever ability from the capability to mobilise the resources to bring about the results of that choice. At stake are the relations between knowledge, social action and positioning. If we fail to understand these relations we can easily become the dirt in the oil that lubricates individualistic ideologies that separate choice, context and resources. As David Simpson puts it at the end of his study on 'situatedness', 'It seems fairly clear that the rhetoric of individualism is riding high, along with a relatively unanalysed assertion of the significance of group identities' (2002: 239).

As discussed throughout the book, acts of self-consciousness and self-monitoring cannot be based upon an abstracted individualism through a narrow focus on the rational calculation of action and psychological reductionism. The individual is not something that is given. In social and political arrangements institutions are nonetheless set up and this leads to a process of abstraction in which there is no connection to experience: 'Individuality in a social and moral sense is something to be wrought out. It means initiative, inventiveness, varied resourcefulness, assumption of responsibility in choice of belief and conduct. These are not gifts, but achievements. As achievements, they are not absolute, but relative to the use that is to be made of them. And this varies with the environment' (Dewey 1957: 194).

The analysis of achievements in terms of environmental variation should not be ignored in the quest for a narrowly conceived scientific status. The result is mere appeasement of ideologies that frame worldviews for the benefit of the minority who prosper from current arrangements (Dorling 2014; Sayer 2015): 'the concentration of wealth leads almost reflexively to concentration of political power which in turn translates into legislation, naturally in the interests of those implementing it' (Chomsky 2012: 55). In the face of such pressures, the social scientific quest should be clear to counter such overblown tendencies, and to create the conditions in which social science and civic life can meet in more sustained and systematic ways.

━━ Box 8.3 ━━━━━━━━━━━━━━━━━━━━━━━━━━━━━━

A new model of social class in the university

People are differentially positioned and that informs their identities and capabilities to mobilise resources and act in different circumstances. Recognition of these issues is informing a reinterpretation of traditional issues of class and social inequality in Great Britain. The Great British Class Survey (GBCS) involved completing a 'class calculator' and was an experiment in doing social science research between an academic team, BBC Lab UK and BBC Current Affairs (Devine and Snee 2015). Acknowledging the influence of Bourdieu's ideas, the GBCS

(Continued)

(Continued)

informs a 'new model of social class which shows how measures of economic, cultural and social capital can be combined to provide a powerful way of mapping contemporary class divisions in the UK' (Savage et al. 2013: 220). Rejecting traditional views on class based only on occupational roles and economic labour, the GBCS was designed to take detailed measures of economic, social and cultural capital. This included: measuring the extent of people's social ties, and their connections to people in different occupations; obtaining information on their income, savings and asset values; and assessing household composition, education, social mobility and political attitudes (see Savage et al. 2015).

The result is an analysis of seven classes in modern Britain: elite, established middle class, technical middle class, new affluent workers, traditional working class, emergent service workers and the precariat. The identification of the elite and the precariat are particularly salient. The elite are the most privileged group in the UK with the highest level of every form of capital, with a mean household income of £89,000. The precariat, on the other hand, is the economically poorest class with a household income of £8000, few assets, often located in old industrial areas and with high levels of insecurity. This 'multi-dimensional analysis reveals the polarisation of social inequality … and the fragmentation of traditional sociological middle and working-class divisions into more segmented forms' (Savage et al. 2013: 246). In incorporating a broader range of factors into ideas of class, positioning becomes a key area of understanding to inform social mobility.

This is an illuminating analysis that raises questions concerning the role of social science in society (May 2015). Within universities both the elite and precariat co-exist in an uneasy and often unacknowledged tension. Looking at economic indices alone the Times Higher Education Pay Survey 2015 is informative here. In 2013–14 the average pay for a vice chancellor in the UK was £240,794; for a university professor, £76,395; and for other academic staff, £42,193. At the same time, less than 10% of higher education institutions in the UK are Living Wage employers. Early career researchers struggle to get off short-term contracts, and move from position to position in search of permanency as casualisation becomes a norm (Lopes and Dewan 2014). What does this tell us about the institutions from which we conduct our work and the positions we hold within them? For Guy Standing (2011: 70), the need for action is urgent in universities, which are responsible for maximising the 'throughput' of students and profits, without considering what kind of graduates are being produced and which class they might enter.

For that purpose, a study of positioning is needed which enables an explanation of how people have, or do not have, the resources to act in the conditions that they find themselves (see Box 8.3). This requires first the movement from practical to discursive knowledge through an analysis of components of agency – that is, the ability to account for actions and the capability to act within given conditions. It also requires focusing upon practice-positioned relations. Our earlier discussions have examined how the world is experienced and constituted within particular sets of conditions. The study of positioning moves into a terrain where individuals and groups are located from a relational viewpoint. Methodologically speaking, the emphasis is between perspectival and relational viewpoints through the production of 'mediating concepts' between lay and social scientific knowledge: 'The mediating system we need is that of the *positions* (places, functions, rules, tasks, duties, rights, etc.) occupied (filled, assumed, enacted, etc.) by individuals, and of the *practices* (activities, etc.) in which, by virtue of their occupancy of these positions (and vice versa), they engage' (Bhaskar 1989: 40–1; original emphasis).

Society exists in our actions and those can be both conscious and unconscious. The consequences of our actions are also the conditions that enable or constrain them and they can be unintended: 'people do not marry to reproduce the nuclear family or work to sustain the capitalist economy' (Bhaskar 1998: 35). Yet we often encounter situations we cannot alter, and in drawing upon objective conditions our practices appear 'ill-adapted because they are attuned to an earlier state of the objective conditions' (Bourdieu 1986: 109). This is part of an 'ontological hiatus' that exists between people and society: 'For the properties possessed by social forms may be very different from those possessed by the individuals upon whose activity they depend. Thus one can allow, without paradox or strain, that purposefulness, intentionality and sometimes self-consciousness characterize human actions but not transformations in the social structure' (Bhaskar 1998: 35).

The hiatus is a feature of the world that varying forms of social scientific activity have attempted to ignore or 'solve' at the level of method or through advancement in the effectiveness of such methods. It informs the content and reception of social scientific accounts in the dynamics between the endogenous and referential reflexivity. Bringing to awareness how contexts inform our positioned-practices always concerns an openness to engage in explanation and reinterpretation. We are dealing with openness to revision in the domain of social life and not closure over a hermetically sealed realm constituted through the scientific gaze. Rather than tackling this issue, empiricism collapses the relations between lay and scientific knowledge, whilst those clinging to more positivist-inspired approaches easily lapse into scientism.

Positioning oneself

The capacity to act is linked to being accepted according to cultural definitions and those, in turn, relate to the attributes that are valued within given fields. To the capacity to belong and how one is positioned must also be added the power to position oneself. A person might, for example, be able to exercise sufficient power via their mobilisation of resources without relying upon cultural expectations within a given social setting. Symbolic acceptance may not then follow and so material power is circumscribed in particular ways. To this extent, symbolic capital refers to sedimentations of power within a field of relations, accumulated by past struggles, that grants recognition of a position and also a capacity to intervene in circumstances when that is threatened (Bourdieu 2000). To analyse this movement requires a consideration of 'how the habitus is transformed from pre-discursive doxa into reflexive, discursive consciousness' (Burkitt 1997: 194). This is why, as we emphasised above, we provided an account of the self that focuses on dialectical relations, rather than collapsing the subject into the social self and from there to social determinants. In this way we can see how social scientific knowledge relates to the realm of practical action.

The capability of an individual to position themselves will relate to how they are accommodated and that, as we have said, relates to issues of recognition which themselves are informed by issues of race, class, gender and sexuality. Here we find a continuum from active embrace and implicit accommodation through to estrangement, hostility and violence. If positioned as dependent a 'cry of pain is hearable as a plea of help'. On the other hand if positioned as dominant 'a similar cry can be heard as a protest or even as a reprimand' (Harré and van Langenhove 1991: 396). To this extent, positions delimit John Austin's idea of speech acts and provide for pre-interpretations of what people say or do (Harré and Slocum 2003). We thus need to understand the attributes of persons and groups within given constellations of social relations or, in Pierre Bourdieu's terminology, 'fields': 'If we only focus our theoretical gaze on abstractions from the bourgeois model of the singular self we will never be able to imagine or understand how value is produced and lived beyond the dominant symbolic and will repeatedly misrecognise, wilfully ignore and de-grade other forms of value practices, person-value and personhood, by default performatively relegating them to the void of the valueless' (Skeggs 2011: 509).

Positioning in fields concerns the distribution of types of capital that are mobilised in the struggles that take place within them. There are those whose actions contribute to conservation (orthodoxy) and those who engage in strategies of heresy. The symbolic forms that place value upon the points of view and the attributes of persons work in an objective sense. They refer to particular objects, but also place evaluative meanings upon those objects, characteristics and attributes from which individuals draw in order to make sense of their environments. As noted, the 'who' 'what' and 'how' can lie within a congruity of meaning or, as Bourdieu puts it, ontological complicity. There is not only the power to confer meaning upon objects, attributes and characteristics (symbolic capital), there are also the skills and knowledges that people possess within a particular field (cultural) and their differential access to wealth and material resources (economic capital).

Individuals experience existential concern in the dialectic between sameness and selfhood, either through their attempts to change those conditions which may persist despite such actions, or by having change imposed in such a way that states of flux and uncertainty result. The process of organisational change is one example whereby previous attributes that were valued may no longer be held in the same esteem. Relations of power are then altered by 'technicians of transformation' (May 1999b, 2006) who are positioned accordingly, with the result that individuals no longer feel valued, but evaluated. To study relations of power requires that the resources that are mobilised within a field are explained in relation to an understanding of the realisation or frustration of actions (see Box 8.4).

If we regard actions as either solely related to a social system, or derived from individual preferences, we remove the connections to struggles in the world through a choice between subjectivism and objectivism. Technicist manoeuvres in social science cut off reflexivity as a property of the world and the ways in which we grasp the relations between past–present and potential futures and how social scientific accounts are part of meaning construction. Self-consciousness is formed in the practical dealings with the world in the relations between the subjective and objective and that creates a confusing excess as a space for referential reflexivity. Mapping the territory in terms of the relations of power that constitute a field enables one to see those spaces and how critical distanciation may be achieved. It is within the examination of not only who and what, but also how and why. Positioning deals with an analysis of knowledge in action in which we act upon a present, with a view of the past and orientation towards the future. The concern is with a relationalism that does not collapse into celebrations of situated subjectivity or over-determination.

■ Box 8.4 ■

Full steam ahead! All change! Full steam ahead!

The pace of change in higher education is extreme. There is a 'litany' of changes in the field of higher education linked to markets and economic pressures, technology, societal expectations, public accountability, demographic change and global forces beyond the control of any one sector (Kezar and Eckel 2002). Yet change strategies have not been particularly helpful in guiding institutions. This is partly because higher education is a distinctive sector, characterised by 'academic tribes' (Becher and Trowler 2001); it is variable in its structure and there are strong disciplinary and cultural norms which may result in 'goal ambiguity' between different members of the organisation. Hence it is argued that transformational change must alter the culture of the institution, and be pervasive, intentional and systematic over time (Kezar and Eckel 2001).

Organisational change is potentially threatening to individuals' narrative identities. Managed badly it can interrupt the reflexive task of maintaining selfhood, whilst equally disrupting professional and personal selves. As our own experiences in Chapter 7 highlight, if context dominates over the content and consequences of social scientific work, reflexivity is subdued. When changes are implemented poorly, dislocation and disruption occur between character, context and commitment, leaving no place of safety from which to engage in reflexive social scientific practice. Managing organisational change in higher education thus also requires reflexivity. Moldaschl et al. (2015) focus on the role of reflexivity in institutional and personal capabilities for innovation. Through concentrating on the co-evolution of epistemic styles they consider how reflexivity can help people and institutions to participate in change processes more effectively: 'a deepening engagement with

(Continued)

(Continued)

reflexivity opens up new perspectives on the complex character of organisational reality. It calls for reimagining usual ideas of innovation and learning, including the questioning of principles of "old modernity" and its model of Weberian purposive rationality' (Moldsachl et al. 2015: 138).

Others focus on the inappropriateness of top-down models of change management within higher education as they fail to take the relational and inter-referential dimensions of reflexivity seriously. Tsoukas and Chia's (2002) work on organisational becoming focuses on micro-practices which lead to change, and similarly an 'ethnoventionist' approach is recommended by Marrewijk et al. (2010). In all cases, it is apparent that reflexivity is a precondition for individuals managing and experiencing change, requiring mediation between individual and collective identities, values and goals, institutional cultures, and potential and actual effects for different groups. The values and consequences of such changes, however, are another matter.

WHY AND HOW MIGHT I PRACTISE?

In analysing relations of power Michel Foucault wrote of the need to examine specific rationalities, as opposed to invoking an over-arching idea of rationalisation. He took this to be a more empirical approach that is attuned to contemporary society: 'Rather than analyzing power relations from the point of view of its internal rationality, it consists of analyzing power relations through the antagonism of strategies' (Foucault 1982b: 210–11). When doxic appearance is ruptured in these antagonisms, the question of whether any resulting resistance is transformative is raised. This latter point tempers the limitations of Foucault's approach for it becomes necessary to move into the terrain of explanation in terms of bringing attention to the conditions under which actions are performed, as well as the limitations that are placed upon forms of power. How this relates to structured antagonisms is a focus of empirical interest and reflexive concern: here are the spaces between practice-in-the-world and the meeting of social scientific knowledge that brings to attention the conditions of actions, resources and potentials.

The transformative potential of social science

In terms of the possibility for social transformation and meeting between forms of knowledge, several factors stand between reading, recognition, illumination and transformation. First, as noted in the previous chapter, there is the power to ignore or dismiss research findings: 'scientific discourse misses the fact that the ability to deny is an amazing human phenomenon, largely unexplained and often inexplicable, a product of the sheer complexity of our emotional, linguistic, moral and intellectual lives' (Cohen 2001: 50). Second, power can work through a process of mis-recognition whereby privilege is ascribed rather than achieved (Bourdieu 1992). In reverse this works for the non-powerful, namely systems of classification position people in particular ways through a dialectic that exists between the classified and classification systems (Hacking 2004): 'Discerning how positioning, movement and exclusion are generated through these systems of inscription, exchange and value is central to understanding how differences (and inequalities) are produced, lived and read' (Skeggs 2004: 4). Third, if we deploy reflexivity to inform engagement, we should not overstretch it, nor reduce it to the exceptionality of character separate from culture via a romantic ideal as we found in the works of Weber. How might a form of analysis then proceed that seeks to examine the forms and limits of power relations in order to unleash the potential for transformation?

Roberto Unger makes a helpful distinction between the logics of routinisation and transgression. He characterises these as 'trance' and 'struggle' respectively (1987: 205). Here, we can take on board issues associated with the subject, including conscious, habitual and unconscious action, as well as unintended consequences. To employ this distinction enables an empirical examination of a 'fit' with objective conditions (Bourdieu), the spaces of agonism between that exist between freedom and power (Foucault), and the dialectical tensions between sameness and selfhood (Ricoeur). Bearing in mind the points made in relation to oscillations and ambivalences within the self, as well as among social scientists in terms of the apparent promises and disappointments of their disciplines, we often act according to two different logics: 'We behave as if we were the passive objects of the formative institutional and imaginative contexts of our societies and the victims or beneficiaries of the tendencies and constraints that shape these frameworks of social life ... however, we sometimes think and act as if our pious devotion to the practical or argumentative routines imposed by these structures has been just a ploy, to be continued until the propitious occasion for more open defiance' (Unger 1987: 202).

An understanding of unstable relations existing between the logics of routinisation and transgression is important here. In exploring transgressions, so too must research communities be open to innovation by turning those tools of investigation back onto themselves: 'The logic of context breaking persists as an inconvenient residue in even the most routinized social situations' (Unger 1987: 203). Paying attention to this aspect enables us to face the weaknesses resulting from the one-sidedness of so many calls to greater reflexivity: 'The Cartesian claim to a "view from nowhere" is to be avoided not just by invocation of the excluded other, nor even by the location of subjects within the realm of concrete experience and social relations, but by the recognition of tension that opens up the possibility of critique and change' (Calhoun 1995: 187). Here we find a project taking place without allusion to simple certainties or celebrations of fragmentation, and the tensions inherent in social life between who we are, how we and others see ourselves, and the formation and consequences of our practice-positioned relations.

An analysis of acts of refusal and resistance is related to the above points in terms of the capability to be effective in such aspirations; all of which permits a study of limits of appropriation of dominant viewpoints in order to expose false necessities. Logics of routinisation are frequently invoked in the service of tidy descriptions of social relations, and in justifying the social organisation of inequalities as 'natural' states of affairs. They may also divert attention, as they have over the course of history, towards particular groups in order to secure the consent of populations. What has been noted as a peculiarity of current times is the extent to which ideas of fairness, democracy and equality are 'invoked *to justify* the channelling of public hostilities towards vulnerable or disadvantaged groups' (Tyler 2013: 212; original emphasis). Equally, we can find ourselves in a state of inoculation born of an instrumental rationalisation saturating our lives and so leading to an emotional appeal to a simple world that negates its effects: 'As an ideological ploy, the trick works best when the image is on some level, profoundly appealing. One is first drawn into the vision of the alternative world, experience a kind of vicarious thrill imagining it – only to ultimately recoil in horror at the implications of one's own desires' (Graeber 2015: 181). Such is the pervasiveness of these forces that they have been characterised as appearing in terms of their opposite: non-ideology (Žižek 2009).

Transgressions are the uncomfortable residues that must be subsumed under generalised accounts. To collapse routinisation and transgression, as well as degrees of willingness into objective locations, is to commit the fallacy of the capitulated self. Presuppositions of homogeneity within cultural traditions, invoking ideas of multi-faceted selves with no point of view, or the totalising capacity of power, are three routes towards this end. A lapse into a celebration of everyday practices to the exclusion of the ways in which such practices are themselves constrained, as well as enabled, by the conditions in which they are enacted, is not a way forward. What is being suggested is that the study of ideas of the self and positioning enables an understanding not only of endogenous reflexivity, but also of the spaces for the potential of referential reflexivity. By producing social scientific accounts sensitive to the issues associated with personal and social identity, alongside explanations of the conditions that given rise to positioning, the potential for transformations in social practices is opened up. The task is to assist research in illuminating those areas of struggle that inhere in everyday circumstances via a fusion of the critical and pragmatic stances (Bénatouïl 1999; Boltanski 2011).

The relationship between the empirical, actual and real is brought forth in terms of the possibilities for transformation given through an explanation of the relations between actions, aspirations, dispositions, and the conditions through which they are enacted. A process of recognition does not imply that self-consciousness of the relations between actions and social conditions is a given; it is a task that seeks to illuminate how our conceptions of the world are themselves social and historical products and so amenable to transformation. In acts of interpretation, issues are then disclosed in such a way that they are recognised. We may then enter into a process of social becoming in which actualities and potentialities are linked across time (Sztompka 1991).

The critical and hermeneutic can be brought together in order that the abstractions often associated with the former become rooted in the idea of tradition that is associated with the latter, whilst also correcting for a tendency to resort to tradition to locate meaning. What operates at this level lies between reflections upon tradition and the anticipation of freedom. It plays upon the strengths of both ideology critique and hermeneutics (Ricoeur 1982). Social becoming sees our acts of retrospection informing present action and thus viewing the potential for difference as a projection into the future. Retrospection acts as a check upon simple allusions to transcendence, whilst at the same time revealing misunderstanding and the potential for greater understanding in the future as a check upon the operation of the status quo.

The issue is reformulated in terms of the 'inner life of hermeneutics' as a dialectic 'between the experience of belonging and alienating distanciation' (Ricoeur 1981: 90). In the process the deception that lies in 'the alleged antinomy between an ontology of prior understanding and an eschatology of freedom is revealed' (1981: 100). Within these reflexive spaces the social sciences work at their best, often unrecognised and requiring the practical efforts of listening, translating and imagining to inform understandings of what we have been, are and may become. In this way, we can agree with Foucault when he wrote, 'in saying that we are much more recent than we believe is not a way of placing all the burden of our history on our shoulders. Rather, it puts within the range of work which we can do to and for ourselves the greatest possible part of what is presented to us an inaccessible' (Foucault 1982a: 35).

The 'subject' 'is not a name for the gap of freedom and contingency that infringes upon the positive ontological order, active in its interstices; rather, "subject" is the contingency that grounds the very positive ontological order, that is, the "vanishing mediator" whose self-effacing gesture transforms the pre-ontological chaotic multitude into the semblance of a positive "objective" order of reality' (Žižek 2008a: 185). Taking us back to Kant's observations, the idea that there is an epistemological limitation to our grasping 'total' reality is now the condition for reality itself (Žižek 2008b). This is not an escape from social conditions or from the role of emotion and embodiment, but a space in which theory–research–practice deliberations generate understandings. An emphasis upon an analysis of relations within the social world and how they bear upon knowledge and action is not an impediment to scientific validity, but informs the ways in which the social world is known. Through the deployment of 'relationalism' we can see how all knowledge is at least partially true: 'It may be genuine or sincere, cynical or manipulative, but it is an authentic expression of the interests, experiences, concerns and circumstances of those in a particular social location' (Scott 1998: 111).

In terms of those social locations, we introduced practice-positioned relations. Where one is positioned has consequences. These positions are not, however, fully determining. As such, we can open up a space in which to reflect on alternative ends and thus the means for their achievement. So we are dealing with the relations between ontology of what exists and an ethic of development. A person's ability and insight are connected to their being able to bring into being their aspirations, or even an alignment of their dispositions with positions within reflexive spaces. Here we encounter the issues of how positions display a tendency to reproduce particular individual and group 'trajectories' that inform and even constrain but do not determine our lives, thus leaving open potential.

Active intermediation

A reflexive practice guards against those who conflate the model of reality with the reality of the model. It also tempers those who take acts of clarification in the endogenous realm of social scientific practice and over-extend them to saturate the domain of resolution in the referential realm. When objectivism is confused with objectivity we can be sure this is happening. The latter has a reflexive recognition of limits and a willingness to learn; the former is born of a disposition that knows no bounds and is reluctant to submit itself to an interrogation of its presuppositions and consequences. When researchers position themselves as experts with ready-made solutions to problems, or when dialogue aimed at understanding is absent, or when those who criticise practices that have institutionally enabled them to take place claim privilege of insight, engagement is being eradicated in praise of partial understanding. What is assumed is that 'being' may be reduced to 'knowing'. The same mistake is repeated in reflective philosophies. Here is the assumption: 'that the thinking subject can absorb into its thinking or appropriate without remainder the object of its thought, that our being can be brought down to our knowledge' (Merleau-Ponty 1989[1962]: 62).

Social scientific research is the systematisation of an understanding of the relations between subject, self and environment in the interactions between endogenous and referential reflexivity. We are situated within socio-cultural milieus and we exhibit varying abilities to submit those to analysis. Social scientific approaches can describe the dynamics that inhere in everyday life and become celebrations of our daily achievements. Yet reflecting back the means of such achievement in social scientific accounts is important. Despite the emphases upon the 'exceptional' and 'entrepreneurial' to which all must apparently aspire, we must be careful in how we draw attention to the mundane and extraordinary ways in which people sustain their lives in difficult circumstances. It is the relation between those circumstances, the resources mobilised and the consequences for our actions and understandings, that comprises the exterior-systemic lenses of social science, but this should not bypass the reflexive gaze due to their apparent detachment from mundane reality.

In the idea of 'habitus' we found a link between these in terms of history as a 'socialised subjectivity'. Embodied in human beings, we find ways of talking, walking and making sense of one's environment. That is a disposition which guides and informs reasons for practices that exhibit tendencies which do not determine those actions. Parallels are apparent with Karl Mannheim's ideas and here we can also draw from the Frankfurt School's and Pierre Bourdieu's important emphases upon the social conditions of knowledge production: 'The rise of the bourgeoisie was attended by an extreme intellectualism. Intellectualism, as it is used in this connection, refers to a mode of thought which either does not see elements in life and in thought which are based on will, interest, emotion, and *Weltanschauung* – or, if it does recognise their existence, treats them as though they were equivalent to the intellect and believes that they may be mastered by and subordinated to reason' (Mannheim 1960[1936]: 108; original emphasis).

What was demanded in these approaches was a 'scientific politics', but one existing alongside state-sponsored free competition and a class struggle that creates a new 'irrational sphere' which is exacerbated by the inability of intellectualism 'to tolerate emotionally determined and evaluative thinking' (Mannheim 1960: 109). Mannheim's aim remains to this day: 'to develop a theory, appropriate to the contemporary situation, concerning the significance of the *non-theoretical conditioning factors* in knowledge ... Only in this way can we hope to overcome the vague, ill-considered, and sterile form of relativism with regard to scientific knowledge' (Mannheim 1970: 109).

Our suggestion is that we draw upon recognition of being situated in a way that gives rise to certain values, and create *mediated spheres* that provide the grounds for understanding of actions in a dynamic between existence and social scientific accounts. The emphasis rests on a co-operative process of generating intelligibility (Shotter 1993). The critical task for social scientists becomes that of boundary-spanning and sense-making between different realms: between science and society, justification and application, epistemic communities and communities of practice, endogenous and referential reflexivity, and belonging and positioning. It also means working in and across different contexts. Our practices have sought to create different opportunities for 'safer spaces' and inter-referential reflexivity (see Chapter 7).

Inspired by debates concerning the contextualisation of science and society and co-production in research, different spaces for reflexive social science are being imagined. In complex social and political settings, reflexivity is needed to 'manage disorderly thinking ... needing new boundary spaces as mediating institutions between different social worlds' (Durose and Richardson 2016: 45). Increasingly there is demand for the development of the 'agora' as a social space in which science is debated and discussed, consisting of 'a highly articulate, well-educated population, the product of enlightened educational systems ... who face multiple publics and plural institutions' (Nowotony et al. 2001: 204–5). In this we also see echoes of Habermas's idea of a public sphere in terms of the deliberative ideal. Gadamer also adds to these ideas, with his notion of 'mediality'. For Gadamer, we are all caught up in the play of forging social relations and making history, neither in full control nor passively swept along. Play is contested and the goal is to keep playing.

Mediation is an active task. Active intermediation is not a solution or reflexive model to be implemented, but a set of practices in the interstitial spaces between research and practice. As such, it represents the active and constant 'agonism' (Mouffe 2005) of engaged social scientific research: there is no state of resolution, rather a set of practices that inform the possibility of producing excellent-relevant knowledge. Active intermediation means working at the boundaries which inform the conduct, context and consequences of social scientific research and shape its transformative potential.

FINAL WORDS

Reflexivity is a condition of good social scientific work which inheres in social life. It can also be experienced as a burden. It is a burden because there are limits to the idea that we can be continually reflexive in our practice and it can easily become non-relational and subject to individualism. Whilst we are expected to monitor our actions at the same time as performing them, the contexts in which our actions take place are removed from the same conditions and wrench us from our social settings in any evaluation of our actions. We have noted that reflexivity has its limits when actions, reasons and events can only be illuminated retrospectively. There have been all sort of attempts to overcome these issues through invoking particular approaches that are based upon an understanding of the subject, the role of language, the relations between knowledge and action, the imagination, and the role of art and literature. As it is in social life itself, so it is in scientific practices.

In this final chapter we have raised a set of issues that are important for a reflexive understanding of the social sciences in society. The production of social scientific findings meets conditions of reception and what we are seeing are shifting boundaries between production and reception. As opposed to viewing this as a topic, we find an over-drawing of the demarcation between expert and lay knowledge with the paradoxical result that the production–transmission–reception dimensions to scientific practices are relatively neglected. Public and policy perceptions need to be addressed if the transformative potential of knowledge is to be released. What is at stake is the opportunity to make good the promise of knowledge-based change with widespread benefits for all, and overcome the dichotomous tensions between excellence and relevance, competition and collaboration, élite advantage and social cohesion that perpetuate contemporary discourses. In placing greater value upon a broader understanding of the contribution of a range of knowledges to socio-economic-political and cultural development, the possibility can emerge for a real 'agora' to be forged. This poses a real challenge, yet has much to offer in the way of improved understandings that go far beyond the simplistic, hypodermic 'solutions' offered by knowledge consultancies and academics peddling their models in the marketplace of ideas.

The question is not only whether the social sciences can rise to such a challenge, but how, under what conditions, utilising what means, and at what cost? There are those who have argued for a re-education of both society and the university itself as to its values via a form of 'pragmatic action research' linking an understanding of needs with the environment in which researchers operate (Greenwood and Levin 2016). Echoes are found here with a call for a 'pragmatic social science' and paying attention to the conditions that enable its production (Stehr 1992; Boltanski 2011). This requires active work: 'We live between the positive and the normative, on the slippery slope of lack, able to climb up it, and indeed to extend it upwards by constructing new forms of flourishing and protection, but we are unable to resist sliding down except by continually climbing back up and defending and seeking to improve our situation' (Sayer 2011: 140).

We cannot overburden reflexivity as an idea that does not require a commitment to engagement with all the practical difficulties that follow. Nor should it be deployed as yet another sword against which to slash at the inadequacy of ambitions that over-extend the boundaries in which work takes place. There is much pleasure to be gained and needs to be met through the very absence of reflexivity and positive feelings of belonging from suspending a consideration of its place. However, when such expressions are constituted through the exclusion of the 'other' we easily see our struggles for recognition spilling over into a demand enacted through exclusion and attribution, with unpleasant and disastrous consequences. There are more mundane and exclusionary mechanisms that are not so spectacular in gaining the public eye, such as the relations between the informal and formal in organisational life, sports clubs and social gatherings. To bring attention to the process that constitutes such exclusions risks being ostracised or met with denial. When these are placed in question and their consequences brought to attention by social scientific explanations, contestation is inevitable.

Criticisms of conditions that inform actions seem like exercises of bad faith by those who have enjoyed their advantages. We can go further and say that it is the positioning enabled by those very conditions, now part of a pre-reflexive acceptance, that permits distance from their effects on others in the first instance. Distanciation is achieved by a set of pre-reflexive conditions that are, for many, the subject of necessity in managing their day-to-day existences. In this sense social science will resonate with the experiences of everyday life but cannot, in general, expect to reflect it in its multi-faceted dimensions. A critical, reflexive social science brings to awareness the effect of conditions on action to provide a vantage point from which to consider the retrospective–prospective link. Without some connection to social life, calls to reflexivity and the potential for transformation are devoid of substance. However, there is no necessary relationship between this illumination and transformation. In considering spaces of dialogue in which research findings and their potential implications for action are considered, there is a fundamental feature of the social world that we encounter in our actions and forms of analysis: the interplay between the processual and structural. Here the endogenous dimension of reflexivity may be seen to inform the referential dimension through a movement from practical to discursive reasoning. This encompasses a movement from reflexivity within actions towards reflexivity upon actions.

The accounts produced in this fusion do not bring forth automatic emancipation. Change is a collective rather than a single act. There may be liberation from self-misunderstanding, but there is a need to combine the politics of personal relations with those of the institutions and systems that rule over us. We may then move from the trance of those forces that exist over and through us, to a place of struggle and ultimately judgement and determination of those forces for the future. We do not move towards absolute truth, but we do move towards better ways of coming to understand ourselves through our relations with others and the social contexts we inhabit.

BIBLIOGRAPHY

Ackoff, R.L. (1979) The future of operational research is past, *Journal of the Operational Research Society*, 30(2): 93–104.

Adkins, L. (2004) Reflexivity: freedom or habit of gender?, in L. Adkins and B. Skeggs (eds), *Feminism After Bourdieu*. Oxford: Blackwell.

Adkins, L. and Lury, C. (eds) (2012) *Measure and Value*. Oxford: Wiley-Blackwell.

Adkins, L. and Skeggs, B. (eds) (2004) *Feminism After Bourdieu*. Oxford: Blackwell.

Adorno, T. (2013) *Aesthetic Theory*. Edited by G. Adorno and R. Tiedemann (eds), translated by H. Hullot-Kentor. London: Bloomsbury.

Adorno, T., Frankel-Brunswik, E., Levinson, D. and Sanford, R. (1950) *The Authoritarian Personality*. New York: Harper Row.

Adorno, T. and Horkheimer, M. (1979[1944]) *Dialectic of Enlightenment*. Translated by J. Cumming. London: Verso.

Afary, J. and Anderson, K.B. (2005) *Foucault and the Iranian Revolution: Gender and the Seductions of Islamism*. Chicago: University of Chicago Press.

Agamben, G. (2007) *Infancy and History: On the Destruction of Experience*. Translated by L. Heron. London: Verso.

Alanen, L. and Witt, C. (eds) (2004) *Feminist Reflections on the History of Philosophy*. Dordrecht/Boston: Kluwer Academic.

Amorós, C. (1994) Cartesianism and feminism: what reason has forgotten: reasons for forgetting, *Hypatia*, 9(1): 147–63.

Andersen, J. (2011) Situating Axel Honneth in the Frankfurt School tradition, in D. Petherbridge (ed.), *Axel Honneth: Critical Essays*. Boston, MA: Brill.

Anderson, H.T. and Atkinson, R. (eds) (2013) *Production and Use of Urban Knowledge: European Experiences*. Dordrecht/London: Springer.

Anderson, J. (2000) The third generation of the Frankfurt School, *Intellectual History Newsletter*, 22: 49–61.

Anderson, R. (1998) Intuitive inquiry: a transpersonal approach, in W. Braud and R. Anderson (eds), *Transpersonal Research Methods for the Social Sciences: Honoring Human Experience*. Thousand Oaks, CA: Sage.

Apel, K.O. (1995[1967]) *Charles S. Peirce: From Pragmatism to Pragmaticism*. Atlantic Highlands, NJ: Humanities Press.

Appelbaum, D. (ed.) (1995) *The Vision of Kant*. Shaftesbury: Element.

Archer, M.S. (2007) *Making Our Way Through the World: Human Reflexivity and Social Mobility*. Cambridge: Cambridge University Press.

Archer, M.S. (2012) *The Reflexive Imperative in Late Modernity.* Cambridge: Cambridge University Press.

Arendt, H. (1998[1958]) *The Human Condition* (2nd edn). Introduction by M. Canovan. Chicago: University of Chicago Press.

Aronowitz, S. (1992) The tensions of Critical Theory: is negative dialectics all there is?, in S. Seidman and D. Wagner (eds), *Postmodernism and Social Theory.* Oxford: Blackwell.

Arvidsson, A. (2012) General sentiment: how value and affect converge in the information economy, in L. Adkins and C. Lury (eds), *Measure and Value.* Oxford: Wiley-Blackwell.

Asante, M.K. (2004) An African origin of philosophy: myth or reality? City Press, July. Available at www.asante.net/articles/26/afrocentricity/

Ashmore, M. (1989) *The Reflexive Thesis: Writing the Sociology of Scientific Knowledge.* Chicago: University of Chicago Press.

Atherton, M. (1994) *Women Philosophers of the Early Modern Period.* Indianapolis, IN: Hackett.

Austin, J. (1976) *How to Do Things with Words.* Oxford: Oxford University Press.

Bain, A.L. and Payne, W.J. (2016) Queer de-participation: reframing the co-production of scholarly knowledge. *Qualitative Research,* 16(3): 330–40.

Baker, G. and May, T. (2002) Auditing as the eternal present: the depoliticising implications of organizational transformation in British higher education, *European Political Science,* 1(3): 12–22.

Banana, E., Chikoti, P., Harawa,C,.Mcgranahan, G., Mitlin, D., Stephen, S., Schermbrucker, N., Shumba, F. and Walnycki, A. (2015) Sharing reflections on inclusive sanitation, *Environment and Urbanisation,* 27(1): 19–34.

Barnes, B. (1974) *Scientific Knowledge and Sociological Theory.* London: Routledge & Kegan Paul.

Barnett, C. (2009) Towards a methodology of postmodern assemblage: adolescent identity in the age of social networking, *Philosophical Studies in Education,* 40: 200–10.

Bauman, Z. (1976) *Towards a Critical Sociology: An Essay on Commonsense and Emancipation.* London: Routledge & Kegan Paul.

Bauman, Z. (1978) *Hermeneutics and Social Science: Approaches to Understanding.* London: Hutchinson.

Bauman, Z. (1989) *Legislators and Interpreters: On Modernity, Post-Modernity and Intellectuals.* Cambridge: Polity.

Bauman, Z. (1991) *Modernity and Ambivalence.* Cambridge: Polity.

Bauman, Z. (1992) *Intimations of Postmodernity.* London: Routledge.

Bauman, Z. (1997) *Postmodernity and its Discontents.* Cambridge: Polity.

Bauman, Z. (2001) *The Individualized Society.* Cambridge: Polity.

Bauman, Z. (2007) Sociology, nostalgia, utopia and mortality: a conversation with Zygmunt Bauman. Interview by M.H. Jacobsen and K. Tester, *European Journal of Social Theory,* 10(2): 305–25.

Bauman, Z. (2014) *What Use Is Sociology? Conversations with Michael Hviid Jacobsen and Keith Tester.* Cambridge: Polity.

Becher, T. and Trowler, P.R. (1989) *Academic Tribes and Territories: Intellectual Enquiry and the Culture of Disciplines*. Buckingham: Society for Research into Higher Education and the Open University Press.

Beck, U. (1992) *Risk Society: Towards a New Modernity*. London: Sage.

Beck, U. (2006) Living in the world risk society, *Economy and Society*, 35(3): 329–45.

Beck, U. and Beck-Gernsheim, E. (2002) *Individualization: Institutionalized Individualism and its Social and Political Consequences*. London: Sage.

Beck, U. and Beck-Gernsheim, E. (2009) Losing the traditional: individualization and precarious freedoms, in A. Elliott and P. du Gay (eds), *Identity In Question*. London: Sage.

Beck, U., Giddens, A. and Lash, S. (1994) *Reflexive Modernization: Politics, Tradition and Aesthetics in the Modern Social Order*. Cambridge: Polity.

Bénatouïl, T. (1999) A tale of two sociologies: the critical and the pragmatic stance in contemporary French sociology, *European Journal of Social Theory*, 2(3): 381–98.

Bendix, R. (1977) *Max Weber: An Intellectual Portrait*. Berkeley, CA: University of California Press.

Benhabib, S. (1986) *Critique, Norm and Utopia: A Study of the Foundations of Critical Theory*. New York: Columbia University Press.

Benhabib, S. (1992) *Situating the Self: Gender, Community and Postmodernism in Contemporary Ethics*. Cambridge: Polity.

Benhabib, S. (2006) *Another Cosmopolitanism: Hospitality, Sovereignty and Democratic Iterations*. Oxford: Oxford University Press.

Benhabib, S., Butler, J., Cornell, D. and Fraser, N. (1995). *Feminist Contentions: A Philosophical Exchange*. London: Routledge.

Bentham, J. (2007) *An Introduction to the Principles of Morals and Legislation*. Originally published in 1780. New York: Dover Publications.

Berger, P.L. and Luckmann, T. (1967) *The Social Construction of Reality: A Treatise in the Sociology of Knowledge*. New York: Anchor.

Bernstein, J.M. (1995) *Recovering Ethical Life: Jürgen Habermas and the Future of Critical Theory*. London: Routledge.

Bernstein, R. (1992) *The New Constellation: The Ethical-Political Horizons of Modernity/ Postmodernity*. Cambridge, MA: MIT Press.

Beynon, H. and Nichols, T. (eds) *Patterns of Work in the Post-Fordist Era: Volume 2*. Cheltenham: Edward Elgar.

Bhaskar, R. (1975). *A Realist Theory of Science*. Leeds: Leeds Books.

Bhaskar, R. (1986) *Scientific Realism and Human Emancipation*. London: Verso.

Bhaskar, R. (1989) *Reclaiming Reality: A Critical Introduction to Contemporary Philosophy*. London: Verso.

Bhaskar, R. (1998) *The Possibility of Naturalism: A Philosophical Critique of the Contemporary Human Sciences* (3rd edn). London: Routledge.

Billig, M. (2001) Humour and hatred: the racist jokes of the Ku Klux Klan, *Discourse and Society*, 12(3): 267–89.

Binkley, S. and Capetillo, J. (2009) *A Foucault for the 21st Century: Governmentality, Biopolitics and Discipline on the New Millennium.* Newcastle: Cambridge Scholars.

Bloor, D. (2011) *The Enigma of the Aerofoil: Rival Theories in Aerodynamics, 1909–1930.* Chicago: University of Chicago Press.

Boltanski, L. (2011) *On Critique: A Sociology of Emancipation.* Translated by G. Elliott. Cambridge: Polity.

Bonneuil, C., Joly, P.B. and Marris, C. (2008) Disentrenching experiment? The construction of GM-crop field trials as a social problem, *Science, Technology and Human Values*, 33(2): 201–29.

Botha, A.P. (2008) *Knowledge: Living and Working with It.* Johannesburg: Juta.

Bottomore, T. and Nisbet, R. (eds) (1979) *A History of Sociological Analysis.* London: Heinemann.

Bourdieu, P. (1986) *Distinction: A Social Critique of the Judgement of Taste.* Translated by R. Nice. London: Routledge.

Bourdieu, P. (1990) *In Other Words: Essays Towards a Reflexive Sociology.* Translated by M. Adamson. Cambridge: Polity.

Bourdieu, P. (1992) *Language and Symbolic Power.* Edited and introduced by J. Thompson, translated by G. Raymond and M. Adamson. Cambridge: Polity.

Bourdieu, P. (1993) *Sociology in Question.* Translated by R. Nice. London: Sage.

Bourdieu, P. (1998) *Practical Reason: On the Theory of Action.* Cambridge: Polity.

Bourdieu, P. (1999) The social conditions of the international circulation of ideas, in R. Shusterman (ed.), *Bourdieu: A Critical Reader.* Oxford: Blackwell.

Bourdieu, P. (2000) *Pascalian Meditations.* Translated by R. Nice. Cambridge: Polity.

Bourdieu, P. (2004) *Science of Science and Reflexivity.* Translated by R. Nice. Cambridge: Polity.

Bourdieu, P. (2007) *Sketch for a Self Analysis.* Translated by R. Nice. (Originally published in 2004 as *Esquisse pour une auto-analyse.*) Cambridge: Polity.

Bourdieu, P. (2008) *Political Interventions: Social Science and Political Action.* Texts selected and introduced by F. Poupeau and T. Discepolo, translated by D. Fernbach. London: Verso.

Bourdieu, P. (2010) *Sociology is a Martial Art: Political Writings by Pierre Bourdieu.* Edited by G. Sapiro, translated by P.P. Ferguson, R. Nice and L. Wacquant. New York: The New Press.

Bourdieu, P. and Wacquant, L.J. (1992) *An Invitation to Reflexive Sociology.* Cambridge: Polity.

Boyle, D. and Harris, M. (2009) The challenge of co-production: how equal partnership between professionals and the public are crucial to improving public services. London: NESTA.

Braidotti, R. (2013) *The Posthuman.* Cambridge: Polity Press.

Branaman. A. (ed.) (2000) *Self and Society.* London: Blackwell.

Braud, W. and Anderson, R. (eds) (1998) *Transpersonal Research Methods for the Social Sciences: Honoring Human Experience.* Thousand Oaks, CA: Sage.

Breazeale, D. and Rockmore, T. (eds) (1994) *Fichte: Historical Contexts/Contemporary Controversies*. Atlantic Highlands, NJ: Humanities Press.

Brenner, N. (2004) *New State Spaces: Urban Governance and the Rescaling of Statehood*. Oxford: Oxford University Press.

Brenner, N. (2012) What is critical urban theory?, in N. Brenner, P. Marcuse and M. Mayer (eds), *Cities for People Not for Profit: Critical Urban Theory and the Right to the City*. London: Routledge.

Brenner, N., Marcuse, P. and Mayer, M. (eds) (2012) *Cities for People Not for Profit: Critical Urban Theory and the Right to the City*. London: Routledge.

Brock, K. and McGee, R. (eds) (2002) *Knowing Poverty: Critical Reflections on Participatory Research and Policy*. London: Earthscan.

Bronner, S. (1994) *Of Critical Theory and Its Theorists*. Oxford: Blackwell.

Brown, J.S. and Duguid, P. (2001) Knowledge and organization: a social-practice perspective, *Organization Science*, 12: 198–213.

Brunkhorst, H. (1992) Culture and bourgeois society: the unity of reason in a divided society, in A. Honneth, M. McCarthy, C. Offe and A. Wellmer (eds), *Cultural-Political Interventions in the Unfinished Project of Enlightenment*. Cambridge, MA: MIT Press.

Bryant, A. and Charmaz, K. (eds) *The SAGE Handbook of Grounded Theory*. London: Sage.

Bryman, A. (1998) Quantitative and qualitative research strategies in knowing the social world, in T. May and M. Williams (eds), *Knowing the Social World*. Buckingham: Open University Press.

Bryson J., Daniels P., Henry N. and Pollard J. (ed.) (2000) *Knowledge, Space, Economy*. London: Routledge.

Bulkeley, H. and Betsill, M.M. (2005) *Cities and Climate Change: Urban Sustainability and Global Environmental Governance*. Hove: Psychology Press.

Burawoy, M. (2004) For public sociology, *American Sociological Review*, 70(1): 4–28.

Burchell, G., Gordon, C. and Miller, P. (eds) (1991) *The Foucault Effect: Studies In Governmentality*. London: Harvester Wheatsheaf.

Burke, P. (2000) *A Social History of Knowledge*. Cambridge: Polity.

Burkitt, I. (1997) The situated social scientist: reflexivity and perspective in the sociology of knowledge, *Social Epistemology*, 11(2): 193–202.

Burton-Jones, A. (2001). *Knowledge Capitalism: Business, Work, and Learning in the New Economy*. Oxford: Oxford University Press.

Butler, J. (1994) Gender as performance: an interview with Judith Butler. Conducted by P. Osborne and L. Segal, *Radical Philosophy*, 67: 32–9.

Butler, J. (2005) *Giving an Account of Oneself*. New York: Fordham University Press.

Butler, J. (2011[1993]) *Bodies that Matter: On the Discursive Limits of 'Sex'*. New York: Routledge.

Button, G. (ed.) (1991) *Ethnomethodology and the Human Sciences*. Cambridge: Cambridge University Press.

Bynner, J. and Stribley, K. (eds) (1979) *Social Research: Principles and Procedures*. Milton Keynes: Open University Press.

Byrne, R.M.J. (2005) *The Rational Imagination: How People Create Counterfactual Alternatives to Reality*. Cambridge, MA: MIT Press.

Cairney, P. (2015) *The Politics of Evidence-Based Policy Making*. London: Palgrave Macmillan.

Calhoun, C. (1995) *Critical Social Theory: Culture, History and the Challenge of Difference*. Oxford: Blackwell.

Calhoun, C. (ed.) (1992) *Habermas and the Public Sphere*. Cambridge, MA: MIT Press.

Calhoun, C., LiPuma, E. and Postone, M. (eds) (1993) *Bourdieu: Critical Perspectives*. Cambridge: Polity.

Cameron, A. and Palan, R. (2004) *The Imagined Economies of Globalization*. London: Sage.

Campbell, H. and Vanderhoven, D. (2016) *Knowledge that Matters: Realising the Potential of Co-Production*, ESRC. Available at www.n8research.org.uk/media/Final-Report-Co-Production-2016-01-20.pdf

Castells, M. (2010) *The Rise of the Network Society. The Information Age: Economy, Society and Culture, Volume 1* (2nd edn). Oxford: Blackwell.

Chappell, V.C. (ed.) (1968) *Hume*. London: Macmillan.

Chatterton, P. (2008) Demand the possible: journeys in changing our world as a public activist-scholar, *Antipode*, 40(3): 421–7.

Chatterton, P. (2013) Towards an agenda for post-carbon cities: lessons from Lilac, the UK's first ecological, affordable cohousing community, *International Journal of Urban and Regional Research*, 37(5): 1654–74.

Chiapello, E. (2014) Capitalism and its criticisms, in P. du Gay and G. Morgan (eds), *New Spirits of Capitalism: Crises, Justifications, and Dynamics*. Oxford: Oxford University Press.

Chomsky, N. (2012) *Occupy*. London: Penguin.

Claxton, G. (1997) *Hare Brain, Tortoise Mind: Why Intelligence Increases When You Think Less*. London: Fourth Estate.

Clegg, N. (2012) Nick Clegg apologies for tuitions fee pledge. *Guardian*, 20 September. Available at www.theguardian.com/politics/2012/sep/19/nick-clegg-apologies-tuition-fees-pledge

Cohen, A.P. (1994) *Self Consciousness: An Alternative Anthropology of Identity*. London: Routledge.

Cohen, S. (2001) *States of Denial: Knowing about Atrocities and Suffering*. Cambridge: Polity.

Collins, F. and Pedersen, D.B. (2013) The Frankfurt School, science and technology studies, and the humanities, *Social Epistemology*, 29(1): 44–72.

Collins, H. (2010) *Tacit and Explicit Knowledge*. Chicago: University of Chicago Press.

Collins, P.H. (1998) *Fighting Words: Black Women and the Search for Justice*. Minneapolis, MN: University of Minnesota Press.

Conard, M.T. (2011) Thus spake Bart: on Nietzsche and the virtues of being bad, in W. Irwin, M.T. Conard and A.J. Skoble (eds), *The Simpsons and Philosophy: The D'oh! of Homer* (Vol. 3). Chicago: Open Court.

Condor, S., Tileaga, C. and Billig, M. (2013) Political rhetoric, in L. Huddy, D.O. Sears and J.S. Levy (eds), *Oxford Handbook of Political Psychology*. Oxford: Oxford University Press.

Cook, J. and Fonow, M. (1990) Knowledge and women's interests: issues of epistemology and methodology in sociological research, in J. McCarl Nielsen (ed.), *Feminist Research Methods: Exemplary Readings In the Social Sciences*. London: Westview.

Cook, S.D. and Brown, J.S. (1999) Bridging epistemologies: the generative dance between organizational knowledge and organizational knowing, *Organization Science*, 10: 381–400.

Cotoi, C. (2011) Neoliberalism: a Foucauldian perspective, *International Review of Social Research*, 1(2): 109–24.

Coulter, J. (1979) *The Social Construction of Mind: Studies in Ethnomethodology and Linguistic Philosophy*. London: Macmillan.

Coulter, J. (1983) *Rethinking Cognitive Theory*. London: Macmillan.

Craib, I. (1998) *Experiencing Identity*. London: Sage.

Craib, I. (1994) *The Importance of Disappointment*. London: Routledge.

Cranmer, S., Dohn, N.B., de Laat, M., Ryberg, T. and Sime, J.A. (eds) (2016) *Proceedings of the Tenth International Conference on Networked Learning*. Lancaster: Lancaster University.

Crawford, M.B. (2015) *The World Beyond Your Head: On Becoming an Individual in an Age of Distraction*. New York: Farrar, Straus and Giroux.

Critchley, S. (2012) *Impossible Objects: Interviews*. Edited by C. Cederström and C. Kesselman. Cambridge: Polity.

Crossley, N. (1996) *Intersubjectivity: The Fabric of Social Becoming*. London: Sage.

Croteau, D. (2005) Which side are you on? The tensions between movement scholarship and activism, in D. Croteau, W. Hoynes and C. Ryan (eds), *Rhyming Hope and History: Activists, Academics and Scholarship*. Minneapolis, MN: University of Minnesota Press.

Croteau, D., Hoynes, W. and Ryan, C. (eds) (2005) *Rhyming Hope and History: Activists, Academics and Scholarship*. Minneapolis, MN: University of Minnesota Press.

Crouch, C. (2011) *The Strange Non-Death of Neoliberalism*. Cambridge: Polity.

Curtis, J. and Petras, J. (eds) (1970) *The Sociology of Knowledge: A Reader*. London: Duckworth.

Cutcliffe, S.H. (2001) The historical emergence of STS as an academic field in the United States, *AfRumentos de Razón 7'écnica*, 4: 281–92. Available at http://institucional.us.es/revistas/argumentos/5/art_11.pdf

Dale, G. (2010) *Karl Polanyi: The Limits of the Market*. Cambridge: Polity.

Dallos, R. and Stedman, J. (2009a) Flying over the swampy lowlands: reflective and reflexive practice, in R. Dallos and J. Stedman (eds), *Reflective Practice In Psychotherapy and Counselling*. Maidenhead: Open University Press.

Dallos, R. and Stedman, J. (eds) (2009b) *Reflective Practice in Psychotherapy and Counselling*. Maidenhead: Open University Press.

Daston, L. and Galison, P. (2010[2007]) *Objectivity*. New York: Zone Books.

De Bono, E. (2009[1970]) *Lateral Thinking: A Textbook of Creativity*. Harmondsworth: Penguin.

De la Mothe, J. (2001) Knowledge, politics and governance, in J. de la Mothe (ed.), *Science, Technology and Governance*. London: Continuum.

Denzin, N.K. (1997) *Interpretive Ethnography: Ethnographic Practices for the 21st Century*. London: Sage.

Derrida, J. (1994) *Specters of Marx: The State of the Debt, the Work of Mourning, and the New International*. Translated by P. Kamuf. London: Routledge.

Derrida, J. (1996) Remarks on deconstruction and pragmatism, in C. Mouffe (ed.), *Deconstruction and Pragmatism*. (With Simon Critchley, Jacques Derrida, Ernesto Laclau and Richard Rorty.) London: Routledge.

Devine, F. and Snee, H. (2015) Doing the Great British Class Survey, *The Sociological Review*, 63(2): 240–58.

Dewey, J. (1957) *Reconstruction in Philosophy* (enlarged edn). Boston, MA: Beacon.

Dewey, J. (2005[1934]) *Art as Experience*. New York: Perigee Books.

Dews, P. (ed.) (1992) *Autonomy and Solidarity: Interviews with Jürgen Habermas* (revised edn). London: Verso.

Donath, J. and Boyd, D. (2004) Public displays of connection, *BT Technology Journal*, 22(4): 71–82.

Doney, W. (ed.) (1967) *Descartes: A Collection of Critical Essays*. London: Macmillan.

Dorling, D. (2014) *Inequality and the 1%*. London: Verso.

Doucet, A. (2008) From her side of the Gossamer Wall(s): reflexivity and relational knowing, *Qualitative Sociology*, 31: 73–87.

Dresner, S. (2001) A comparison of RTD structures in EU Member States, in S. Dresner and N. Gilbert (eds), *The Dynamics of European Science and Technology Policies*. Aldershot: Ashgate.

Dreyfus, H. and Rabinow, P. (1982) *Michel Foucault: Beyond Structuralism and Hermeneutics*. Chicago: University of Chicago Press.

Dreyfus, H. and Rabinow, P. (1993) Can there be a science of existential structure and social meaning?, in C. Calhoun, E. LiPuma and M. Postone (eds), *Bourdieu: Critical Perspectives*. Cambridge: Polity.

Dreyfuss, R., Zimmerman, D.L. and First, H. (eds) (2001) *Expanding the Boundaries of Intellectual Property*. Oxford: Oxford University Press.

Du Gay, P. and Morgan, G. (eds) (2014) *New Spirits of Capitalism: Crises, Justifications, and Dynamics*. Oxford: Oxford University Press.

Dunne, S., Harney, S., Parker, M. and Tinker, T. (2008) Discussing the role of the business school, *Ephemera: Theory and Politics in Organization Interviews*, 8(3): 271–83.

Durkheim, E. (1992[1899]) Review article on F.S. Merlino's 'Formes et essences du socialisme', in M. Gane (ed.), *The Radical Sociology of Durkheim and Mauss*. London: Routledge.

Durose, C., Beebeejaun, Y., Rees, J., Richardson, J. and Richardson, L. (2011) Towards co-production in research with communities. Available at www.ahrc.ac.uk/documents/project-reports-and-reviews/connected-communities/towards-co-production-in-research-with-communities/

Durose, C. and Richardson, L. (2015) *Designing Public Policy Through Coproduction: Theory, Practice and Change*. Bristol: Policy.

Eberly, D. and Streeter, R. (2002) *The Soul of Civil Society: Voluntary Associations and the Public Value of Moral Habits: Voluntary Associations and the Cultivation of Moral Habit*. Lanham, MD: Lexington.

Edwards, G. (2009) Habermas and social movement theory, *Sociology Compass*, 3(3): 381–93.

Elliott, A. and du Gay, P. (eds) (2009) *Identity in Question*. London: Sage.

Elliott, H., Ryan, J. and Hollway, W. (2011) Research encounters, reflexivity and supervision, *International Journal of Social Research Methodology*, 15(5): 433–44.

England, K. (1994) Getting personal: reflexivity, positionality and feminist research, *The Professional Geographer*, 46(1): 80–9.

Erion, G.J. and Smith, B. (2002) Skepticism, morality and *The Matrix*, in W. Irwin (ed.), *The Matrix and Philosophy: Welcome to the Desert of the Real*. Chicago: Open Court.

Etzkowitz, H. and Leydesdorff, L. (2000) The dynamics of innovation: from national systems and 'Mode 2' to a triple helix of university–industry–government relations, *Research Policy*, 29(2): 109–23.

Evans, J. and Karvonen, A. (2014) 'Give me a laboratory and I will lower your carbon footprint!' Urban laboratories and the pursuit of low carbon futures, *International Journal of Urban and Regional Research*, 38(2): 413–30.

Evans, J., Karvonen, A. and Raven, R. (eds) (2016) *The Experimental City*. Abington: Routledge.

Express Online (2015) Eighty per cent of Britains 'hate the meddling nanny state', 27 December. www.express.co.uk/news/uk/548848/Government-should-stop-sin-taxes-on-alcohol-and-tobacco-products

Faberman, H.A. (1991[1985]) The foundations of symbolic interactionism: James, Cooley and Mead, in K. Plummer (ed.), *Symbolic Interactionism, Volume 1: Foundations and History*. Aldershot: Edward Elgar.

Facer, K. and Enright, B. (2016) Creating living knowledge: The Connected Communities Programme, community–university relationships and the participatory turn in the production of knowledge. Available at https://connected-communities.org/wp-ontent/uploads/2016/04/Creating-Living-Knowledge.Final.pdf

Fairclough, N. (2000) *New Labour, New Language?* London: Routledge.

Fay, B. (1987) *Critical Social Science: Liberation and its Limits*. Ithaca, NY: Cornell University Press.

Ferrara, A. (1998) *Reflective Authenticity: Rethinking the Project of Modernity*. London: Routledge.

Fichte, J.G. (1994) *Introductions to the Wissenschaftslehre and Other Writings (1797–1800)*. Edited and translated by D. Breazeale. Indianapolis: Hackett.

Figgou, L. and Condor, S. (2007) Categorising category labels in interview accounts about the 'Muslim minority' in Greece, *Journal of Ethnic and Migration Studies*, 33(3): 439–59.

Finlay, L. (2002) Negotiating the swamp: the opportunity and challenge of reflexivity in research practice, *Qualitative Research*, 2(2): 209–30.

Finlayson, J.G. (2005) *Habermas: A Very Short Introduction*. Oxford: Oxford University Press.

Flick, U., von Kardorff, E. and Steinke, I. (eds) (2004) *A Companion to Qualitative Research*. London: Sage.

Flood, M., Martin, B. and Dreher, T. (2013) Combining academia and activism: common obstacles and useful tools, *Australian Universities Review*, 55(1): 17–26.

Forst, R. (2014a) *Justification and Critique*. Translated by C. Cronin. Cambridge: Polity.

Forst, R. (2014b) Justifying justifications: a reply to my critics, in R. Forst (ed.), *Justice, Democracy and the Right to Justification: Rainer Forst in Dialogue*. London: Bloomsbury.

Foucault, M (1977) *Discipline and Punish*. Translated by A. Sheridan. New York: Vintage.

Foucault, M. (1982a) The subject and power, in H. Dreyfus and P. Rabinow (eds), *Michel Foucault: Beyond Structuralism and Hermeneutics*. Chicago: University of Chicago Press.

Foucault, M. (1982b) Is it really important to think? An interview translated by Thomas Keenan. *Philosophy and Social Criticism*, 9(1): 29–40.

Foucault, M. (1984a) *The Foucault Reader*. Edited by P. Rabinow. Harmondsworth: Penguin.

Foucault, M. (1984b) Le pouvoir, comment s'exerce-t-il?, in H.L. Dreyfus and P. Rabinow (eds), *Michel Foucault: Un Parcours Philosophique*. Paris: Gallimard.

Foucault, M. (1988) Truth, power, self: an interview, in L.H. Martin, H. Gutman and P.H. Hutton (eds), *Technologies of the Self: A Seminar with Michel Foucault*. London: Tavistock.

Foucault, M. (1989a) *Foucault Live: Collected Interviews 1961–1984*. Edited by E. Lotringer and translated by J. Johnston. New York: Semiotext(e).

Foucault, M. (1989b[1969]) *The Archaeology of Knowledge*. Translated by A.M. Smith. London: Routledge.

Foucault, M. (1991a) *Remarks on Marx: Conversations with Duccio Trombadori*. Translated by R.J Goldstein and J. Cascaito. New York: Semiotext(e).

Foucault, M. (1991b) Questions of method, in G. Burchell, C. Gordon and P. Miller (eds), *The Foucault Effect: Studies In Governmentality*. London: Harvester Wheatsheaf.

Foucault, M. (1992[1970]) *The Order of Things: An Archaeology of the Human Sciences*. London: Routledge.

Foucault, M. (1997) *Ethics: Subjectivity and Truth. The Essential Works, Volume 1*. Edited by P. Rabinow and translated by R. Hurley et al. London: Allen Lane/Penguin.

Foucault, M. (1998) *Aesthetics, Method, and Epistemology: The Essential Works, Volume 2*. Edited by J. Faubion and translated by R. Hurley et al. London: Allen Lane/Penguin.

Foucault, M. (2001) Qui êtes-vous professeur Foucault?, in *Dits et Ecrits, Vol. 1*. Paris: Gallimard.

Fowler, B. (ed.) *Reading Bourdieu on Society and Culture*. Oxford: Blackwell.

Fransman, J. (2013) Researching academic literacy practices around Twitter: performative methods and their onto-ethical implications, in R. Goodfellow and M.R. Lea (eds), *Literacy in the Digital University: Critical Perspectives on Learning, Scholarship and Technology*, Society for Research into Higher Education (SRHE) series. Abingdon: Routledge.

Fraser, N. (1989) *Unruly Practices: Power, Discourse and Gender in Contemporary Social Theory*. Cambridge: Polity.

Fraser, N. (1995) 'False Antitheses', in S. Benhabib, J. Butler, D. Cornell and N. Fraser (eds), *Feminist Contentions: A Philosophical Exchange*. London: Routledge.

Fraser, N. (1997) *Justice Interruptus: Critical Reflections on the 'Postsocialist' Condition.* London: Routledge.

Fraser, N. and Honneth, A. (2003) *Redistribution or Recognition? A Political-Philosophical Exchange.* London: Verso.

Freire, P. (1970) *Pedagogy of the Oppressed.* New York: Herder & Herder.

Freud, S. (1938) *Psychopathology of Everday Life.* Harmondsworth: Penguin.

Frisby, D. and Featherstone, M. (eds) (1997) *Simmel on Culture: Selected Writings.* London: Sage.

Fromm, E. (1997[1976]) *To Have or to Be?* London: Continuum.

Fromm, E. (1999[1942]) *The Fear of Freedom.* London: Routledge.

Fuggle, S., Lanci, Y. and Tazzioli, M. (eds) (2015) *Foucault and the History of Our Present.* Basingstoke: Palgrave Macmillan.

Fuller, S. (2000) *The Governance of Science: Ideology and the Future of the Open Society.* Buckingham: Open University Press.

Fuller, S. (2004) In search of vehicles for knowledge governance: on the need for institutions that creatively destroy social capital', in N. Stehr (ed.), *The Governance of Knowledge.* New Brunswick, NJ: Transaction.

Funtowicz, S.O. and Ravetz. J.R. (1993) Science for the post normal age, in L. Westra and J. Lemons (eds), *Perspectives on Ecological Integrity*, pp. 146–61. Dordrecht: Springer. Available at www.uu.nl/wetfilos/wetfil10/sprekers/Funtowicz_Ravetz_Futures_1993.pdf

Furedi, F. (2017) *What's Happened to the University? A Sociological Exploration of its Infantilisation.* London: Routledge.

Gadamer, H.G. (1975[1960]) *Truth and Method.* London: Sheed & Ward.

Gadamer, H.G. (1977) *Philosophical Hermeneutics.* Translated and edited by D.E. Linge. Berkeley, CA: University of California Press.

Gane, M. (ed.) (1992) *The Radical Sociology of Durkheim and Mauss.* London: Routledge.

Garfinkel, H. (1967) *Studies in Ethnomethodology.* Englewood Cliffs, NJ: Prentice-Hall.

Garfinkel, H. (1991) Respecification: evidence for locally produced, naturally accountable phenomena of order, logic, reason, meaning, method, etc. in and as of the essential haecceity of immortal ordinary society, (1) – an announcement of studies', in G. Button (ed.), *Ethnomethodology and the Human Sciences.* Cambridge: Cambridge University Press.

Garland, D. (2014) What is a 'history of the present'? On Foucault's genealogies and their critical preconditions, *Punishment and Society*, 16(4): 365–84.

Garry, A. and Pearsall, M. (eds) (1992) *Women, Knowledge and Reality: Explorations in Feminist Philosophy.* London: Routledge.

Gellner, E. (1968) *Words and Things.* Penguin: Harmondsworth.

Gellner, E. (1987) *Culture, Identity and Politics.* Cambridge: Cambridge University Press.

Gergan, K.J. (2000) The saturated self, in A. Branaman (ed.), *Self and Society.* London: Blackwell.

Gerth, H. and Mills, C. W. (eds) (1970) *From Max Weber: Essays in Sociology.* London: Routledge & Kegan Paul.

Gherardi, S. (2000) Practice-based theorizing on learning and knowing in organizations, *Organization*, 7: 211–24.

Gibbons, M. (2001) Governance and the new production of knowledge, in J. de la Mothe (ed.), *Science, Technology and Governance*. London: Continuum.

Gibbons, M., Limoges, C., Nowotny, H., Schwartaman, S., Scott, P. and Trow, M. (1994) *The New Production of Knowledge: The Dynamics of Science and Research in Contemporary Societies*. London: Sage.

Gibson-Graham, J.K. (1996) *The End of Capitalism (As We Knew It): A Feminist Critique of Political Economy*. Oxford: Blackwell.

Giddens, A. (1989) A reply to my critics, in D. Held and J.B. Thompson (eds), *Social Theory of Modern Societies: Anthony Giddens and His Critics*. Cambridge: Cambridge University Press.

Giddens, A. (1991) *Modernity and Self-Identity: Self and Society in the Late Modern Age*. Stanford, CA: Stanford University Press.

Giddens, A. (1996) *In Defence of Sociology: Essays, Interpretations and Rejoinders*. Cambridge: Polity.

Giddens, A. (2009) *The Politics of Climate Change*. Cambridge: Polity.

Gieryn, T. (1999) *Cultural Boundaries of Science: Credibility on the Line*. Chicago: University of Chicago Press.

Gilbert, A. and Sliep, Y. (2009) Reflexivity in the practice of social action: from self- to inter-relational reflexivity, *South African Journal of Psychology*, 39(4): 468–79.

Gilligan, C., Spencer, R., Weinberg, K. and Bertsch, T. (2005) On the listening huide: a voice-centered relational method, in S. Hesse-Biber and P. Leavy (eds), *Emergent Methods in Social Research*. Thousand Oaks, CA: Sage.

Gitlin, A.D. (ed.) *Power and Method: Political Activism and Educational Research*. New York: Routledge.

Glendinning, S. (1998) *On Being with Others: Heidegger – Derrida – Wittgenstein*. London: Routledge.

Goffman, E. (1971) *Relations in Public: Microstudies of the Public Order*. Harmondsworth: Penguin.

Goffman, E. (1974) *Frame Analysis: An Essay on the Organization of Experience*. New York: Harper & Row.

Goffman, E. (1984[1959]) *The Presentation of Self in Everyday Life*. Harmondsworth: Penguin.

Goldacre, B. (2012) *Bad Pharma: How Medicine Is Broken, and How We Can Fix It*. London: Fourth Estate.

Goodfellow, R. and Lea, M.R. (eds) (2013) *Literacy in the Digital University: Critical Perspectives on Learning, Scholarship and Technology*, Society for Research into Higher Education (SRHE) series. Abingdon: Routledge.

Gouldner, A. (1971) *The Coming Crisis of Western Sociology*. London: Heinemann.

Gouldner, A. (1975) *For Sociology: Renewal and Critique in Sociology Today*. Harmondsworth: Penguin.

Graeber, D. (2011) *Revolutions in Reverse: Essays on Politics, Violence, Art, and Imagination.* London: Minor Compositions.

Graeber, D. (2015) *The Utopia of Rules: On Technology, Stupidity, and the Secret Joys of Bureaucracy.* London: Melville House.

Graham, M. and Dutton, W.H. (eds) (2014) *Society and the Internet: How Networks of Information and Communication are Changing Our Lives.* Oxford: Oxford University Press.

Graham, S. and Marvin, S. (2001) *Splintering Urbanism: Networked Infrastructures, Technological Mobilities and the Urban Condition.* London: Routledge.

Greenwood, D. and Levin, M. (1998). Action research, science, and the co-optation of social research. *Studies in Cultures, Organisations and Societies,* 4: 237–61.

Greenwood, D. and Levin, M. (2006) *Introduction to Action Research: Social Research for Social Change* (2nd edn). London: Sage.

Greenwood, D. and Levin, N. (2016) *Creating a New Public University and Reviving Democracy: Action Research in Higher Education.* New York: Berghahn.

Griffiths, M. and Whitford, M. (eds) (1988) *Feminist Perspectives in Philosophy.* London: Macmillan.

Habermas, J. (1981) Towards a reconstruction of historical materialism, in K. Knorr-Cetina and A. Cicourel (eds), *Advances in Social Theory and Methodology: Towards an Integration of Micro and Macro Theories.* London: Routledge & Kegan Paul.

Habermas, J. (1982) A reply to my critics, in J.B. Thompson and D. Held (eds), *Habermas: Critical Debates.* London: Macmillan.

Habermas, J. (1984) *The Theory of Communicative Action. Vol. 1: Reason and the Rationalization of Society.* Translated by T. McCarthy. London: Heinemann.

Habermas, J. (1987) *The Theory of Communicative Action. Vol. 2: Lifeworld and System: A Critique of Functionalist Reason.* Translated by T. McCarthy. Cambridge: Polity.

Habermas, J. (1989a[1968]) *Knowledge and Human Interests.* Translated by J.J. Shapiro. Cambridge: Polity.

Habermas, J. (1989b) *The Structural Transformation of the Public Sphere.* Translated by T. Berger and F. Lawrence. Cambridge, MA: MIT Press.

Habermas, J. (1990[1970]) *On the Logic of the Social Sciences.* Translated by S.W. Nicholsen and J.A. Stark. Cambridge: Polity.

Habermas, J. (1991) A reply, in A. Honneth and H. Joas (eds), *Communicative Action: Essays on Jürgen Habermas's The Theory of Communicative Action.* Translated by J. Gaines and D.L. Jones. Cambridge, MA: MIT Press.

Habermas, J. (1992a) *Postmetaphysical Thinking: Philosophical Essays.* Translated by W.M. Hohengarten. Cambridge, MA: MIT Press.

Habermas, J. (1992b) *The Philosophical Discourse of Modernity: Twelve Lectures.* Cambridge: Polity.

Habermas, J. (1993) *Justification and Application: Remarks on Discourse Ethics.* Translated by C. Cronin. Cambridge: Polity.

Habermas, J. (1994) *The Past as Future.* Interviews by M. Haller, translated and edited by M. Pensky. Cambridge: Polity.

Habermas, J. (2001) *On the Pragmatics of Social Interaction: Preliminary Studies in the Theory of Communication Action.* Translated by B. Fultner. Cambridge: Polity.

Habermas, J. (2006) *Time of Transitions.* Edited and translated by C. Cronin and M. Pensky. Cambridge: Polity.

Hacking, I. (2004) Between Michel Foucault and Erving Goffman: between discourse in the abstract and face-to-face interaction, *Economy and Society*, 33(3): 277–30.

Haklay, M. (2003) Public access to environmental information: past, present and future, *Computers, Environment and Urban Systems*, 27(2): 163–80.

Hall, J.R. (1999) *Cultures of Inquiry: From Epistemology to Discourse in Sociohistorical Research.* Cambridge: Cambridge University Press.

Hanley, R.P. (2012) Political economy and individual liberty, in E. Grace and C. Kelly (eds), *The Challenge of Rousseau.* Cambridge: Cambridge University Press.

Hann, C. and Hart, K. (2011) *Economic Anthropology.* Cambridge: Polity.

Haraway, D. (1997) *Modest_Witness@Second_Millennium. FemaleMan©_Meets_OncomouseTM.* New York: Routledge.

Harding, S. (1991) *Whose Science? Whose Knowledge? Thinking from Women's Lives.* Milton Keynes: Open University Press.

Harding, S. (ed.) (1987) *Feminism and Methodology.* Milton Keynes: Open University Press.

Harding, S. (2006) *Science and Social Inequality: Feminist and Postcolonial Issues.* Urbana, IL: University of Illinois Press.

Harloe, M. and Perry, B. (2004) Universities, localities and regional development: the emergence of the Mode 2 university?, *International Journal of Urban and Regional Research*, 28(1): 212–23.

Harré, R. (1998) *The Singular Self.* London: Sage.

Harré, R. and Moghaddam, F. (eds) *The Self and Others: Positioning Individuals in Personal, Political, and Cultural Contexts.* London: Praeger.

Harré, R. and Slocum, N. (2003) Disputes as complex social events: on the uses of positioning theory, in R. Harré and F. Moghaddam (eds), *The Self and Others: Positioning Individuals in Personal, Political, and Cultural Contexts.* London: Praeger.

Harré, R. and van Langenhove, L. (1991) Varieties of positioning, *Journal for the Theory of Social Behaviour*, 21(4): 393–407.

Hartsock, N. (1987) The feminist standpoint: developing the ground for a specifically feminist historical materialism, in S. Harding (ed.), *Feminism and Methodology.* Milton Keynes: Open University Press.

Harvey, D. (2012) *Rebel Cities: From the Right to the City to the Urban Revolution.* London: Verso.

Harvey, D. (2014) *Seventeen Contradictions and the End of Capitalism.* London: Profile.

Harvey, M. and McMeekin, A. (2007) *Public or Private Economies of Knowledge? Turbulence in the Biological Sciences.* Cheltenham: Edward Elgar.

Hawthorn, G. (1976) *Enlightenment and Despair: A History of Sociology.* Cambridge: Cambridge University Press.

Hayek, F. A. (1968) The legal and political philosophy of David Hume, in V.C. Chappell (ed.), *Hume*. London: Macmillan.

Heelas, P., Lash, S. and Morris, P. (eds) (1996) *Detraditionalization: Critical Reflections on Authority and Identity*. Oxford: Blackwell.

Hegel, G.W.F. (1991) *The Philosophy of History*. Translated by J. Sibree. Buffalo, NY: Prometheus.

Heidegger, M. (1961[1953]) *An Introduction to Metaphysics*. New York: Anchor.

Held, D. and Thompson, J. (eds) (1989) *Social Theory of Modern Societies: Anthony Giddens and His Critics*. Cambridge: Cambridge University Press.

Heller, A. (1984) *Everyday Life*. Translated by G. Campbell. London: Routledge & Kegan Paul.

Hellström, T. and Jacob, M. (2000) The scientification of politics or the politicisation of science? Traditionalist science-policy discourse and its quarrels with Mode 2 epistemology, *Social Epistemology*, 14(1): 69–75.

Hellström, T. and Ramen, S. (2001) The commodification of knowledge about knowledge: knowledge management and the reification of epistemology, *Social Epistemology*, 15(3): 139–54.

Henkel, M. (2005) Academic identity and autonomy in a changing policy environment, *Higher Education*, 49: 155–76.

Henneberry J. (ed.) (2016) *Transience and Permanence in Urban Development*. Chichester: Wiley.

Hesse-Biber, S. and Leavy, P. (eds) (2005) *Emergent Methods in Social Research*. Thousand Oaks, CA: Sage.

Hill, C. (1997[1965]) *Intellectual Origins of the English Revolution Revisited*. Oxford: Oxford University Press.

Hobbs, R. and May, T. (eds) (1993) *Interpreting the Field: Accounts of Ethnography*. Oxford: Oxford University Press.

Hobsbawm, E. (1962) *The Age of Revolution: 1789–1848*. London: Weidenfeld & Nicolson.

Hobsbawm, E. (1975) *The Age of Capital: 1848–1875*. London: Weidenfeld & Nicolson.

Hochschild, A.E. (2003) *The Commercialization of Intimate Life: Notes from Home and Work*. Berkeley, CA: University of California Press.

Hogan, B. and Wellman, B. (2014) The relational self-portrait: selfies meet social Networks', in M. Graham and W.H. Dutton (eds), *Society and the Internet: How Networks of Information and Communication are Changing Our Lives*. Oxford: Oxford University Press.

Hollingdale, R.J. (ed.) (1977) *A Nietzsche Reader*. Translated by R.J. Hollingdale. Harmondsworth: Penguin.

Holloway, J. (2010) *Crack Capitalism*. London: Pluto.

Holton, R. and Turner, B. (1990) *Max Weber on Economy and Society*. London: Routledge.

Holub, R. (1991) *Jürgen Habermas: Critic in the Public Sphere*. London: Routledge.

Honneth, A. (1991) *The Critique of Power: Reflective Stages in a Critical Social Theory*. Translated by K. Baynes. Cambridge, MA: MIT Press.

Honneth, A. (1996) *The Struggle for Recognition: The Moral Grammar of Social Conflicts*. Translated by J. Anderson. Cambridge, MA: MIT Press.

Honneth, A. (2007) *Disrespect: The Normative Foundations of Critical Theory*. Cambridge: Polity.

Honneth, A. and Joas, H. (1988) *Social Action and Human Nature*. Cambridge: Cambridge University Press.

Honneth, A. and Joas, H. (eds) (1991) *Communicative Action: Essays on Jürgen Habermas's The Theory of Communicative Action*. Translated by J. Gaines and D.L. Jones. Cambridge, MA: MIT Press.

Honneth, A., McCarthy, M., Offe, C. and Wellmer, A. (eds) (1992) *Cultural-Political Interventions in the Unfinished Project of Enlightenment*. Cambridge, MA: MIT Press.

Hopkins, N. and Kahani-Hopkins, V. (2004) The antecedents of identification: a rhetorical analysis of British Muslim activists' constructions of community and identity, *British Journal of Social Psychology*, 43: 41–57.

Horkheimer, M. (1972) *Critical Theory: Selected Essays*. Translated by M.J. O'Connell and others. New York: Herder & Herder.

Hosking, D.M. and Pluut, B. (2010) (Re)constructing reflexivity: a relational constructionist approach, *The Qualitative Report*, 15(1): 59–75.

House of Commons (2011) www.publications.parliament.uk/pa/cm201012/cmselect/cmpubadm/902/902.pdf

Hoy, D.C. (1998) Foucault and Critical Theory, in J. Moss (ed.), *The Later Foucault: Politics and Philosophy*. London: Sage.

Hoy, D.C. (ed.) (1986) *Foucault: A Critical Reader*. Oxford: Basil Blackwell.

Hoy, D.C. and McCarthy, T. (1994) *Critical Theory*. Oxford: Blackwell.

Huddy, L., Sears, D.O. and Levy, J.S. (eds) *Oxford Handbook of Political Psychology*. Oxford: Oxford University Press.

Huschke, S. (2014) Giving back: activist research with undocumented migrants in Berlin, *Medical Anthropology: Cross-Cultural Studies In Health and Illness*, 34(1): 54–69.

Hutchinson, P., Read, R. and Sharrock, W. (2008) *There Is No Such Thing as a Social Science: In Defence of Peter Winch*. Aldershot: Ashgate.

Irwin, W. (ed.) (2002) *The Matrix and Philosophy: Welcome to the Desert of the Real*. Chicago: Open Court.

Irwin, W., Conard, M.T. and Skoble, A.J. (eds) (2001) *The Simpsons and Philosophy: The D'oh! of Homer (Vol. 3)* Chicago: Open Court.

James, W. (2002[1909]) *The Meaning of Truth*. Mineola, NY: Dover.

Jasanoff, S. (ed.) (2004) *States of Knowledge: The Co-production of Science and Social Order*. London: Routledge.

Jasanoff, S. (2005) *Designs on Nature: Science and Democracy in Europe and the United States*. Princeton, NJ: Princeton University Press.

Jasanoff, S. (2010) A new climate for society, *Theory, Culture and Society*, 27(2–3): 233–53.

Jeter, G. (2014) Burke's *Philosophical Enquiry*: towards a corporeal epistemology and politics, *The CEA Critic*, 76(3): 239–45.

Joas, H. (1993) *Pragmatism and Social Theory*. Chicago: University of Chicago Press.

Joas, H. (1996) *The Creativity of Action*. Translated by J. Gaines and P. Keast. Cambridge: Polity.

Joas, H. (1997) *G.H. Mead: A Contemporary Re-Examination of His Thought*. Translated by R. Meyer. Cambridge, MA: MIT Press.

Joas, H. (1998) The autonomy of the self: the median heritage and its postmodern challenge, *European Journal of Social Theory*, 1: 7–18.

Jones, O. (2014) *The Establishment: And How They Get Away with It*. London: Allen Lane.

Jordan, K. (2016) Academics' online connections: characterising the structure of personal networks on academic social networking sites and Twitter, in S. Cranmer, N.B. Dohn, M. de Laat, T. Ryberg and J.A. Sime (eds), *Proceedings of the Tenth International Conference on Networked Learning*. Lancaster: Lancaster University.

Kahneman, D. (2011) *Thinking, Fast and Slow*. London: Macmillan.

Kant, I. (2009[1781]) *Critique of Pure Reason*. Translated by J.M.D. Meiklejohn. New York: Dover.

Kargon, R.H. and Molella, A.P. (2008) *Invented Edens: Techno-Cities of the Twentieth Century*. Cambridge, MA: MIT Press.

Karvonen, A. and van Heur, B. (2014) Urban laboratories: experiments in reworking cities, *International Journal of Urban and Regional Research*, 38: 379–92.

Kearney, H. (1971) *Science and Change: 1500–1700*. London: Weidenfeld & Nicolson.

Kearney, R. (ed.) (1996) *Paul Ricoeur: The Hermeneutics of Action*. London: Sage.

Keller Fox, E. (2010) *The Mirage of a Space Between Nature and Nurture*. Durham, MD: Duke University Press.

Kelly, A. and Burrows, R. (2012) Measuring the value of sociology: some notes on performative metricization in the contemporary academy, in L. Adkins and C. Lury (eds), *Measure and Value*. Oxford: Wiley-Blackwell.

Kelly, M. (ed.) (1994) *Critique and Power: Recasting the Foucault/Habermas Debate*. Cambridge, MA: MIT Press.

Kezar, A. and Eckel, P. (2002) The effect of institutional culture on change strategies in higher education: universal principles or culturally responsive concepts?, *Journal of Higher Education*, 73(4): 435–60.

Kirkup, G. (2010) Academic blogging: academic practice and academic identity, *London Review of Education*, 8(1): 75–84.

Knoblauch, H. (2004) The future prospects of qualitative research, in U. Flick, E. von Kardorff and I. Steinke (eds), *A Companion to Qualitative Research*. London: Sage.

Knorr-Cetina, K. (1981) *The Manufacture of Knowledge: An Essay on the Constructivist and Contextual Nature of Science*. Oxford: Pergamon.

Knorr-Cetina, K. (1999) *Epistemic Cultures: How the Sciences Make Knowledge*. Cambridge, MA: Harvard University Press.

Knorr-Cetina, K. and Cicourel, A. (eds) (1981) *Advances in Social Theory and Methodology: Towards an Integration of Micro and Macro Theories*. London: Routledge & Kegan Paul.

Knorr-Cetina, K.D. and Mulkay, M.J. (eds) (1985) *Science Observed: Perspectives on the Social Study of Science.* London: Sage.

Koch, M. (2012) *Capitalism and Climate Change: Theoretical Discussion, Historical Development and Policy Responses.* Basingstoke: Palgrave Macmillan.

Lamont, M. (2009) *How Professors Think: Inside the Curious World of Academic Judgement.* Cambridge, MA: Harvard University Press.

Larrabee, M.J. (ed.) (1993) *An Ethic of Care: Feminist and Interdisciplinary Perspectives.* London: Routledge.

Lash, S. (1993) Pierre Bourdieu: cultural economy and social change', in C. Calhoun, E. LiPuma and M. Postone (eds), *Bourdieu: Critical Perspectives.* Cambridge: Polity.

Lash, S. (1999) *Another Modernity, A Different Rationality.* Oxford: Blackwell.

Latour, B. (1985) Give me a laboratory and I will raise the world, in K.D. Knorr-Cetina and M.J. Mulkay (eds), *Science Observed: Perspectives on the Social Study of Science.* London: Sage.

Latour, B. (1993). *We Have Never Been Modern.* Translated by C. Porter. London: Harvester Wheatsheaf.

Latour, B. (2004a) *Politics of Nature: How to Bring the Sciences into Democracy.* Translated by C. Porter. Cambridge, MA: Harvard University Press.

Latour, B. (2004b) Why has critique run out of steam? From matters of fact to matters of concern, *Critical Inquiry*, 30(2): 225–48.

Latour, B. and Woolgar, S. (1979) *Laboratory Life: The Social Construction of Scientific Facts.* Princeton, NJ: Princeton University Press.

Lave, R. (2012) Neoliberalism and the production of environmental knowledge, *Environment and Society: Advances in Research*, 3: 19–38.

Law, J. (2004) *After Method: Mess in Social Science Research.* London: Routledge.

Lawler, S. (2014) *Identity: Sociological Perspectives.* Cambridge: Polity.

Lawson, H. (1986) *Reflexivity: The Postmodern Predicament.* London: Hutchinson.

Lazzarato, M. (2014) *Signs and Machines: Capitalism and the Production of Subjectivity.* Los Angeles: Semiotext(e).

Le Grand, J. and New, B. (2015) *Government Paternalism? Nanny State or Helpful Friend?* Cambridge, MA: Princeton University Press.

Lemert, C. (1997) *Postmodernism Is Not What You Think.* Oxford: Blackwell.

Lenz, J.W. (1966) Hume's defence of causal inference, in V.C. Chappell (ed.), *Hume.* London: Macmillan.

Levin, K., Cashore, B., Bernstein, S. and Auld, G. (2012) Overcoming the tragedy of super wicked problems: constraining our future selves to ameliorate global climate change, *Policy Sciences*, 2: 123–52.

Lloyd, G. (1992) The man of reason, in A. Garry and M. Pearsall (eds), *Women, Knowledge and Reality: Explorations in Feminist Philosophy.* London: Routledge.

Longino, H. (1990) *Science as Social Knowledge: Values and Objectivity in Scientific Inquiry.* Princeton, NJ: Princeton University Press.

Longino, H. (2002) *The Fate of Knowledge*. Princeton, NJ: Princeton University Press.

Lopes, A. and Dewan, I. (2014) Precarious pedagogies? The impact of casual and zero-hour contracts in higher education, *Journal of Feminist Scholarship*, 7(8): 28–42. Available at http://eprints.uwe.ac.uk/26825

Lovell, T. (2000) Thinking feminism with and against Bourdieu, in B. Fowler (ed.), *Reading Bourdieu on Society and Culture*. Oxford: Blackwell.

Löwith, K. (1993) *Max Weber and Karl Marx* (new edn). Preface by B.S. Turner, edited with an introduction by T. Bottomore and W. Outhwaite. London: Routledge.

Luhmann, N. (1982) *The Differentiation of Society*. Translated by S. Holmes and C. Larmore. New York: Columbia University Press.

Lukes, S. (1981) *Emile Durkheim: His Life and Work: A Historical and Critical Study*. Harmondsworth: Penguin.

Lustig, R. (2013) *Fat Chance: The Hidden Truth About Sugar, Obesity and Disease*. London: HarperCollins.

Lynch, M. (2000) Against reflexivity as an academic virtue and source of privileged knowledge, *Theory, Culture and Society*, 17(3): 26–54.

Lyotard, J.F. (1984[1979]) *The Postmodern Condition: A Report on Knowledge*. Translated by G. Bennington and B. Massumi, foreword by F. Jameson. Manchester: Manchester University Press.

MacIntyre, A. (1985) *After Virtue: A Study in Moral Theory* (2nd edn). London: Duckworth.

Macmurray, J. (1969[1957]) *The Self as Agent*. London: Faber and Faber.

Magnusson, R. and Griffiths, P. (2015) Who's afraid of the nanny state? Introduction to a symposium, *Public Health*, 129(8): 1017–20.

Mail Online (2015) Only nanny state Britain could turn this glorious sunshine into a national crisis, 1 July. www.dailymail.co.uk/debate/article-3145328/QUENTIN-LETTS-nanny-state-Britain-turn-glorious-sunshine-national-crisis.html

Mannheim, K. (1960[1936]) *Ideology and Utopia*. Preface by L. Wirth. London: Routledge & Kegan Paul.

Mannheim, K. (1970) The sociology of knowledge, in J. Curtis and J. Petras (eds), *The Sociology of Knowledge: A Reader*. London: Duckworth.

Marcuse, H. (1966) *Eros and Civilization: A Philosophical Inquiry into Freud* (2nd edn). Boston, MA: Beacon.

Marcuse, H. (1968) *One Dimensional Man: The Ideology of Industrial Society*. London: Sphere.

Marcuse, H. (1969) *Reason and Revolution: Hegel and the Rise of Social Theory*. London: Routledge & Kegan Paul.

Marrewijk, Van, A., Veenswijk, M. and Clegg, S. (2010) Organizing reflexivity in designed change: the ethnoventionist approach. *Journal of Organizational Change Management*, 23(3): 212–29.

Martin, L.H., Gutman, H. and Hutton, P.H. (eds) (1988) *Technologies of the Self: A Seminar with Michel Foucault*. London: Tavistock.

Marx, K. (1963[1956]) *Selected Writings in Sociology and Social Philosophy.* Edited by
T.B. Bottomore and M. Rubel. Harmondsworth: Penguin.

Marx, K. (1979) *Marx's Grundrisse.* Edited and translated by D. McLellan. London: Paladin.

Marx, K. (1980) Preface to a contribution to the critique of political economy, in
K. Marx and F. Engels (eds), *Selected Works In One Volume.* London: Lawrence &
Wishart.

Marx, K. (1981) *Economic and Philosophical Manuscripts of 1844.* London: Lawrence & Wishart.

Marx, K. (1983) *Capital: A Critique of Political Economy. Volume 1: The Process of Production
of Capital.* Edited by F. Engels, translated by S. Moore and E. Aveling. (English edition
first published in 1887.) London: Lawrence & Wishart.

Marx, K. and Engels, F. (1953) *Selected Correspondence: 1843–1895.* London: Lawrence &
Wishart.

Mauthner, N. and Doucet, A. (1998) Reflections on a voice centered relational method of
data analysis: analysing maternal and domestic voices, in J. Ribbens and
R. Edwards (eds), *Feminist Dilemmas in Qualitative Research: Private Lives and Public
Texts.* London: Sage.

Mauthner, N. and Doucet, A. (2003) Reflexive accounts and accounts of reflexivity in
qualitative data analysis, *Sociology,* 37(3): 413–31.

May, T. (1991) *Probation: Politics, Policy and Practice.* Maidenhead: Open University Press/
McGraw-Hill.

May, T. (1997) When theory fails? The history of American sociological research methods,
History of the Human Sciences, 10(1): 147–56.

May, T. (1998) Reflexivity in the age of reconstructive social science, *International Journal of
Methodology: Theory and Practice,* 1(1): 7–24.

May, T. (1999a) Reflexivity and sociological practice, *Sociological Research Online.* Special
section on 'The Future of Sociology', 4(3): 23. Available at www.socresonline.org.uk/
socresonline/4/3/may.html

May, T. (1999b) From banana time to just-in-time: power and resistance at work, *Sociology,*
33(4): 767–83.

May, T. (2000) The future of critique: positioning, belonging and reflexivity, *European
Journal of Social Theory,* 3(2): 157–73.

May, T. (2001) Power, knowledge and organizational transformation: administration as
depoliticisation, Special Issue on 'Social Epistemology and Knowledge Management',
Social Epistemology, 15(3): 171–86.

May, T. (2005) Transformations in academic production: context, content and
consequences, *European Journal of Social Theory,* 8(2): 193–209.

May, T. (2006) Transformative power: a study in a human service organization, in
H. Beynon and T. Nichols (eds), *Patterns of Work in the Post-Fordist Era: Volume 2.*
Cheltenham: Edward Elgar.

May, T. (2011a) *Social Research: Issues, Methods and Process* (4th edn). Maidenhead: Open
University Press/McGraw-Hill.

May, T. (2011b) Urban knowledge arenas: dynamics, tensions and potentials, *International Journal of Knowledge-Based Development*, 2(2): 132–47.

May, T. (ed.) (2012) *Qualitative Research in Action*. London: Sage.

May, T. (2015) Symptomatic social science: reflexivity, recognition and redistribution in the Great British Class Survey, *Sociological Review*, 63(2): 400–14.

May, T. (forthcoming) Urban governance: bonfire of vanities to find opportunity in the ashes, *Urban Studies*.

May, T. and Perry, B. (eds) (2006) Special edition: universities in the knowledge economy: places of expectation/spaces for reflection?, *Social Epistemology*, 20 (3–4).

May, T. and Perry, B. (2006) Cities, knowledge and universities: transformations in the image of the intangible, *Social Epistemology*, 20 (3–4): 259–82.

May, T. and Perry, B. (2011a) Contours and conflicts in scale: science, knowledge and urban development, *Local Economy*, 26(8): 715–20.

May, T. and Perry, B. (2011b) Urban research in the knowledge economy: content, context and outlook, *Built Environment*, 37(3): 352–68.

May, T. and Perry, B. (2013) Universities, reflexivity and critique: uneasy parallels in practice, *Policy Futures in Education*, 11(5): 505–14.

May, T. and Perry, B. (2016) Cities, experiments and the logics of the knowledge economy, in J. Evans, A. Karvonen and R. Raven (eds), *The Experimental City*. Oxford: Routledge.

May, T. and Perry, B. (2017) *Cities and Knowledge: Promise, Politics and Possibility*. Oxford: Routledge.

May, T. and Perry, B. (2018) *Social Research: Issues, Methods and Process* (5th edn). Maidenhead: McGraw-Hill.

May, T. and Powell, J. (2008) *Situating Social Theory* (2nd edn). Maidenhead: Open University Press/McGraw-Hill.

May, T. with Perry, B. (2011) *Social Research and Reflexivity: Content, Consequences and Context*. London: Sage.

May, T. and Williams, M. (eds) (1998) *Knowing the Social World*. Buckingham: Open University Press.

Maynard, M. (1998) Feminists knowledge and the knowledge of feminisms: epistemology, theory, methodology and method, in T. May and M. Williams (eds), *Knowing the Social World*. Buckingham: Open University Press.

McCabe, J. and Holmes, D. (2009) Reflexivity, critical qualitative research and emancipation: a Foucauldian perspective, *Journal of Advanced Nursing*, 65(7): 1518–26.

McCarl Nielsen, J. (ed.) (1990) *Feminist Research Methods: Exemplary Readings in the Social Sciences*. London: Westview.

McCarthy, T. (1991) *Ideals and Illusions: On Reconstruction and Deconstruction in Contemporary Critical Theory*. Cambridge, MA: MIT Press.

McCarthy, T. (1994) The critique of impure reason, in M. Kelly (ed.), *Critique and Power: Recasting the Foucault/Habermas Debate*. Cambridge, MA: MIT Press.

McGettigan, A. (2013) *The Great University Gamble: Money, Markets and the Future of Higher Education*. London: Pluto.

McKee, K. (2009) Post-Foucauldian governmentality: what does it offer critical social policy analysis?, *Critical Social Policy*, 29(3): 465–86.

McNay, L. (2000) *Gender and Agency: Reconfiguring the Subject in Feminist and Social Theory*. Cambridge: Polity.

McNay, L. (2008) *Against Recognition*. Cambridge: Polity.

McPherson, M., Budge, K. and Lemon, N. (2015) New practices in doing academic development: Twitter as an informal learning space, *International Journal for Academic Development*, 20(2): 126–36.

Mead, G.H. (1938) *The Philosophy of the Act: Works of George Herbert Mead*, Volume 3. Edited and introduced by C.W. Morris. Chicago: University of Chicago Press.

Mead, G.H. (1964) *Selected Writings: George Herbert Mead*. Edited by A.J. Reck. Chicago: University of Chicago Press.

Mead, G. H. (1982). *Individual and the Social Self: Unpublished Work of George Herbert Mead*. Edited and introduced by D. Miller. Chicago: Chicago University Press.

Meeker, K. (2013) *Hume's Radical Scepticism and the Fate of Naturalized Epistemology*. New York: Palgrave Macmillan.

Merleau-Ponty, M. (1974) *Phenomenology, Language and Sociology: Selected Essays*. Edited by J. O'Neill. London: Heinemann.

Merleau-Ponty, M. (1989[1962]) *Phenomenology of Perception*. Translated by C. Smith. London: Routledge.

Merton, R. (1976) *Sociological Ambivalence and Other Essays*. New York: Free.

Mespoulet, M. (ed.) *Universite et Territoires*. Rennes: Presses Universitaires de Rennes.

Mill, J.S. (1974[1859]) *On Liberty*. Harmondsworth: Penguin.

Miller, D.L. (ed.) (1982) *The Individual and the Social Self: Unpublished Essays by G.H. Mead*. Chicago: University of Chicago Press.

Mills, C. (1963) *The Marxists*. Harmondsworth: Penguin.

Mills, C. (1997) *The Racial Contract*. Ithaca, NY: Cornell University Press.

Mirowski, P. (2014) *Never Let a Serious Crisis Go to Waste: How Neoliberalism Survived the Financial Meltdown*. London: Verso.

Mistra Urban Futures (2016a) *Realising Just Cities through Co-Production?* Gothenburg: Chalmers University.

Mistra Urban Futures (2016b) *Co-production in Action: Towards Realising Just Cities*. Gothenburg: Mistra Urban Futures.

Mitlin, D. (2008) With and beyond the state, *Environment and Urbanization*, 20(2): 339–60.

Moldaschl, M.F., Hallensleben, T. and Wörlen, M. (2015) Editorial – special issue on institutional and personal reflexivity, *International Journal of Work Innovation*, 1(2): 137–42. Available at www.inderscience.com/editorials/f711128110425369.pdf

Moore, H. (2007) *The Subject of Anthropology: Gender, Symbolism and Psychoanalysis*. Cambridge: Polity.

Morgan, G. (1983a) Knowledge, uncertainty and choice, in G. Morgan (ed.), *Beyond Method: Strategies for Social Research*. London: Sage.

Morgan, G. (ed.) (1983b) *Beyond Method: Strategies for Social Research*. London: Sage.

Morgan, K. (2001) The exaggerated death of geography: localised learning, innovation and uneven development. Paper presented at The Future of Innovation Studies Conference, The Eindhoven Centre for Innovation Studies, Eindhoven University of Technology, Netherlands.

Morozov, E. (2013) *To Save Everything, Click Here: Technology, Solutionism and the Urge to Fix Problems that Don't Exist*. London: Allen Lane.

Moser, P. (2013) Integrating urban knowledge, in H.T. Anderson and R. Atkinson (eds), *Production and Use of Urban Knowledge*. Dordrecht: Springer.

Moss, J. (ed.) (1998) *The Later Foucault: Politics and Philosophy*. London: Sage.

Mouffe, C. (ed.) (1996) *Deconstruction and Pragmatism*. (With Simon Critchley, Jacques Derrida, Ernesto Laclau and Richard Rorty.) London: Routledge.

Mouffe, C. (2005) *On the Political*. London: Routledge.

Mounce, H.O. (1997) *The Two Pragmatisms: From Peirce to Rorty*. London: Routledge.

Mruck, K. and Mey, G. (2007) Grounded theory and reflexivity, in A. Bryant and K. Charmaz (eds), *The SAGE Handbook of Grounded Theory*. London: Sage.

Nagel, T. (1986) *The View from Nowhere*. Oxford, Oxford University Press.

Nicholson, G. (2009) *The Lost Art of Walking: The History, Science, Philosophy and Literature of Pedestrianism*. New York: Riverhead.

Nietzsche, F. (1968) *The Will to Power*. New York: Vintage.

Nietzsche, F. (1977) *A Nietzsche Reader*. Selected and translated by R.J. Hollingdale. Harmondsworth: Penguin.

Nkulu-N'Sengha, M. (2005) African epistemology, in M.K. Asante and A. Mazama (eds), *Encyclopaedia of Black Studies*. Thousand Oaks, CA: Sage.

Nordhagen, S., Calverley, D., Foulds, C.,Thom, L.L. and Wang, X. (2012) Credibility in climate change research: a reflexive view, Tyndall Centre for Climate Change research working paper 152. Available at www.tyndall.ac.uk/sites/default/files/twp152.pdf

Norris, C. (2014) What strong sociologists can learn from critical realism: Bloor on the history of aerodynamics, *Journal of Critical Realism*, 13(1): 3–37.

Nowotny, H., Scott, P, and Gibbons, M. (2001) *Re-thinking Science: Knowledge and the Public in an Age of Uncertainty*. Cambridge: Polity.

Nuyen, A. T. (1990) Truth, method, and objectivity: Husserl and Gadamer on scientific method, *Philosophy of the Social Sciences*, 20(4): 437–52.

Nyamnjoh, F. (2012) Blinded by sight: divining the future of anthropology in Africa, *Africa Spectrum*, 47(2–3): 63–92.

O'Connor, J. (1987) *The Meaning of Crisis: A Theoretical Introduction*. Oxford: Basil Blackwell.

O'Flynn, M. and Panayiotopoulos, A. (2015) Activism and the academy in Ireland: a bridge for social justice, *Studies in Social Justice*, 9(1): 54–69.

O'Mara, M.P. (2005) *Cities of Knowledge: Cold War Science and the Search for the Next Silicon Valley*. Princeton, NJ: Princeton University Press.

O'Neill, J. (1972) *Sociology as a Skin Trade: Essays Towards a Reflexive Sociology*. London: Heinemann.

O'Neill, J. (1995) *The Poverty of Postmodernism*. London: Routledge.

Oakley, A. (2000) *Experiments in Knowing: Gender and Method in the Social Sciences*. Cambridge: Polity.

Ollman, B. (1979) *Social and Sexual Revolution: Essays on Marx and Reich*. London: Pluto.

Opezzo, M. and Schwartz, D.L. (2014) Give your ideas some legs: the positive effect of walking on creative thinking, *Journal of Experimental Psychology: Learning, Memory and Cognition*, 40: 1142–52.

Osborn, R. (1937) *Freud and Marx: A Dialectical Study*. Introduction by J. Strachey. London: Gollancz.

Osborne, S.P., Radnor, Z. and Strokosch, K. (2016) Co-production and the co-creation of value in public services: a suitable case for treatment?, *Public Management Review*, 18(5): 639–53.

Ostrom, E. (1996) Crossing the great divide: coproduction, synergy, and development, *World Development*, 24 (6): 1073–87.

Outhwaite, W. (1986) *Understanding Social Life: The Method Called Verstehen* (2nd edn). Lewes: Jean Stroud.

Owen, D. (1997) *Maturity and Modernity: Nietzsche, Weber, Foucault and the Ambivalence of Reason*. London: Routledge.

Pahl, K. (2014) The aesthetics of everyday literacies: home writing practices in a British-Asian household, *Anthropology and Education Quarterly*, 45(3): 293–311.

Parham, S. (2015) *Food and Urbanism: Towards the Convivial City and a Sustainable Future*. London: Bloomsbury.

Pariser, E. (2012) *The Filter Bubble: What the Internet Is Hiding from You*. London: Penguin.

Park, P.K.J. (2013) *Africa, Asia, and the History of Philosophy: Racism in the Formation of the Philosophical Canon, 1780–1830*. Albany, NY: State University of New York Press.

Parker, M. and Jary, D. (1995) The McUniversity: organization, management and academic subjectivity, *Organization*, 2(2): 319–38.

Parsons, T. (1965) An outline of the social system, in T. Parsons, E. Shils, K.D. Naegele and J.R. Pitts (eds), *Theories of Society: Foundations of Modern Sociological Theory*. New York: Free.

Parsons, T., Shils, E., Naegele, K.D. and Pitts, J.R. (eds) (1965) *Theories of Society: Foundations of Modern Sociological Theory*. New York: Free.

Patai, D. (1994) (Response)When methods become power, in A.D. Gitlin (ed.), *Power and Method: Political Activism and Educational Research*. New York: Routledge.

Patel, Z., Greyling, S., Parnell, S. and Pirie, G. (2015) Co-producing urban knowledge: experimenting with alternatives to 'best practice' for Cape Town, South Africa, *International Development Planning Review*, 37(2): 187–203.

Peirce, C.S. (1931) *The Collected Papers of Charles Sanders Peirce*, Volumes 1–6. Edited by C. Hartshorne and P. Weiss, volumes 7 and 8 edited by A.W. Burks. Cambridge, MA: Harvard University Press.

Pels, D. (2003) *Unhastening Science: Autonomy and Reflexivity in the Social Theory of Knowledge*. Liverpool: Liverpool University Press.

Perry, B. (2007) The multi-level governance of science policy in England, *Regional Studies*, 41(8): 1051–67.

Perry, B. (2010) Academic knowledge and urban development: theory, policy and practice, in T. Yigitcanlar, K. Velibeyoglu and S. Baum (eds), *Knowledge-Based Urban Development: Planning and Applications in the Information Era*. New York: Information Science Reference.

Perry, B. (2012) Science frictions and fictions in the north west of England: excellence, relevance and the university, in R. Pinheiro, P. Benneworth and G. Jones (eds), *Universities and Regional Development: A Critical Assessment of Tensions and Contradictions*. London: Routledge.

Perry, B. (2016) *Let the Band Play: Reflections on Co-Production*, video diary. Available at www.youtube.com/channel/UCYJWfTHhISqZLFJCGPky1RA (uploaded 1 July 2016).

Perry, B. and May, T. (2006) Excellence, relevance and the university: the 'missing middle' in socio-economic engagement, *Journal of Higher Education in Africa*, 4(3): 69–92.

Perry, B. and May, T. (eds) (2007) Governance, science policy and regions: an introduction, in special edition on 'Governance, Science Policy and Regions', *Regional Studies*, 41(8): 1039–50.

Perry, B. and May, T. (2010) Taking urban knowledge exchange seriously: devilish dichotomies and active intermediation, *International Journal of Knowledge-Based Development*, 1(1–2): 6–24.

Perry, B. and May, T. (2015) Context matters: the English science cities and visions for knowledge-based urbanism, in J. Tian Miao, P. Benneworth and N. Phelps (eds), *Making 21st Century Knowledge Complexes: Technopoles of the World 20 Years After*. London: Routledge.

Perry, B., Smith, K. and Warren, S. (2015) Revealing and re-valuing cultural intermediaries in the 'real' creative city: insights from a diary-keeping exercise, *European Journal of Cultural Studies*, 18(6): 1–17.

Perry, B., Walsh, V. and Barlow, C. (2016) Navigating the rapids of urban development: lessons from the Biospheric Foundation, Salford, UK, in J. Henneberry (ed.), *Transience and Permanence in Urban Development*. Chichester: Wiley.

Perry, B., Wharton, A., Hodson, M. and May, T. (2012) *Mapping the Urban Knowledge Arena*. Report of the Greater Manchester Local Interaction Platform. Salford: Mistra Urban Futures. Available at www.mistraurbanfutures.org/sites/default/files/mapping_the_urban_knowledge_arena_report_2012_0.pdf

Pfeffer, J. and Sutton, R.I. (2000) *The Knowing–Doing Gap: How Smart Companies Turn Knowledge into Action*. Boston, MA: Harvard Business School.

Pillow, W. (2003) Confession, catharsis, or cure? Rethinking the uses of reflexivity as methodological power in qualitative research, *International Journal of Qualitative Studies in Education*, 16(2): 175–96.

Pinheiro, R, Benneworth, P. and Jones, G. (eds) (2012) *Universities and Regional Development: A Critical Assessment of Tensions and Contradictions*. London: Routledge.

Platt, J. (1996) *A History of Sociological Research Methods in America 1920–1960*. Cambridge: Cambridge University Press.

Plummer, K. (ed.) (1991) *Symbolic Interactionism, Volume 1: Foundations and History*. Aldershot: Elgar.

Pohl, C., Rist, S., Zimmermann, A., Fry, P., Gurung, G.S., Schneider, F., Speranza, C.I., Kiteme, B., Boillat, S., Serrano, E., Hadorn, G.H. and Wiesmann, U. (2010) Researchers' roles in knowledge co-production: experience from sustainability research in Kenya, Switzerland, Bolivia and Nepal, *Science and Public Policy*, 37(4): 267–81.

Polanyi, M. (1962) *Personal Knowledge: Towards a Post-Critical Philosophy*. London: Routledge.

Polanyi, K. (2001[1944]) *The Great Transformation: The Political and Economic Origins of our Time* (2nd edn). Foreword by J.E. Stiglitz. Boston, MA: Beacon.

Polanyi, M. (1983[1966]) *The Tactic Dimension*. Gloucester, MA: Peter Smith.

Polk, M. (ed.) (2015) *Co-producing Knowledge for Sustainable Cities: Joining Forces for Change*. Abingdon: Routledge.

Polk, M. and Kain, J.H. (2015) Co-producing knowledge for sustainable futures, in M. Polk (ed.), *Co-producing Knowledge for Sustainable Cities: Joining Forces for Change*. Abingdon: Routledge.

Poovey, M. (1998) *A History of the Modern Fact: Problems of Knowledge in the Sciences of Wealth and Society*. Chicago: University of Chicago Press.

Popper, K.R. (1968[1959]) *The Logic of Scientific Discovery* (revised edn). London: Hutchinson.

Puppin, G. (2014) Advertising and China: how does a love/hate relationship work?, in A. Hulme (ed.), *The Changing Landscape of China's Consumerism*. Oxford: Elsevier.

Putnam, H. (1981) *Reason, Truth and History*. Cambridge: Cambridge University Press.

Quiddington, P. (2010) *Knowledge and Its Enemies: Towards a New Case for Higher Learning*. Amherst, NY: Cambria.

Raco, M. (2003) Governmentality, subject-building, and the discourses and practices of devolution in the UK, *Transactions of the Institute of British Geographers*, 28(1): 75–95.

Raffnsøe, S., Gunmand-Høyer, M. and Thaning, M.S. (eds) (2016) *Michel Foucault: A Research Companion*. Basingstoke: Palgrave Macmillan.

Rasmussen, D. (1996a) Rethinking subjectivity: narrative identity and the self, in R. Kearney (ed.) *Paul Ricoeur: The Hermeneutics of Action*. London: Sage.

Rasmussen, D. (ed.) (1996b) *Handbook of Critical Theory*. Oxford: Blackwell.

Reason, P. and Bradbury, H. (2001) *Handbook of Action Research: Participative Enquiry and Practice*. London: Sage.

Research Excellence Framework (2014) Available at http://results.ref.ac.uk/

Ribbens, J. and Edwards, R. (eds) *Feminist Dilemmas in Qualitative Research: Private Lives and Public Texts*. London: Sage.

Ricoeur, P. (1982) *Hermeneutics and the Human Sciences: Essays on Language, Action and Interpretation*. Edited, translated and introduced by J.B. Thompson. Cambridge: Cambridge University Press.

Ricoeur, P. (1994) *Oneself as Another*. Translated by K. Blamey. Chicago: University of Chicago Press.

Ricoeur, P. (2005) *The Course of Recognition*. Translated by Pellauer, D. Cambridge, MA: Harvard University Press.

Rittel, H.W.J. and Webber, M.M. (1973) Dilemmas in a general theory of planning, *Policy Sciences*, 4(2): 155–69.

Ritzer, G. (1999) *Enchanting a Disenchanted World: Revolutionizing the Means of Consumption*. Thousand Oaks, CA: Pine Forge.

Ritzer, G. (2015) *The McDonaldization of Society* (8th edn). London: Sage.

Robbins, D. (2012) *French Post-War Social Theory*. London: Sage.

Roberts, J.M. (2014) *New Media and Public Activism: Neoliberalism, the State and Radical Protest in the Public Sphere*. Bristol: Policy.

Roberts, N. (2000) Wicked problems and network approaches to resolution, *International Public Management Review*, 1(1). Available at http://journals.sfu.ca/ipmr/index.php/ipmr/article/view/175

Rock, P. (1979) *The Making of Symbolic Interactionism*. London: Macmillan.

Rockmore, T. (1994) Antifoundationalism, circularity, and the spirit of Fichte, in D. Breazeale and T. Rockmore (eds), *Fichte: Historical Contexts/Contemporary Controversies*. Atlantic Highlands, NJ: Humanities.

Rogers, K.M. (ed.) (1979) *Before Their Time: Six Women Writers of the Eighteenth Century*. New York: Unger.

Rose, G. (1993) *Feminism and Geography: The Limits of Geographical Knowledge*. Cambridge: Polity.

Ross, D. (1992) *The Origins of American Social Science*. Cambridge: Cambridge University Press.

Roth, M.S. (1981) Foucault's 'History of the Present', *History and Theory*, 20(1): 32–46.

Rothenburg, M.A. (2010) *The Excessive Subject: A New Theory of Social Change*. Cambridge: Polity.

Rousseau, J.-J. (1922[1782]) *The Reveries of the Solitary Walker*. Translated with an introduction by C.E. Butterworth. Indianapolis, IN: Hackett.

Routledge, P. and Driscol Derickson, K. (2015) Situated solidarities and the practice of scholar-activism, *Environment and Planning D Society and Space*, 33(3): 391–407.

Rowe, D. (2011) *The Successful Self*. London: HarperCollins.

Ruivo, B. (1994) 'Phases' or 'paradigms' of science policy?, *Science and Public Policy*, 21(3): 157–64.

Russell, B. (2009[1946: Nov.]) Philosophy for laymen, in *Universities Quarterly*, 1. Reproduced in *Unpopular Essays*. London: Routledge.

Russell, B. (1955) *History of Western Philosophy and its Connection with Political and Social Circumstances from the Earliest Times to the Present Day* (5th impression). London: George, Allen & Unwin.

Russell, B. (1983[1912]) *Problems of Philosophy* (11th impression). Oxford: Oxford University Press.

Russell, B. (2004[1935]) *In Praise of Idleness*. London: Routledge.

Russell, B. (2015) Beyond activism/academia: militant research and the radical climate and climate justice movement(s), *Area*, 47(3): 222–9.

Ryan, A. (1986) *Property and Political Theory*. Oxford: Basil Blackwell.

Ryan, A. (ed.) (1973) *The Philosophy of Social Explanation*. Oxford: Oxford University Press.

Ryan, T.G. (2005) *The Reflexive Classroom Manager*. Calgary: Temeron Books/Detselig.

Ryle, G. (2000[1949]) *The Concept of Mind*. Harmondsworth: Penguin.

Sandywell, B. (1996) *Reflexivity and the Crisis and Western Reason: Logological Investigations, Volume 1*. London: Routledge.

Saper, C. (2006) Blogademia, *Reconstruction*, 6(4): 1–15. Available at http://reconstruction.eserver.org/064/saper.shtml9

Sassen, S. (2011) *Cities in a World Economy* (4th edn). Thousand Oaks, CA: Sage.

Savage, M., Cunningham, N., Devine, F., Friedman, S., Laurison, D., McKenzie, L., Miles, A., Snee, H. and Wakeling, P. (2015) *Social Class in the 21st Century*. London: Pelican.

Savage, M., Devine, F., Cunningham, N., Taylor, M., Li, Y., Hiellbrekke, J., Le Roux, B., Friedman, S. and Miles, A. (2013) A new model of social class? Findings from the BBC's Great British Class Survey Experiment, *Sociology*, 47(2): 219–50.

Sayer, A. (2005) *The Moral Significance of Class*. Cambridge: Cambridge University Press.

Sayer, A. (2011) *Why Things Matter to People: Social Science, Values and Ethical Life*. Cambridge: Cambridge University Press.

Sayer, A. (2015) *Why We Can't Afford the Rich*. Bristol: Policy.

Scarborough, H. (2001) Knowledge à la mode: the rise of knowledge management and its implications for views of knowledge production, *Social Epistemology*, 15(3): 201–13.

Schelling, F.W.J. (1992[1936]) *Philosophical Inquiries into the Nature of Human Freedom*. Translated and introduced by J. Gutmann. La Salle, IL: Open Court.

Schlembach, R. (2015) Negation, refusal and co-optation: the Frankfurt School and Social Movement Theory, *Sociology Compass*, 9(11): 987–9.

Schlesinger, H.J. (2008) *Promises, Oaths, and Vows: On the Psychology of Promising*. New York: Analytic.

Schlosberg, D. (2006) Communicative action in practice: intersubjectivity and new social movements, *Political Studies*, 43(2): 291–311.

Schön, D.A. (1971) *Beyond the Stable State*. New York: Random House.

Schön, D.A. (1991) *The Reflective Practitioner: How Professionals Think in Action*. San Francisco, CA: Jossey Bass.

Schutz, A. (1970) *Alfred Schutz on Phenomenology and Social Relations: Selected Writings.* Edited and introduced by H.R. Wagner. Chicago: University of Chicago Press.

Schutz, A. (1973) Problems of interpretative sociology, in A. Ryan (ed.), *The Philosophy of Social Explanation.* Oxford: Oxford University Press.

Schutz, A. (1979) Concept and theory formation in the social sciences, in J. Bynner and K. Stribley (eds), *Social Research: Principles and Procedures.* Milton Keynes: Open University Press.

Scott, J. (1998) Relationism, cubism, and reality: beyond relativism, in T. May and M. Williams (eds), *Knowing the Social World.* Buckingham: Open University Press.

Seidman, S. and Wagner, D. (eds) (1992) *Postmodernism and Social Theory.* Oxford: Blackwell.

Seigfried, C.H. (1996) *Pragmatism and Feminism: Reweaving the Social Fabric.* London: University of Chicago Press.

Shalin, D. (2010) Hermeneutics and prejudice: Heidegger and Gadamer in their historical setting, *Russian Journal of Communication*, 3(1–2): 7–24.

Shotter, J. (1993) *Cultural Politics of Everyday Life: Social Constructionism, Rhetoric and Knowing of the Third Kind.* Buckingham: Open University Press.

Shusterman, R. (ed.) (1999) *Bourdieu. A Critical Reader.* Oxford: Blackwell.

Siedentop, L. (2015) *Inventing the Individual: The Origins of Western Liberalism.* London: Penguin.

Silver, N. (2013) *The Signal and the Noise: The Art and Science of Prediction.* London: Penguin.

Silverman, D. and Torode, B. (2011[1980]) *The Material World: Some Theories of Language and its Limits.* London: Routledge.

Simmel, G. (1964[1950]) *The Sociology of Georg Simmel.* Translated, edited and introduced by K.H. Wolff. New York: Free.

Simpson, D. (2002) *Situatedness, or, Why We Keep Saying Where We're Coming From.* Durham, NC: Duke University Press.

Skeggs, B. (1997) *Formations of Class and Gender: Becoming Respectable.* London: Sage.

Skeggs, B. (2002) Techniques for telling the reflexive self, in T. May (ed.), *Qualitative Research in Action.* London: Sage.

Skeggs, B. (2004) *Class, Self, Culture.* London: Routledge.

Skeggs, B. (2011) Imagining personhood differently: person value and autonomist working class value practices, *Sociological Review*, 59(3): 496–513.

Skeggs, B. (2015) Introduction: stratification or exploitation, domination, dispossession and devaluation?, *Sociological Review*, 63(2): 205–22.

Slaughter, S. and Leslie, L.L. (1997) *Academic Capitalism: Politics, Policies, and the Entrepreneurial University.* Baltimore, MD: Johns Hopkins University Press.

Sloterdijk, P. (2011[1998]) *Spheres. Volume 1: Bubbles – Microspherology.* Translated by W. Hoban. Los Angeles: Semiotext(e).

Smith, D.E. (1988) *The Everyday World as Problematic: A Feminist Sociology.* Milton Keynes: Open University Press.

Smith, D.E. (1996[1990]) *Conceptual Practices of Power: A Feminist Sociology of Power*. Toronto: Toronto University Press.

Smith, D.E. (2002) Institutional ethnography, in T. May (ed.), *Qualitative Research in Action*. London: Sage.

Smith, D.E. (2005) *Institutional Ethnography: A Sociology for People*. Oxford: AltaMira.

Smith, D.L. (2007) *Why We Lie: The Evolutionary Roots of Deception and the Unconscious Mind*. London: Macmillan.

Sontag, S. (2001[1966]) *Against Interpretation*. London: Vintage.

Soros, G. (1998) *The Crisis of Global Capitalism (Open Society Endangered)*. London: Little, Brown and Company.

Soros, G. (2010) *The Soros Lectures*. New York: Public Affairs.

Soros, G. (2013) Fallibility, reflexivity, and the human uncertainty principle, *Journal of Economic Methodology*, 20(4): 309–29.

Spivak, G.C. (1984–85) Criticism, feminism and the institution, *Thesis Eleven*, 10(11): 175–89.

St. Pierre, E. (1997) Methodology in the fold and the irruption of transgressive data, *International Journal of Qualitative Studies in Education*, 10(2): 175–89.

Standing, G. (2011) *The Precariat: The New Dangerous Class*. London: Bloomsbury.

Stanley, L. (ed.) (1990) *Feminist Praxis: Research, Theory and Epistemology in Feminist Sociology*. New York: Routledge.

Stehr, N. (1992) *Practical Knowledge: Applying the Social Sciences*. London: Sage.

Stehr, N. (ed.) (2004) *The Governance of Knowledge*. London: Transaction.

Sternberg, R. J. (ed.) *Handbook of Creativity*. Cambridge: Cambridge University Press.

Sternberg, R.J. and Lubart, T.L. (1999) The concept of creativity, in R.J. Sternberg (ed.), *Handbook of Creativity*. Cambridge: Cambridge University Press.

Stokoe, E. (2000) Toward a conversation analytic approach to gender and discourse, *Feminism and Psychology*, 10: 552–63.

Stout, A.K. (1967) The basis of knowledge in Descartes, in W. Doney (ed.), *Descartes: A Collection of Critical Essays*. London: Macmillan.

Strasser, S. (1985) *Understanding and Explanation: Basic Ideas Concerning the Humanity of the Human Sciences*. Pittsburgh, PA: Duquesne University Press.

Strober, M. (2010) *Interdisciplinary Conversations: Challenging Habits of Thought*. Stanford, CA: University of Stanford Press.

Strydom, P. (2000) *Discourse and Knowledge: The Making of Enlightenment Sociology*. Liverpool: Liverpool University Press.

Strydom, P. (2002) *Risk*. Buckingham: Open University Press.

Summers, M. (2007) Rhetorically self-sufficient arguments in Western Australian parliamentary debates on lesbian and gay law reform, *British Journal of Social Psychology*, 46: 839–58.

Sustainable Development Commission (2010) *The Future Is Local: Empowering Communities to Improve Their Neighbourhoods*. Available at www.sd-commission.org.uk/data/files/publications/SDC_TFiL_report_w.pdf

Suzuki, D. and Mayorga, E. (2014) Scholar-activism: a twice told tale, *Multicultural Perspectives,* 16(1): 16–20.

Swyngedouw, E. (2009) The antinomies of the postpolitical city: in search of a democratic politics of environmental production, *International Journal of Urban and Regional Research,* 33(3): 601–20.

Symons, J. and Perry, B. (2016) *Maximising What's Already There: Increasing Research Impact in Communities Using the Ordsall Method.* Manchester: University of Salford.

Sztompka, P. (1991) *Society in Action: The Theory of Social Becoming.* Cambridge: Polity.

Talwar, V. and Lee, K. (2008) Social and cognitive correlates of children's lying behaviour, *Child Development,* 79(4): 866–81.

Taylor, B. (2013) The 'Big Society' and the politics of paternalism: Edmund Burke's influence on the government is clear. http://blogs.lse.ac.uk/politicsandpolicy/edmund-burke-the-big-society-and-the-politics-of-paternalism/

Taylor, C. (1981) Understanding in human science, *Review of Metaphysics,* 34: 25–38.

Taylor, C. (1985) *Philosophy and the Human Sciences: Philosophical Papers: Volume 2.* Cambridge: Cambridge University Press.

Taylor, C. (1986) Foucault on freedom and truth, in D.C. Hoy (ed.), *Foucault: A Critical Reader.* Oxford: Basil Blackwell.

Taylor, C. (1992) *Sources of the Self: The Making of the Modern Identity.* Cambridge: Cambridge University Press.

Taylor, C. (1995) *Philosophical Arguments.* Cambridge, MA: Harvard University Press.

Taylor, M. (2007) Community participation in the real world: opportunities and pitfalls in new governance spaces, *Urban Studies,* 44(2): 297–317.

Telegraph Online (2009) Climate change: this is the worst scientific scandal of our generation, 28 November. www.telegraph.co.uk/comment/columnists/christopherbooker/6679082/Climate-change-this-is-the-worst-scientific-scandal-of-our-generation.html

Thayer, H. S. (1981) *Meaning and Action: A Critical History of Pragmatism* (2nd edn). Indianapolis, IN: Hackett.

Thompson, E.P. (1968) *The Making of the English Working Class* (revised edn). Harmondsworth: Penguin.

Thompson, J.B. (1981) *Critical Hermeneutics: A Study in the Thought of Paul Ricoeur and Jürgen Habermas.* Cambridge: Cambridge University Press.

Thompson, J.B. (1993) *Fiction, Crime and Empire: Clues to Modernity and Postmodernism.* Chicago: University of Illinois Press.

Thompson, J.B. and Held, D. (eds) (1982) *Habermas: Critical Debates.* London: Macmillan.

Thrift, N. (2005) *Knowing Capitalism.* London: Sage.

Tian Miao, J., Benneworth, P. and Phelps, N.A. (eds) (2015) *Making 21st Century Knowledge Complexes: Technopoles of the World Revisited, Regions and Cities.* London: Routledge.

Times Higher Education, The (2015) Pay Survey 2015. Available at www.timeshighereducation.com/features/times-higher-education-pay-survey-2015/2019360.article

Titmuss, R. (1976) *Commitment to Welfare* (2nd edn). Introduction by B. Abel-Smith. London: George Allen & Unwin.

Tostevin, B. (2010) *The Promethean Illusion: The Western Belief in Human Mastery of Nature.* Jefferson, NC: MacFarland & Co. Inc.

Toulmin, S. (2003) *Return to Reason.* Cambridge, MA: Harvard University Press.

Tsoukas, H. and Chia, R. (2002) On organizational becoming: rethinking organizational change, *Organization Science*, 13(5): 567–82.

Turkle, S. (2012) *Alone Together: Why We Expect More from Technology and Less from Each Other.* New York: Basic.

Turner, B.S. (1981) *For Weber: Essays on the Sociology of Fate.* London: Routledge & Kegan Paul.

Turner, B.S. (ed.) (1990) *Theories of Modernity and Postmodernity.* London: Sage.

Turner, C. (1990) Lyotard and Weber: postmodern rules and neo-Kantian values, in B.S. Turner (ed.), *Theories of Modernity and Postmodernity.* London: Sage.

Turner, S. (2003) *Liberal Democracy 3.0: Civil Society in an Age of Experts.* London: Sage.

Tyler, I. (2013) *Revolting Subjects: Social Abjection and Resistance in Neoliberal Britain.* London: Zed.

Unger, R.M. (1987) *Social Theory: Its Situation and Its Tasks: A Critical Introduction to Politics, A Work in Constructive Social Theory.* Cambridge: Cambridge University Press.

Unger, R.M. (2009) *The Self Awakened: Pragmatism Unbound.* Cambridge, MA: Harvard University Press.

Van Marrewijk, A., Veenswijk, M. and Clegg, S. (2010) Organizing reflexivity in designed change: the ethnoventionist approach, *Journal of Organizational Change Management*, 23(3): 212–29.

Vico, G. (1990[1709]) *On the Study Methods of Our Time.* Translated and introduced by E. Gianturco. Ithaca, NY: Cornell University Press.

Visker, R. (1995) *Michel Foucault: Genealogy as Critique.* Translated by C. Turner. London: Verso.

Wacquant, L. (1992) The structure and logic of Bourdieu's sociology, in P. Bourdieu and L. Wacquant (eds), *An Invitation to Reflexive Sociology.* Cambridge: Polity.

Wacquant, L. (2007) Territorial stigmatization in the age of advanced marginality, *Thesis Eleven*, 91(1): 66–77.

Wade Hands, D. (2013) Introduction to symposium on 'reflexivity and economics: George Soros's theory of reflexivity and the methodology of economic science', *Journal of Economic Methodology*, 20(4): 303–8.

Wallas, G. (2014[1926]) *The Art of Thought.* Tunbridge Wells: Solis.

Wallerstein, I. (ed.) (1996) *Open the Social Sciences: Report of the Gulbenkian Commission on the Restructuring of the Social Sciences.* Stanford, CA: Stanford University Press.

Watson, V. (2014) Co-production and collaboration in planning – the difference, *Planning Theory and Practice*, 15(1): 62–76.

Watt, D. (2007) On becoming a qualitative researcher: the value of reflexivity, *The Qualitative Report*, 12(1): 82–101.

Weber, M. (1949) *The Methodology of the Social Sciences*. Edited by E. Shils and H. Finch. Glencoe, IL: Free.

Weber, M. (1964[1947]) *The Theory of Social and Economic Organization*. Translated by A. Henderson and T. Parsons, edited with an introduction by T. Parsons. Glencoe, IL: Free.

Weber, M. (1985[1930]) *The Protestant Ethic and the Spirit of Capitalism*. London: Counterpoint.

Weber, M. (1994[1919]) The profession and vocation of politics, in *Political Writings*. Cambridge: Cambridge University Press.

Wetherell, M. (2012) *Affect and Emotion: A New Social Science Understanding*. London: Sage.

Wiggershaus, R. (1995) *The Frankfurt School: Its History, Theories and Political Significance*. Translated by M. Robertson. Cambridge: Polity.

Williams, A. (1990) Reading feminism in fieldnotes, in L. Stanley (ed.), *Feminist Praxis: Research, Theory and Epistemology in Feminist Sociology*. New York: Routledge.

Williams, M. and May, T. (1996) *Introduction to the Philosophy of Social Research*. London: University College of London Press.

Winch, P. (1990[1958]) *The Idea of a Social Science and its Relation to Philosophy* (2nd edn). London: Routledge.

Winter, R. (2009) Academic manager or managed academic? Academic identity schisms in higher education, *Journal of Higher Education Policy and Management*, 31(2): 121–31.

Witt, C. (1996) How feminism is re-writing the philosophical canon. The Alfred P. Stiernotte Memorial Lecture in Philosophy at Quinnipiac College, 2 October. Available at www.uh.edu/~cfreelan/SWIP/Witt.html

Witt, C. and Shapiro, L. (2016) Feminist history of philosophy, *The Stanford Encyclopedia of Philosophy* (Spring), edited by E.N. Zalta. Available at http://plato.stanford.edu/archives/spr2016/entries/feminism-femhist/

Wittgenstein, L. (1922) *Tractatus Logico – Philosophicus*. London: Routledge & Kegan Paul.

Wittgenstein, L. (1953) *Philosophical Investigations*. Oxford: Blackwell.

Wolff, K. H. (1979) Phenomenology and sociology, in T. Bottomore and R. Nisbet (eds), *A History of Sociological Analysis*. London: Heinemann.

Wolin, S. (2004) *Politics and Vision: Continuity and Innovation in Western Political Thought* (expanded edn). Princeton, NJ: Princeton University Press.

Woolgar, S. (1998) *Knowledge and Reflexivity: New Frontiers in the Sociology of Knowledge*. Beverly Hills, CA: Sage.

Wright, C. (2013) Against flourishing: wellbeing as biopolitics and the psychoanalytic alternative, *Health, Culture and Society*, 5(1): 20–35.

Wright, C. (2014) Happiness studies and wellbeing: a Lacanian critique of contemporary conceptualisations of the cure, *Culture Unbound: Journal of Current Cultural Research*, 6: 791–813.

Wynne, B. (1992) Misunderstood misunderstanding: social identities and public uptake of science, *Public Understanding of Science*, 1(3): 281–304.

Yigitcanlar, T., Velibeyoglu, K. and Baum, S. (eds) (2010) *Knowledge-Based Urban Development: Planning and Applications in the Information Era*. New York: Information Science Reference.

Youtie, J., and Shapira, P. (2008) Building an innovation hub: a case study of the transformation of university roles in regional technological and economic development, *Research Policy*, 37(8): 1188–204.

Žižek, S. (2008a[1999]) *The Ticklish Subject: The Absent Centre of Political Ontology*. London: Verso.

Žižek, S. (2008b[1989]) *The Sublime Object of Ideology*. London: Verso.

Žižek, S. (2009) *First as Tragedy, Then as Farce*. London: Verso.

Žižek, S. (2012) *Less than Nothing: Hegel and the Shadow of Dialectical Materialism*. London: Verso.

AUTHOR INDEX

SUBJECT INDEX